"Talk about having 'your cheese moved'! This memoir is an extraordinary example of how you can survive and thrive in the face of unfair change."

—Spencer Johnson, MD
Author of *Who Moved My Cheese?* and
coauthor of *The One Minute Manager*

"The human spirit inspires all of us to help another, with the benefit of our own experiences, trials, and tribulations. Lucinda's book is an honest, open, quieting story that so many spouses and family members who have lost loved ones, or experienced extreme tragedy, will learn from. Love and honesty with one another is what improves us all, and Lucinda does just that in *Truth Be Told*. It is so worth reading!"

—Delilah
National radio personality and author

"*Truth Be Told* tells an intimate, powerful, and riveting story of success and loss. Everyone has tragedies in their lives; it is what one does with them that matters most. This book will be an inspiration to many, especially to anyone who has lost a loved one to suicide. I highly recommend it."

—Daniel G. Amen, MD
Author of *Change Your Brain, Change Your Life* and
Unleash the Power of the Female Brain

"In this brilliantly courageous and candid book, Lucinda opens up about topics of pain that are so taboo most people choose to keep them in the closet. These are the 'unspeakable topics' that people do not want to address; child sexual abuse and suicide. In this bold, powerful memoir, not only does Lucinda address these topics, but she demonstrates the power of the human spirit to move beyond the suffering. This inspiring book will help anyone who has been traumatized by either to understand that healing is possible."

—Arlene Drake, PhD
Expert/Adult Survivors Sexual Abuse

"Lucinda Bassett's life journey will inspire others to move beyond extreme pain and find peace again. I recommend this book to anyone who has experienced loss and heartbreak—and that would be just about everyone."

—Kenny Loggins
Grammy®-winning singer, songwriter, guitarist, and author

"These are difficult times, and many people are experiencing tremendous anxiety, loss, and tragedy. This compelling memoir is a timely reminder that hope, loved ones, patience, and strong conviction and belief in your own ability to survive, and eventually thrive again, will ultimately get you through and absolutely make you stronger. An excellent, intimate, and highly motivating read."

—George J. Pratt, PhD
Coauthor of *Code to Joy* and past chairman of psychology
at Scripps Memorial Hospital, La Jolla, CA

"This is an incredibly moving and candid story of one the most loving and successful couples in direct-response television who made it their business to help people. In this powerful memoir, Lucinda has chosen once again to use her pain and struggle to help others heal. A beautiful tribute to her husband, and an inspiring read for anyone who has experienced tragedy or loss."

—Bill Guthy
Cofounder of Guthy-Renker

"Having been honored to review Lucinda Bassett's remarkable memoir, this day ends with a feeling of gratitude and peace. Lucinda's capacity for love, empathy, and forgiveness is her key. . . . I believe that destiny follows from a life that touches fellow travelers in those shared moments of love and beauty that transcend the inevitable losses that intrude in this gift of being."

—Owen Stanley Surman, MD
Psychiatrist at Massachusetts General Hospital and
associate professor of psychiatry at Harvard Medical School

Truth Be Told

Truth Be Told

A MEMOIR OF
SUCCESS, SUICIDE, AND SURVIVAL

Lucinda Bassett

STERLING
New York

STERLING
New York

An Imprint of Sterling Publishing
387 Park Avenue South
New York, NY 10016

ISBN 978-1-4027-7987-9

Some of the names and details have been changed to protect people's privacy.

Distributed in Canada by Sterling Publishing
c/o Canadian Manda Group, 165 Dufferin Street
Toronto, Ontario, Canada M6K 3H6

For information about custom editions, special sales, and premium and
corporate purchases, please contact Sterling Special Sales at 800-805-5489
or specialsales@sterlingpublishing.com.

Manufactured in the United States of America

2 4 6 8 10 9 7 5 3 1

www.sterlingpublishing.com

Contents

DEDICATION

This book is dedicated to my best friend, life partner, and my biggest fan . . .
David. Thank you for giving me two beautiful children, a wonderful family
life, and for helping me to build an amazing career. Thank you for showing
all of us through all the years we had you, how a man should love a woman,
and how a father should love his children. Thank you for believing in me and
helping me to find my star while helping millions of people all over the world.
We still greatly struggle with the fact that you left us, but as I am learning,
that was your journey. Our duty to you and to ourselves is to continue to live
well, in spite of your choice. That is the challenge we face. We all miss you so
much it hurts every single day, almost every single moment, honestly. I will
always love you, and I doubt I'll find another man like you. You were such a
giver. Until we meet again . . .

What would happen if one woman told the truth about her life? The world would split open.

—Muriel Rukeyser

June 8, 2011

THE IRONY IS THAT my biggest fear for many years was a fear of going crazy, fear of losing my mind. Who would have thought that twenty-five years later, my partner, lover, and best friend, one of the most together, sane people I knew, would lose his.

Two days ago was the three-year anniversary of my husband David's death, and no matter how much time goes by, it is still excruciatingly painful. And the worst part is I really have no one to share the grief with. My kids have decided to ignore it or disown it, all in an attempt to forget it. Right.

The two people who I should have been sharing the grieving process with on this painful day, my two children, Brittany and Sammy, simply can't deal with the horrific memory of that day when David took his life. If he had died in a car accident, of a heart attack, or from some disease, it would be so different. But when someone you love commits suicide, when someone chooses to leave you, there is a huge amount of guilt, blame, anger, and shame that goes with it—so much that it's unbearable.

You would think after three years, *three years* . . . you could at least talk about it.

When I called my daughter to remind her what day it was, she broke into tears, got angry with me, and said, "Don't bring it up again."

Okay. If that's the reaction I got from her, I told myself, I'd best not say anything to remind my son. Instead, I poured a glass of wine and sat at my laptop flipping through files of family photos—pictures of David: the father, the husband, on ski trips, at graduations, with friends, with his dog, at Christmases, in family portraits, and on camping trips . . . all gone now. I cried. I kept crying. I wanted to throw up. What was he thinking?

I'm trying very hard to keep the tender, loving memories of this beautiful man alive in my heart and in my children's hearts, in spite of the fact that he killed himself. There are pictures around my home of him holding my children, loving and happy, pictures of him holding me.

In my children's defense, on the anniversary of his death it's extremely difficult not to get lost in the guilt-blame-anger-and-shame thing all over again. Most of all, we get overwhelmed by the feelings of such "unfair" incredible loss and depression that come when someone we loved and counted on to always be there for us, and needed the way we needed him, kills himself. That said, the year David died, in an attempt to memorialize him and create a place to "visit" him, I donated a beautiful bench to a local park, where David used to coach softball and soccer for Sammy's teams. The bench has an inscription: *In Memory of David Bassett, Loving Father to Brittany and Sammy, Devoted Husband to Lucinda.* I comforted myself to some degree with the thought that we would go there every year on the anniversary of his death, say a prayer, and share some memories and kind words about David.

Not happening.

The kids refuse to go to the bench. The way back to life after death of a loved one from suicide is such an ugly monster. No matter how much time passes, you're angry. It's like a dark cloud that continuously hangs over you. You get mad at every event where there are complete and *intact* families: every Father's Day celebration out in a restaurant with large families, holidays, family reunions, school events—any event where there is a father in tow.

Worse yet, suicide haunts you as something to hide, something to be ashamed of, something that keeps reminding you that your family is damaged, scarred, almost white trash. It's a dark, ugly secret that you don't want to share. Whose fault is it, anyway? Mine, someone else's . . . his? Why did he *really* do it? That's what people are thinking, and you know it. And the way people *do* react when they find out how he died.

Suicide is like AIDS. It scares people. They don't want to touch someone who has been associated with it. Surely there is a hidden reason the person took his or her life. And they look at you all squinty-eyed. What do you know that we don't know? According to a very bright psychiatrist friend of mine, "There is only one reason someone takes their life: they are mentally ill. Period."

But try telling your children that. And that's supposed to make them feel . . . better?

"Your dad was mentally ill." Yeah, that makes them feel better.

In fact, try finding anything on dealing with suicide that makes you feel better. I went in search of books for myself and for my children with some type of "light at the end of the very dark tunnel of suicide." There weren't any. Tried suicide support groups. They were depressing.

The real truth is that suicide and the reasons for it are complicated. Sometimes people who are suicidal are inappropriately treated and end up on the wrong medication. Sometimes they are agitated and overwhelmed by certain situations, and they can't see a way out. Sometimes there is a genetic predisposition to mood disorders that can be triggered by outside stressors. All of the above are part of David's story, which means they are part of my story as well.

As I moved through the overwhelmingly challenging months that followed the tragedy of his death, I became aware of several major connecting themes in my life, the most significant being experiences that recreated the cycle of guilt, blame, anger, and shame. Cycles of emotions ripped at my insides, penetrated my soul, and immersed me in anxiety, fear, and feelings of despair that I was forced once again to face head-on. In addition, I have always had a deep-seated need to "fix" people—alas, my "unchosen" mission in life.

That said, one of the most important recurring themes is that I am one of those people who—by God's hand, I believe—is at various times in my life brought to my knees, humbly and with complete and utter surrender, only to be pushed once again, to find my way, and yes, survive. And then, I believe, as demonstrated to me universally and by divine intervention, I am supposed to share what I have learned with others. Others who stand in fear, unable to function, destroyed by some unbearable trauma, believing there is no light at the end of the tunnel—no help, no hope, no happiness. So here I stand once again, humbled and open, sharing my life experience with you . . . for it is now an open book. If I can come out sane and grateful to be here, you can, too.

Brought to My Knees

IT WAS A NIGHT THAT will be etched in my memory forever. In fact, I recount it over and over again, wondering what I could have said differently, done differently. On June 6, 2008, my husband, David, and I had come home from an evening out with our twenty-two-year-old daughter, Brittany, and her boyfriend, Justin. Sammy, our sixteen-year-old son, was in his room. As we got ready for bed, I tried to reassure myself that the loving, pleasant evening we had just shared meant my deep concerns earlier in the afternoon were unfounded. David had smiled and talked right along with the rest of us as we enjoyed a wonderful dinner and time at Brittany's by the fireplace.

"Mom," she had said, "why don't you and Dad stay here tonight? Just sleep here."

"That's odd," I thought to myself. She had never requested that before. We didn't live that far away. I must tell you, I have regretted that we didn't stay ever since.

For almost a year, the man who had been everything to me—my husband, my children's father, my business partner, my best friend, and my lover—had been struggling with mental illness. Before the symptoms of this devastating disease began to change him, he was the man who went to the store to get my favorite ice cream before I even asked for it, made sure that there was oil in my daughter's car, and did Tarzan calls when my son's team scored points at a water polo game.

He was a wonderful father and an adoring husband. As the smart and capable president of our company, the Midwest Center for Stress and Anxiety, he had steered us to success. From the moment we met, he believed in me and loved me unconditionally. He was my biggest fan and a big part of the reason I have become successful in my life and my career. For our twenty-five years of marriage, he was always with me as we worked together and brought up our children together. We took great pleasure in our life as a couple. We loved each other deeply and completely, and spent most of our time together. My mother used to say, "If you're not with him, you're on the phone with him." He was my best friend. Watching him slip into psychosis was the most wrenching experience my children and I had ever been through.

The irony was not lost on me that I, a recognized expert in the field of anxiety and depression, could not help the man who had always been the proverbial wind beneath my wings. As I came to realize, there's a big difference between anxiety disorder and psychosis. I'm not a psychiatrist, so I vowed I would get David the very best psychiatric care possible. Unfortunately, the doctors prescribed various medications that were not right for him. The medications caused intolerable side effects, and I believe an initial unsuccessful attempted suicide. As a result, David was hospitalized in early 2008. Nothing worked. He was getting steadily worse instead of better. I begged his doctor to try lithium, because it was the only thing that worked for his grandfather, but that never happened. I am convinced to this day that he was on the wrong medication, and that it was greatly responsible for the events I am about to share with you.

This time in my life was so overwhelming and painful, so traumatic, humbling, and devastating, that I thought I would never recover. If someone had told me back then that we would eventually come through this horrible period and begin to live again, I would never have believed it. If someone had told me that we would find moments of joy again and even laugh again, I would not have been able to see it. If someone had told me

16

we could eventually begin to move beyond even the grief and feelings of extreme loss, I would have said, "Never." But we are moving in that direction. If someone had told me that three years later I would be writing this book to help others move through their extreme trauma, I would have said, "Not possible. I have nothing to give." But I do, or at least, I do now.

If I can get through that intensely tragic time in my life and continue to not only survive, but thrive, possibly my journey toward self-discovery and recovery can help others. In fact, that is the only way it makes sense to me about why I went through it—to help others. For my own healing, I have no choice but to use it in this way. But this is only the beginning of the story.

I know God will not give me anything I can't handle.
I just wish that He didn't trust me so much.

—Mother Teresa

CHAPTER 1

My Father's Legacy

WHEN I WAS A LITTLE GIRL, we lived in a small, ugly, pink brick house not far from Main Street in Findlay, Ohio. Findlay, "Flag City, USA," is a blue-collar Midwestern town about fifty miles south of Toledo and a hundred miles north of Dayton. The city was home to factories and assembly plants, including RCA, Whirlpool, and Cooper Tire. The "high-class" people worked at Marathon Oil, also headquartered in Findlay, and lived in expensive homes on the edge of town. They wore fancy clothes and shopped at Macy's.

We, the Redicks, were not "those people." There were seven of us in my family: my mother, my father, three brothers and a sister—David, the oldest; Gary, the second oldest; Donna, who was two years younger than Gary; then Michael—and me. I was the youngest.

We were poor. We bought our clothes at Goodwill and our food with food stamps. Every Friday, my mom did our grocery shopping at the old A&P, and when I was little, it was usually Mike, Donna, and I who went along. I would run loose through the market with my brother and sister while my mom pushed the cart. As she walked around, she kept track of what she was buying with a little clicker; she had to be very careful to stay within her food-stamp allowance.

We were a big family, so cheap protein was the only protein we got. Mom bought lots of hot dogs and hamburger. In my head I can still smell the fresh-baked cakes and cookies that were off-limits, foods that other people who were also in the store—Marathon Oil people—put into their carts without even thinking about it. Mostly, though, I remember running my hands longingly over the boxes of doughnuts and breakfast cereals, and especially over the fresh fruits—foods I knew I could not have. We were barely getting by, even with food stamps.

When the shopping was done, my mother pushed our grocery cart all the way home from the A&P to the ugly pink house. The cart went *clickety, click, click* as it rolled along the uneven sidewalks of South Main Street. I was little enough to ride in the top section, facing my mother. I thought it was great fun. When you're four, a ride in a grocery cart isn't much different from a ride in a little red wagon—not that I had a little red wagon.

I remember kicking my feet as we went along, and thinking how pretty my mom looked. People would drive by, honk and yell. I thought they were doing that because we were so cool, but while I was happy and having a wonderful time, my sister and brother were dying of shame. They knew it was anything but cool to be seen pushing a grocery cart down Main Street, and they were painfully aware that the folks driving by were making fun of us. Mike would sometimes scatter and hide, and my sister, Donna, would hold her head down while we walked, like she was afraid of something. And what she was afraid of was that someone would recognize her.

There was no more money at Christmastime than there was at any other time of year. We were one of those "less fortunate" families that made people feel good about giving. I remember my mother opening the front door and taking Christmas gift boxes of food and presents from strangers and saying thank you. She never asked them in. There was no welcome mat at our front door, because we never knew who was going to show up.

Not outside the house. *Inside.*

We were poor and dysfunctional, and alcoholism was the ugly monster crouching at the door, putting us all in a constant state of flight, fight, or freeze. Would Daddy be lying on the floor drunk? Would he embarrass us in front of our friends? Would he be ranting and raving, and possibly violent? His drinking ruined everything, from holidays to homework assignments to regular days and nights that were supposed to be just "normal." For us, chaos *was* normal.

Alcohol was at the core of our family dynamic, and the reason why outsiders weren't welcome. How could we invite people into our house when we ourselves wanted so badly to be out of it . . . somewhere else—*anywhere* else? Whenever we could, we spent a lot of time out of doors. On hot summer days I chased my brothers and sister around the exterior of the house. I chased the rescue cat. My brother Mike and I played with the hose, catching lightning bugs and swatting mosquitoes on hot summer nights. We stayed outside for as long as we could, even though the acrid smell of rubber from Cooper Tire hung heavy in the air. We stayed outside long after it got dark, creating our own denial of the chaos that was ever present inside our home. Anything not to have to go inside to confront the monster Dad became when he got drunk.

They called my father Ikey. I'm not sure where it came from, but his real name was Roy. Except, it wasn't, really. He was adopted, and, according to him, he never actually knew what his name was. Years later, I found out my father's adopted name was Joseph Schoebinger—at least, that was the name on his military service records.

When he was sober, my father ruled the world. He was charming. He was sophisticated in a way that I think is just inborn. We didn't have money, but on special occasions he would buy us the finest chocolates, and even once in a while take us to the local restaurant for dinner. He barely worked as a used-car salesman. That was his job Monday through Friday, but on the weekends he played the fiddle, tap-danced, and had a band. He was well known around town, and when he played at the armory, every seat was filled. I would sit in the front row with my mother, swinging my feet, so happy that everyone loved my daddy. I'd be wearing my best dress—probably bought for Easter. That was the only time we bought anything new.

Back to Ikey. My father was the life of the party, the one who made everyone laugh. He was handsome, witty, and full of jokes, and I loved him. I actually believed and hoped I was his favorite. After all, he took me with him on Sunday mornings to buy the paper, sometimes with a bonus of sticky buns. I loved to hear him whistle when he walked, and he called me Windy Cindy. When he was sober, he was fun and playful. I loved him so when he was sober. But he was like the little girl with the little curl on her forehead: when he was good, he was very, very good, but when he was bad, he was horrid. My father was a serious alcoholic. When he drank, which was often, he got drunk. And when he drank, he was mean. The father I loved just melted away. Dr. Jekyll turned into Mr. Hyde.

I remember one birthday. I don't remember whose. Not mine, but it doesn't matter—since all birthdays were the same, just about cake and ice cream. There were no presents. That night we were all waiting for Dad to come home so we could have our celebration, but he was late. Again. And because he was late, all of us were sitting around the old Formica kitchen table, worried and anxious, our sweaty legs sticking to the vinyl chairs. Again. It was a familiar and destructive pattern that was repeated over and over, year after year, after year; holiday after holiday.

When he finally got home that night, he was drunk. No birthday surprise there. After he made his grand entrance, my brother Michael got mouthy with him, so Dad picked him up and heaved him across the kitchen table. So much for the cake and ice cream.

My father's daytime beverage of choice was beer—Rolling Rock—and he bought it by the case. It used to be that he'd wait till the sun was down before he'd start drinking, or at least till the afternoon, but there were more and more days when he'd wake up and head straight for the Rolling Rock. Breakfast for him was a few beers and Valium, and whatever he could scavenge from the fridge. Breakfast of Champions. At night it was whiskey, straight up. Sometimes he didn't even bother using a glass.

I suppose you could say that he was trying to numb a lot of pain, and there was a lot of pain because there were a lot of secrets—dark secrets—surrounding his birth. The story I was told was that back in the 1920s, some mystery woman put my father in a basket when he was a baby and left him on my grandfather's doorstep. She knocked on the door and asked him to watch her son, saying she'd be back the next day. She never returned.

What I believe happened is that Grandpa's wife got pregnant by another man. Back then no one wanted to talk about that sort of thing, so they just made up the story that my father had been left on the doorstep.

I think in his heart he knew the truth. Maybe that's why he drank. Maybe that's why he was angry and mean. After all, there's always a reason for alcoholism . . . isn't there? He told me that when he was growing up, his father treated him badly. If Grandpa was angry because he was stuck raising his wife's bastard child as his own, that would explain a lot.

My mother's name was Kay. She was pretty, and she was the glue that held the family together, both emotionally and financially. She worked all day on the assembly line at RCA, and then started her second shift when she got home. When she came in the door, she'd say, "I just need to lay down for half an hour." After that, she'd get up and put dinner on the table for five kids. Usually it consisted of fried chicken or hamburgers, some canned vegetable, and lettuce with bottled dressing on top. Then she stood for hours ironing clothes while we did our homework in front of the television set.

Many nights it was just Mom and the five of us at the table, and when Dad wasn't home for dinner, we all knew what that meant. I remember lying awake and fearful in bed. He seemed to know how to be gone long enough for us all to be more worried about him than mad at him. My sister, Donna, was worried, too. We shared a tiny bedroom. It was green, and in the winter it was the warmest bedroom in the house. Because the creaky old furnace was no match for Ohio winters, my mother would light the oven and leave the oven door open as a backup heater. Donna and I were the biggest beneficiaries, because our bedroom was right off the kitchen.

I stared at the ceiling, eyes wide open, waiting to hear the car door slam and the reckless stumble of his footsteps to the door. When he finally got inside, he would curse, then fart and belch, and then raid the refrigerator. He'd stand there in his underwear, swaying unsteadily back and forth and hanging on the refrigerator door, lit by the little bulb inside the fridge. Truth to tell, the door was holding him up while he tried to decide what to chew on. Usually it was leftover meat or some old-man type of smelly cheese, like Limburger. He stank, and what he was eating stank. The stench permeated the kitchen and wafted on the heat from the oven into our bedroom. It was disgusting.

I sometimes wondered why I loved him. I wondered even more why my mother loved him, but according to her and her grandiose memories of what they once had, the relationship between them started off as an amazing love story. They'd been high school sweethearts, madly in love. When he enlisted in the army and was stationed in St. Louis, they couldn't stand being apart. She went off on a train to meet him. They ended up getting married and having their first baby, my brother David.

And that's where the fairy tale ended.

My father shipped out to Hawaii during World War II. Pearl Harbor. He saw a lot of his buddies get shot at close range. They died right before his eyes, and I don't think he ever got over it.

When he returned home from the war, he came back as someone else. My mother's loving, handsome Prince Charming turned into an angry alcoholic chain-smoker with weird ideas about sex. At least, she thought they were weird. After that, they never got along. She stuck with him, according to her, because she "didn't want us not to have a father." The truth was, she was afraid to be without him, a legacy of behavior she left to me as well. All I remember about their relationship was that they fought, but she was really no match for him. Often, instead of confronting him, she would retreat into the bathroom and sit on the toilet with the lid down, feeling sorry for herself. And cry.

That was my cue. Send in the clowns.

Ever since I was about five, I saw it as my job in the family to make people feel better—especially my mother. I was the one who tried to smooth things over and fix it all. Whenever my mother took refuge in the bathroom, I would wander in, crawl up on her lap, and wipe away her tears. "It's going to be okay, Mommy. Don't worry. Don't cry." And then I would tell jokes and make her laugh.

It worked. Making my mother and sometimes even my brothers and sister feel better became a skill I honed throughout my life. Comforting others made me feel good, and I was good at it, even when I was a child.

Little did I know I was establishing the building blocks for a career path of healing. Eventually I became an expert at it. How could I show others how to get through hell if I hadn't done it myself? Practice. Practice. Practice. Thus, the story of my life. Back then, one of the first lessons I learned was that the threat of violence was ever present in our home. Maybe that was why my mother hid in the bathroom so often. All of us lived in fear of my father's temper when he'd been drinking. The smallest thing—a wrong word or glance, or an overturned glass of milk—could set him off. Sometimes what set him off was quite literally nothing.

Many nights my mother and I would go around the kitchen and hide the knives before he got home, for fear that he might use one on us in a moment of rage. (No wonder I was afraid of knives most of my life.) On one unforgettable night, though, it wasn't a knife that caused the nightmare.

It was a cold, snowy night in Ohio. Mike, Donna, and I were sitting watching *The Honeymooners* on TV. Mike and I were just two years apart, and Donna was seven years older than me. Anyway, I loved to watch that show because Dad kind of reminded me of Jackie Gleason. My mother was ironing. David and Gary were hanging out with friends somewhere. It was late, so we all knew Dad would probably come home drunk. I didn't care. I just wanted him to come home, period. He was, after all, my father, and despite everything, I loved him.

Finally he came staggering in, gross, stinking drunk, and the toxic shouting match began.

"You are drunk again!" my mother shouted at him. "Where have you been?"

Honestly, what she did barely qualified as shouting. My mother had a very weak voice and a temperament to match. That night, she cowered in a corner of the living room, arms crossed defensively in front of her body, attempting to show her anger. What came out of her mouth was a feeble, shaking, quiet voice. Weakness.

My father, in contrast, had a huge, booming voice. Anger would come thundering out of him at the top of his lungs. "Shut up!" he spewed. Even when he was slurring his words, he was still intimidating. "Leave me alone!" he roared.

"Where were you?" my mother demanded again. She tried to yell, but as she was yelling her voice trembled, and she trembled along with it.

Mouse versus lion. No contest.

My mother was a good, kind, loving mother, but against my father, she had no moxie. It was pathetic to watch. Oddly enough, because he was strong and had all the power, throughout the years I identified more with him than I did with her. She was a wimp, and I didn't want to ever be like that.

"Jesus Christ! You're a saint, aren't you?" he sneered. Even though I don't recall him ever laying a hand on my mother, he was extremely verbally abusive to her, and never more so than when he was drunk. "You just do everything right, don't you? We are all so goddamned lucky to have you to take care of us, because we'd all *die* if you weren't around." His voice oozed sarcasm. All us kids turned to mush and went into shutdown mode. We tried to make ourselves invisible. If we just sat still and sat quietly, maybe he would calm down and come back to being "normal."

Although there were still traces of the handsome man he used to be, all that beer had made him obese. He was bloated, big from overeating and overdrinking, and he waddled when he walked. On this particular night, he waddled out to the kitchen, careening like a pinball from one piece of furniture to another, until he reached the refrigerator. As usual, he hung on the door as he opened it and started rummaging, looking for something to eat.

My mother followed after him. "You're a mess—how can you do this in front of your children? You are disgusting!"

Game on.

"Kay Redick. Kay Redick. Let's all get down on our knees and pray to Kay Redick." He spat out the words between mouthfuls, and bits of cheese flew out with every syllable. "You're just fuckin' perfect, aren't you? *"AREN'T YOU?!"* With that, he yanked fiercely on the open door of the fridge, pulling the entire refrigerator over. It hit the floor with a loud, violent crash, and everything in it came spilling or tumbling out. A pale peach river of milk and juice flowed across the kitchen floor. Eggs—what few didn't break—rolled into the corners. There was shattered glass everywhere.

"Get out!" my mother screamed in a panic. "GET OUT NOW!"

My father turned red, then purple as rage colored his face. "Shut up, Saint Kay," he said menacingly. "Shut up. Or I'm gonna shut you up, you stupid bitch."

I remember trembling and hating him, yet at the same time praying for Daddy to straighten up and go back to being the man who took me to the store for sticky buns. . . . Where was he now? *Who* was he now? Maybe if I sat real still and prayed real hard, he would calm down and turn back into Daddy again.

Prayer not answered. Not even close. Seemingly out of nowhere, my father pulled out a handgun and pointed it at my mother's face. None of us had seen it when he came in. He must have hidden it somewhere in his clothing. "I'm gonna kill you!" he thundered as he reeled toward her.

In a panic, my mother reached down and grabbed my and my brother Michael's hands—we were the two littlest. She frantically dragged us out the door, screaming for Donna to follow. "RUN!" she cried. "To the neighbors. Run!"

We fled out of our tiny house into the cold night air. I was wearing my favorite nightgown. It was soft and pink, with little roses on it, but it was worn and tattered and no protection from the cold. We went running out of the house in our bare feet, out into the snow, to the perfect neighbors' house next door. They were Catholic. They went to church on Sundays. They were "normal."

After they let us in I heard my mother on the phone, speaking in quiet, anxious tones. "He's got a gun," she said.

We all stood shivering. Why can't we just go home? I wondered. Daddy will calm down. It will be okay. Then I heard a police siren blaring in the distance. It got louder and louder as the police car got closer. I was shivering as I was watching out the window, my feet numb and frozen with melting snow. The squad car screeched to a stop in front of our tiny pink house. The red light on top kept going round and round as the officers jumped out and ran for the front door.

My heart was pounding as the policemen stormed into my imperfect home. When they came back out, my daddy was in handcuffs and they were dragging him away. What are they doing? I wondered. Wait, he sounds better now. He was okay. Things would be okay. But they pulled at him and threw him in the car . . . and took him away.

From *me*.

I had to run to him. I had to save him. I could fix it if they would just let me. I could fix him. I bolted out of the perfect neighbors' perfect house, back into the frigid night air. My small, frozen, bare feet ran after the police car as it drove away. I was terrified, so terrified I peed myself. I remember worrying about ruining my favorite nightgown.

"STOP!" I screamed as I was running. "Leave my daddy alone! Please, please!" I begged through my tears. "PLEASE," I screamed again. "DADDY, DADDY! NO . . . !"

As far as I knew, all that was left of my father were two tiny red taillights vanishing into the distance. Where were they taking him? Would he ever come back?

What did I do? What didn't I do that I should have done? I was only five, so I had no idea that this was a common pattern: children of alcoholics often torment themselves, thinking they are somehow to blame.

My mother came running after me. She scooped me up and brought me back into the neighbors' house. My pee-soaked nightgown clung to my legs. I was afraid I'd ruined it for good.

Daddy was in jail for three days. When he got home, he was nasty, and angry that my mother had called the cops on him. After that, she told him to get out. He did, but it was only temporary. They must have split up and got back together about twenty times while I was a child.

The legacy of growing up in that toxic environment was visited on all of us Redicks in various ways. Each of us was damaged. I struggled with anxiety and depression for a good part of my life, along with extreme fear of abandonment and fear of being alone. I also had a tendency to be drawn to charming, sarcastic, unstable men. Men who needed fixing. Men who, too often, couldn't be fixed.

CHAPTER 2

Dead-End Street

THE LONG LINE OF men who needed fixing started, of course, with my father. One day, in the summer of 1962, he came home beaming, and, for a change, absolutely sober. There was a twinkle in his eye and an unusual sense of excitement in his attitude—now *this* was the Daddy I knew was really in there, the Daddy I loved. "Hey, you kids, get your butts in the car. I've got somethin' to show ya. Come on, now. Kay, let's go!"

Mom looked puzzled and wary. "Where?" she demanded.

"Just trust me this once, goddammit. Can't ya just get in the goddamned car? Jesus Christ! Now let's go." Even though he was cursing, he was "cursing and happy," if that makes any sense at all. We all piled into the Brougham LTD—the "boat on wheels" from the used-car dealership that he worked at. One of the few perks of being a used-car salesman: we may have been living in a pink rented shithole of a house, but Daddy always had a nice set of wheels.

After we jammed ourselves in, he drove us across town, past Main Street, across several sets of railroad tracks, around a big curve, and down a little narrow side road. *All* the way down, all the way to the fence and the Dead End sign, by the railroad tracks.

Dad wheeled the Brougham into the gravel driveway, stones and dust flying everywhere, and brought the big, floaty car to a stop. There it was:

a small, two-story, brown-shingled house at 900 Central Avenue. There was nothing "central" about the street; the railroad tracks were maybe two hundred feet away.

"Get out, all of you. This is our new house!" he said proudly. He pulled himself out of the car, stood back with pride, and lit a Camel.

There was a chorus of oohs and aahs from all of us in the backseat. It may have been a small, ugly-ass, brown-shingled house, but it was the most beautiful thing I had ever seen. We pushed our way out of the car, jumping and climbing over each other with excitement. All of us were taken completely by surprise. My mother was the most surprised of all. Her mouth dropped open. She just sat in the car and shook her head in disapproval.

"What did you do here, Ikey?" she questioned in a suspicious voice.

"Get out of the goddamned car, Kay. Jesus Christ, didn't you hear what I said? This is your new house. Now get out and take a look. Goddammit, why do you have to ruin everything I try and do?"

"Wow! This is ours?" Michael asked, looking at Dad. The rest of us kids were running around the yard, screaming and laughing. We ran up onto the old wooden front porch, oohing and aahing some more—about the porch, about the house, about the size of the yard, and about the apple tree out front. Who cared that it was just a stone's throw from a railroad track? Why, that could even be fun, couldn't it?

"Yes, it *is* ours," Dad replied. "Come on now. Let's go inside."

We were all so excited. We ran into the house, opening doors and closets and touching the walls of our new home. You'd have thought we were royalty—Marathon Oil people or something. We had never owned anything before. To us, this brown-shingled house was a palace, a Ritz-Carlton.

Even my brother David, the oldest, loved it. "We have to take care of things," he said. "We have to take care of the carpet and the front porch, and we have to take our shoes off."

We all sat on the living room floor in disbelief. The carpet was dingy gold and sort of hard, flat, and abrasive, with a weird-shaped leaf design carved into the pile. The walls were covered in various types of outdated wallpaper, every room in the house. The wallpaper in the living room was gold, with a floral print to match the carpet. It was as dingy as the carpet, but to us it was beautiful.

The house had been moved onto the dead-end empty lot from God-knows-where. My father had bought it for six thousand dollars, and he announced that it was the promise of a new life—for all of us.

As part of that promise, he swore things were going to change. "We're Somebodies now. Our life is gonna get better. I'm gonna make things better for us," he vowed.

I was the happiest seven-year-old in Findlay, Ohio. "We're going to be a real family now. I can have friends come over to play and not be afraid here!" I thought to myself.

Although we were still living on food stamps, Goodwill, and hand-me-downs, things did seem to get better for a while. There was a little more money. My mother was no longer working on the RCA assembly line in the factory. She was promoted to the front office and was working as a secretary. That gave her a little more confidence about herself; she started dressing up a bit, and she and Dad started hanging out with his friends and going out to the armory at night.

On the trips to the A&P, there was now enough money to sometimes stop at Dietsch's Ice Cream on the way home. It is still there today, and it's still my favorite candy and ice-cream store. They make everything by hand. Sometimes we'd have ice cream; other times Mom would buy candy—the ones with soft buttery cream centers or chewy centers with nuts. When we got home, it was my job to divide the candy into little cups, one for each of us. I always begged my brother Gary for his share. Most times, he gave it to me.

The "new" old brown house had three bedrooms—two upstairs and one downstairs. David, Gary, and Mike shared the one little bedroom on the second floor at the top of the stairs. Donna and I got the other one, right beside it, right through the door. The stairs themselves were steep and narrow; they were rickety and squeaked really bad. Our room had a window that looked out on the front yard and at the Dead End sign. There was also a big open field at the side of the house, opposite the railroad tracks. There was a big old crabapple tree in the backyard where Mike and I eventually built a tree house. It was just old boards and a pole we'd climb to get up there, but it was our little hideaway.

It wasn't much, but we finally had a home.

Our parents' bedroom was the one downstairs. It was also the only one with a bathroom, and it was the only bathroom in the house. Unfortunately, the only way to get to it was to go through their bedroom.

Right away, this became a problem. We kids were told that it was an absolute rule for us never to open our parents' bedroom door. Not ever. If you had to pee first thing in the morning and their door was shut, too bad. You were walled off from the bathroom. You either had to hold it or figure out another solution. Right away, this became a problem. We kids were told that it was an absolute rule for us never to open our parents' bedroom door. Not ever. If you had to pee first thing in the morning and their door was shut, too bad. You were walled off from the bathroom. You either had to hold it or figure out another solution. Sometimes that solution was just to pee outside.

Why was it a rule for us to keep out if the door was closed? Because more than likely, Dad would either be lying in bed drunk, or they'd be having that weird sex Mom seemed to feel obligated to participate in but was turned off by.

For me, it was the beginning of a lifetime of bathroom issues. I became extremely self-conscious about it, to the point where I couldn't go if someone was in the room or even within earshot. Whether he was drunk or sober, I didn't want my father to hear me pee. I didn't want him to hear me on the toilet at all. Sometimes I had to go so bad I would go outside. Other times I'd get really sick with diarrhea, and I'd sit on the toilet and break out in sweats for fear he could hear me go to the bathroom. I suppose it's not surprising that I've had irritable bowel syndrome since I was a child.

Still, life in the brown-shingled house was, for the most part, better. Good times were few, but the ones we had were nice memories. During the summer, we'd go for Sunday picnics at the lake with Mom's sister, Auntie

Jean; Uncle John, her husband; and their kids. Mom and Dad would make fried chicken, potato salad, and kick-ass baked beans. Then all of us would pile into the LTD and head for the lake, Lake Erie. We'd play in the sand, and my father would lie there like a beached whale. Us kids would swim in the water, have our little picnic, and at the end of a long summer day, pile into the backseat of the car for the trip home to Findlay. On the way home we'd be all huddled up in the backseat, flopped all over each other—no one used seat belts back then—and fall asleep. It was a simple pleasure, but it was fun.

Mom's new job made it possible for us to actually have a real Christmas, sort of, with a tree and everything. Mom even had an old plastic Santa head that she would hang on the front door. Daddy decided to play Santa Claus, drunk off his ass. Ho. Ho. Ho. Each of us would get a present, just one. I still remember getting a doll once. It wasn't much, but it beat the hell out of perfect strangers coming to the door of the pink house, bearing handouts.

We even had real Thanksgivings, when Mom would cook turkey, and homemade mashed potatoes, and even pumpkin pie. She was always stressed, though. I'm sure it was her salary that was carrying the mortgage. Because he was drinking more, Dad was probably making even less money, and he was coming home drunk more often than ever—if he came home at all. And when he was home, his drinking actually got worse.

Sunday mornings were good, though, and a week full of bad nights would almost be worth it for the special Sunday mornings when Daddy was good. I remember waking up to the sound of Dad whistling, and to the delicious smell of Swiss steak baking in the oven. It was Dad's specialty, and he made family dinner for us almost every Sunday. Cooking made him happy, so he whistled. His whistle was distinctive; it had a little vibrato to it. In the pink house I rather liked it, but the older I got the more I hated it. By the time I was a teenager, I couldn't stand to be around anyone who whistled, and now, whistling—well, it's like fingernails on a chalkboard to me.

On several Sundays, we brought home a kite in addition to the Sunday newspaper and the sticky buns. Mike and I would fly it in the field next door. This was after church—it was my mom who started taking us there. Dad stayed home. The United Methodist Church was a big, beautiful building on the other end of town, where the Marathon Oil people lived. I loved the huge stained-glass window of Jesus at the front. During Sunday service, light streamed through that window in rainbow colors, making patterns on the floor and on the well-dressed people in the pews.

Well dressed didn't include us. From the moment we walked up the stairs and into the church, we looked exactly like what we were—people from the wrong side of the tracks. Literally. You could tell we Redicks didn't fit in with the rest of the congregation. We didn't talk to anybody, and nobody talked to us; we didn't socialize with the other churchgoers. I didn't want it to be that way. I wanted it to be so much more warm and inviting than it was. Church was pretty and it felt good to walk into it on Sunday mornings, but God was "up there" judging me. I knew He knew I didn't belong there.

Church to me was a place where you went to sing songs, or it should have been. We had an amazing choir, and I would have loved to be in that choir, but we weren't joiners. Not at church. Not anywhere. In fact, we never officially became members.

The Redicks didn't play sports, either. We didn't have money for sports equipment. We didn't play football. We weren't cheerleaders. We didn't play musical instruments. We never went to the dentist and seldom went to the doctor. We didn't take college prep courses. Heck, we barely made it through school, period.

No one helped us with our homework. No one made sure we actually did our homework, which meant that most of the time, we didn't. No one went to parent-teacher conferences. No one made sure we understood the importance of good grades, of doing well in high school or going to college. No one had a grand plan for us. Dad was too drunk to care, and my mother didn't have time to get involved. For her, it was all she could do to put one foot in front of the other—work, come home, cook dinner, and keep Dad "happy." Life was simply about survival.

She had a job, and she was the only real wage earner in the family. She left the house early every morning and went to RCA. Gary had moved out, and David left for the navy. Donna was working full time at the phone company. That meant Mike and I had to get ready for school by ourselves. Essentially, Mike and I were latchkey kids. We were seven and nine at the time. We had to get ourselves up, get dressed, pack our own lunches, and walk to Jacobs School, more than a mile away, rain, snow, or shine. If I got sick or if there was an event at school, I was on my own.

No one came to see me in a play, not that I was in many. In the one I remember, my job was to hold up the moon and sing, "K-K-K-Katie, beautiful Katie . . ." After the play was over, everyone ran out into the audience to find their family members who had come to see them. I ran out with the other kids, but nobody was there. No one from my family came to see me. I was standing there all by myself, fighting back tears, alone.

Things were no better in class. One day I got so sick I couldn't speak. The teacher, Mrs. Kappelhoff, said, "What's the matter with you? The cat got your tongue?" My throat was on fire. My stomach felt queasy, too. "I'm sick," I whispered. That was as much sound as I could make.

I guess Mrs. Kappelhoff didn't believe me, because she started making fun of me in the classroom. Soon, I couldn't hold it anymore. I puked all over my desk, all over the floor. Mrs. Kappelhoff sent me to the nurse's office. I sat there all day, because there was no one to come get me and take me home. At the end of the school day, I walked back to the brown-shingled house, alone.

One of the parts of the dead-end house that always upset me the most was the basement. It was musty and cold and more than a little sinister, with a wobbly, creaky old staircase that led down to a cold, damp, smelly little brick room with a cement floor. And I will always connect it with Kitty. Kitty was the generic name I gave to a homeless, skinny orange cat that I adopted. I would bring home every sick or stray animal I found—I was always the one who wanted to fix everyone or everything that hurt. Kitty had been with me a while. I found her when we were still living at the pink house and brought her along to the brown-shingled house when we moved. She was just an alley cat, but I really loved her. She was soft and loving, and she would purr when I held her. She was very important to me, and I found comfort in holding her. She slept with me at night.

I remember that it was Thanksgiving. As usual at holiday time, my father was raving drunk . . . again . . . and calling my mother a saint . . . again. He waddled into the living room and sat in his old worn-out La-Z Boy. Mom was trying to make Thanksgiving dinner, but she was shaking so much that she could hardly cook. She stood there working on the turkey. The kitchen windows were covered in steam from the stove. I could smell the fixings for the stuffing sautéing in a pan. If I faked it, I could pretend things were good, so I floated around the house pretending things were "normal" and that we were a normal family.

I was trying to stay below the radar, and I was looking for Kitty. I couldn't find her. After searching all over the house, I bravely went to look in the basement. I don't know why. Kitty didn't like it down there, and neither did I. But, for some reason, I thought I needed to go looking there. The smell of mildew smacked me in the face as soon as I started creeping down those stairs. It was cold and damp and dark. But there, lying on the floor, breathing heavily, was Kitty. She was limp, and I immediately ran over to her and picked her up. She was alive, but she meowed pitifully. Clearly she was sick. Very sick. Probably had pneumonia. I gently laid her down and went running upstairs in a panic.

My heart was pounding. I couldn't breathe. I thought I was going to be sick. "Mom! MOM! Kitty's sick," I cried. "We have to take Kitty to the vet. She's, she's crying. Mom, come and see her! PLEASE!" I paced back and forth, expecting my mom to come running.

She didn't.

"Not now, Cindy. Now go away. I have to make dinner here."

"Mom! Please . . . ," I begged. I began to panic again; I broke out into a sweat, headed toward the basement, and then ran back to my mother. "Come see her, Mom. She is so sick. We have to take her to the doctor!"

I could see she was upset, but she wouldn't look at me. "We don't have the money, Cindy," she said dismissively, like there was nothing she could do. As far as my mother was concerned, it was out of the question. If there wasn't enough money to go to the dentist, there certainly wasn't enough to spend on doctor bills for a cat.

"Please. I'll pay for it, Mommy. I'll find a way. We have to take her now."

"No," she said as she looked down at me with sadness in her face. "We don't have that kind of money. Now you need to run along. Kitty will be okay. I need to make dinner here."

I ran out of the kitchen, crying. What was she doing? What was she thinking? Kitty was sick! My heart was pounding; my mind was racing; I couldn't breathe; I wanted someone to help me, save me, save Kitty, take us away, and make us safe.

I think this was the first real panic attack I ever had. It's the first one I remember, anyway. I was afraid I was dying. I didn't know where to go or what to do. I was so panicked and full of fear, but I couldn't leave Kitty. I moved very hesitantly, shaking and apprehensive, along the dark, damp cellar walls, down the stairs, across the floor, over to where Kitty lay. I picked her up and held her in my arms, sobbing. "You'll be okay. I know you're scared," I said to her, but really to myself I knew she was dying, and I thought I was going to die with her. I trembled and cried. I was cold and scared, and I felt like I was going to shrivel up and die right there.

All of a sudden, I hated that brown house, I hated my mother, I hated my father, I hated everything. There I sat, all by myself, down in that cold cellar, holding my sick, soft, warm, comfortable, familiar little cat, for what seemed like hours. No one cared. There I was, at the tender age of eight years old, alone. She died in my arms. No one would help me. Abandonment. I will never, ever forget that experience and all the fear, abandonment, loss, and sense of having no control over a situation, that came with it—another pattern of experiences that would repeat itself often in my life. After that, the basement was taboo. Satan, death, and secrets were down there, and I would never go down there again.

And the promise of a "new" life in the "new" old house—well, that was just a lie.

(top left) Mom and Dad in 1945.

(top right) The five Redick children. From left to right: David, Gary, Donna, Michael, and the baby of the family, me, "Cindy."

(middle) A trip to Niagara Falls. From left to right: Michael, Mom, me, with issues related to the molestation apparent on my face, and Donna.

(bottom left) My brother Mike and me on Easter Sunday in our new Easter best.

(bottom right) Mom and Dad at Cedar Point in Sandusky, Ohio, around 1966.

CHAPTER 3

Dirty Little Secret

I GREW UP SURROUNDED by secrets. The secret of my father being left as a baby on Grandpa Redick's doorstep—or not. The secret of my father's drinking. The secret of his sleeping with other women. The secret of how poor we really were. These were secrets we didn't want anyone outside the family to know, but everyone in the family knew them. We Redicks all shared the burden of keeping quiet.

But there was one secret that was mine alone, and the burden of carrying it all by myself was almost too much to bear.

As a grown-up, whenever I spoke about my childhood, I told people that I couldn't really remember much about the time in my life between seven and nine years of age. I used to call it the "blackout time." It started about a year after we moved into the brown-shingled house, and it was the reason why the promise of a new life was such a hideous lie.

"It" was molestation. From the time I was seven till I was about nine, I was sexually abused. Repeatedly. Weekly. Sometimes daily.

And if that wasn't ugly enough, it had a satanic twist to it. Out of respect for the person's family, I'm not going to name him or go into detail. That's one secret I'll continue to keep. But I know what you're thinking, and it was not my father. My father may have been a lot of things, but he was not a child molester—at least not that I am aware of. In fact, the perpetrator was not an immediate family member.

By this time, my brothers David and Gary were both out of the house. David went into the navy, and Gary took off to go on the road with his band. Shortly after that, he got married, began having babies, and moved to Kentucky. My sister Donna spent as little time at home as she could. While she was still in high school, she worked part time as an operator for the phone company, but when she got out, she got a job at—can you believe it?—Marathon Oil.

Donna was on the road to respectability. She'd leave the house early in the morning, dressed to the nines. When she wasn't working, she was off with her boyfriend. Donna had started dating Bob, who also worked at Marathon Oil. Bob was a lovely guy who looked like Michael Nesmith of the Monkees—at least, I thought he did. We called him "Motorcycle Man." I'd hang out at the big old window in our bedroom, waiting to hear the throaty growl of his motorcycle as he roared down the street. Bob might have looked like Michael Nesmith, but he reminded me a lot of our brother David. Gentle. Good-hearted. Kind. Steady.

When he came to pick Donna up, he almost never came inside. She rushed out the door as soon as she heard the bike. Donna wouldn't think of inviting him in—or any of her other friends, for that matter. She couldn't, not when the house smelled like urine. Not when they'd have to step over Dad passed out on the floor in his underwear.

One by one, the oldest Redick children fled that brown-shingled house at the end of the dead-end street as fast as they could. They escaped in search of something better. I couldn't blame them, except that it meant I was left behind. There was no escape for me. I was left at home without parental supervision. A lot. Mom was always working, and Dad was never around or drunk. Same thing. Especially when school was out for the summer, as soon as Mom left for work I became prey.

The abuse was presented to me as a game, but it was sick, and there was something satanic about it. I knew it was wrong. I tried running up to the bedroom and closing the door, but it was no use. There were no locks. Even when I tried to hide, he would find me.

I was afraid of staying in the house, and I started pleading with my mother not to leave—anything to keep from being left at home and vulnerable. "Mommy, please don't leave me here! *Pleeeease* say you're not going out tonight!" I begged.

"You know we don't have enough money for a babysitter," she'd say. "I need to go. It won't be that long. You'll be fine."

The game was on, and the predator seemed to know when I was alone. It happened often. I felt dirty, inside and out. I started having nightmares. My abuser threatened me, saying he would hurt me. Worse yet, he said he would tell my mother and say it was my idea.

That threat worked. I remember my mom coming home from work on a day when I had been abused. All I could think about was wanting to tell her, followed by the awful realization of what he promised would happen to me if I did—that I would get blamed.

And maybe it *was* my fault? I really did blame myself. This was the beginning of a long cycle of guilt, blame, anger, and shame. I felt guilty about being molested. I wanted to tell my mother about my abuser, but I couldn't. I was scared, and I was too ashamed to say anything.

Eventually I developed genital warts. I had what looked like a cauliflower growing on my private parts. This was one of the few occasions when my mother took me to the doctor. He gave me a cream to get rid of them, and then asked if I'd been sexually molested. "Absolutely not," my mother answered quickly, before I could even think about whether to say anything, so I didn't.

I sat there in the doctor's office, shaking, wanting so badly to tell him what was happening and not being able to get the words out. I couldn't get any words out at all. I was too frightened, too ashamed. I was afraid no one would believe me. I also was afraid I really was guilty—after all, I *did* go along with it, didn't I? Guilt. Blame. Anger. Shame.

The doctor chose to pay no attention to the scared little girl quaking in front of him. He didn't talk to me, but to my mother. I was a nonperson. "Well," he said offhandedly, "sometimes you can get these off toilet seats."

Idiot.

Genital warts are contagious, spread by sexual contact. The doctor must have known that. I was violated in the worst possible way, but I was left to carry the burden of my shameful secret all by myself. There was nobody I could tell.

Not even God. But He already knew, and I was sure something awful was going to happen to me because of the terrible, dirty, sinful thing I had done.

I remember sitting there in my hand-me-down clothes in Sunday school, surrounded by "good" kids from the right side of the tracks, kids from Marathon Oil families—waiting for my own personal thunderbolt from the Almighty. "He" knew the truth. He knew I was bad. He was going to punish me.

I was dirty and sinful, too dirty to be in Sunday school. "God knows everything," I said to myself inside my head. No surprise there—they said it to us every week in Sunday school, too. "I am going to be greatly punished for what I have done." I became obsessed, repeating it over and over. I didn't know exactly what God was going to do to me, but I was as sure as I could be that God was going to get me, punish me.

The idea that God is love didn't register with me. Neither did the idea of God's forgiveness—that was something I did not deserve. At the time, everything I knew about God was about fear and righteous vengeance—Old Testament stuff. I got no comfort from going to church, only fear—fear that I was going to rot in hell, with Satan by my side. Eternally.

My obsessive fear of God and fear of being punished by Him was just the beginning. The abuse stopped when I was nine, but the guilt, blame, anger, and shame had only just begun. Those obsessive, guilt-ridden fears stayed with me for years—decades—to come. Waves of scary thoughts followed me everywhere. They were magnified by every spooky sound outside the window. They multiplied in dark closets and above all in the darkest recesses of my brain—there was nothing I could do to keep them from taking over my life. And they got worse.

I started having panic attacks regularly, as well as horrific scary thoughts. I became certain that something horrible was about to take place. It wasn't maybe going to happen. It was for sure going to happen, and soon—at any moment. My whole body reacted. My heart would start beating really fast; my hands would get sweaty. I was a deeply frightened, petrified little girl who felt like everything was closing in, like I couldn't breathe.

Not surprisingly, fear of being home alone was at the root of many of my attacks. I was afraid of the trains and the tracks nearby, and I was even more afraid of the bums or hobos who might be on them. About six times a day those long freight trains would go rumbling by, and when trains came through, the whole house shook on its foundation from top to bottom. The noise was deafening, not just of the trains themselves but of the rattling of the house and everything in it. The trains were slow moving, and while the house was shaking I'd look out the window. I imagined I saw rough-and-tumble men hiding in the boxcars. Because the tracks were so close, I thought I could see their faces.

That scared me. If I could see them, they could see me. I was afraid that, at any minute, one of them would come through the front door and kill me, or worse yet, rape me. Soon, my child's already frightened mind blew up that thought into fear of *anyone* coming through the front door. Or any*thing*. I became obsessed with the idea that Martians were coming for me. Logic and common sense were no match for this kind of unreasoning fear. I was sure the Martians were coming because they were looking in the windows, and their hands—which were actually our gloves—were hanging on the clothesline in the backyard.

I would lie in my bed shaking, or sometimes I'd take my scary, obsessive thoughts downstairs and lie on the sofa instead. One night I was down there and I heard a noise at the front door. Bums or Martians, this time they were really coming for me. Scarier still, they were calling my name: "Cindy! Let me in!"

I went to the screen door. I looked at the feet and the bell-bottom trousers—most un-Martianlike—and then my eyes followed all the way up the legs, to the peacoat, to the laughing face . . . to the jaunty sailor hat on top. "DAVID!" I screamed with joy as I unlatched the door and flung myself around my brother David's six-foot–two-inch frame.

David was home on leave before shipping out for Vietnam. He was so handsome—whatever they'd done to him in basic training had turned him into a man. I'll never forget how he smelled, and how strong he felt. David made me feel safe. I wanted to tell him everything about my fears and obsessions, and about being molested, but I just couldn't.

After he left to go back to the service, my obsessions started to expand. To distract myself from my fear of being punished by God, I began to obsess that my food was being poisoned. Whenever I picked up something to eat, it got stuck in my esophagus. Our family took a rare vacation to Niagara Falls, and all the way there I sat in the car thinking of the ways that God was going to punish me. We got to a restaurant; everyone else was digging hungrily into hamburgers and french fries. These happy family occasions were so rare—I just wanted to enjoy myself and be in the moment. I watched my brother take a bite and I said to myself, "I can do that!"

But I couldn't.

I took a bite of hamburger. As soon as I swallowed, it turned into a golf ball in my throat. Stuck. I tried to wash it down with water, but it just stayed there. I set the burger back down and just stared at the plate.

"You need to eat," my mother said. "What is wrong with you?"

What could I say? Could I tell her I was scared of dying, of being poisoned, of Martians, of being molested by bums? Could I tell her I was sexually abused, and God was going to get me? The words stuck in my throat, just like that golf ball of hamburger. A restaurant in Niagara Falls was not a very good place for blurting out the truth, or at least, not *that* truth. To this day, if I'm obsessing or worried, I can't eat.

Part of my fear of eating was that I was afraid I would choke or vomit. I had a severe fear of vomiting, and then I became afraid of people watching me eat. By this time I was already stick thin, and I was getting even thinner. I became so skinny—my arms were little spindles, no bigger around than my wrist. People thought I was anorexic, and I probably was, but it had nothing to do with wanting to be slender. I was thin because I was afraid to eat, and I was afraid to eat because I was afraid I would vomit, and because everything I swallowed hurt like hell going down—*if* it went down, which it didn't.

Fear begets fear. I knew I wasn't normal, and I was afraid I was getting worse. I *knew* I was getting worse. And then the fear of going crazy began. I was ten, almost eleven, and I would lie in bed and worry that I was losing my mind. I didn't know what that meant, exactly, at least not medically. What I *did* know was that on TV, whenever someone went crazy, it was understood that they never got better. They never got un-crazy. They just got weird.

Crazy was permanent.

I began to worry about going crazy a lot. Maybe *this* would be God's way of punishing me—and I already knew that going nuts was a life sentence. But then something happened that solidified the possibility and made it even more real.

I remember driving to Toledo with my mother. She had an old, white, piece-of-shit Oldsmobile with a fender that blew in the wind. It was a rainy, cold December day, but still, the trip was special. Toledo was the "big city." I loved any outing with my mother, but this was special because we were going into Toledo to do some Christmas shopping. We had just reached the outskirts of town, headed for Kmart, when there was an accident. We got detoured off the main highway. At about the same time, the sky darkened to a threatening grayish black. Icy rain started coming down in sheets. The windshield wipers couldn't keep up. Hail the size of ice cubes was falling. It was kind of spooky, and I remember being very cold and feeling anxious.

We found ourselves on a local backstreet that I had never seen before. When we pulled up to a traffic light, I looked out and saw this big, looming, ugly brick building with bars on the windows. It was like something out of an Alfred Hitchcock movie. The rain and the black sky made it even more ominous. An involuntary shiver went down my spine. Even without knowing what it was, it was the scariest building I'd ever seen.

"What is that, Mom?" I asked.

"That old building? Well, that's the mental hospital. That's where they put people that go crazy," she said.

"Can you get out?"

"Oh, no!" Mom replied. "That's why there are bars on the windows."

Oh my God.

In that moment, the image of that creepy building was seared into my brain forever, and it set off a whole new round of obsessive thoughts about going crazy. "What if I end up in there—how would I ever get out? What if I get locked up and no one ever sees me again? What if no one ever cares, like when I was in the cellar with Kitty?" I became convinced that there was a bed in there with my name on it, waiting . . . just waiting.

It wasn't too long after that when my friend Cheryl's mom took us to see *Night of the Living Dead.* What the hell was she thinking? To me, this wasn't just a horror film. It was out-and-out gruesome, with graphic scenes of ghouls and zombies feasting on human flesh. The lone survivor gets shot in the head at the end—nobody human gets out of that movie alive. I walked out of the theater in shock. Before seeing the movie I was scared. Now, I was terrified.

I tried to talk to my mother about it. "Mom, I'm scared I'm going to get possessed by zombies or by the devil," I said.

"If you think it's going to happen, it will," she replied.

My mother told me that often, about lots of different subjects. I think for her it had the effect of cutting off any further conversation. It worked. I would simply walk away convinced that whatever I believed, I would conceive. If I thought about going crazy, then I'd make myself go crazy. If I worried about someone breaking into the house, that's what would happen. If I worried about getting possessed, it would guarantee that I would.

Great.

My doom was preordained—by me. Now I wasn't safe even inside my own head. I was scared to death of my own thoughts.

This set the stage for a lifetime of worrying and obsessing about losing my mind. About losing control. Fear of fear. And, alas, anxiety, depression, and panic attacks.

I didn't have a lot of friends to share any of this with. Cheryl was one. Darlene was another. Darlene lived in my neighborhood, through an alley, just two minutes' running distance from me. She was blonde, with green eyes, and funny. Darlene was my partner in crime. On Christmas we'd run through the alleys between each other's houses, zooming back and forth in the snow to see what each of us got. Not much. But we'd watch *A Charlie Brown Christmas* together, and old episodes of *Lucy*, and, of course, *That Girl*. I would fantasize that maybe I could even be That Girl someday.

Darlene was about the only friend I could let into the house. She understood. Her father was a raging alcoholic, just like mine. Her dad was violent, just like mine. The only difference between her dad and mine was that hers took a gun and shot himself in the head. What kind of person does *that* to his family?

Life is strange.

All my life I believed my anxiety and panic attacks had come from the fact that my father was a violent alcoholic. All my life I blamed much of my fear, obsessive thinking, and scary thoughts on life with him. Looking back now, it's clear that a large part of my fears and obsessions stemmed from being molested, and from the fact that I couldn't share what had happened to me with anyone. As a result, I never dealt with it. It was something I just pushed out of my head, or tried to, for years. And yes, lapses of memory—what I called "blackout time"—are very common among children who have been abused.

I focused instead on being the adult child of an alcoholic to distract myself from the unbearable, unthinkable, disgusting, horrific, dirty, anti-God, sinning, going-to-hell behavior that is sexual abuse to a young child. Except that, as a child, and even well into adulthood, I never thought of it as abuse. Instead it was something that I let happen, something that I blamed myself for participating in. Something I would be punished for by God.

Guilt. Blame. Anger. Shame. I carried that awful weight alone. I never talked about it. Never confronted my abuser. Never told my husband. Never told my children—until now.

All my life this was a secret I chose to keep, but harboring that dirty little secret created torture and torment and grief and issues that, had I been able to talk about it sooner, might have been avoided. And that's why I am sharing it now. Maybe you or someone you know is a victim.

How old was I when I finally understood that I was a victim? Fifty-five. Secrets suck.

What follows is the poem I wrote to the perpetrator when I was about fourteen years old:

Poem to Molester

It's you I blame for feeling sad and these things I can't explain,
And all my times of doing bad.
I'd like to get away from you, you make me see things dark and gray,
You make me hate to smile, you seem to chase the sun away.
You make me hate the things I do.
If only you weren't so unreal, if you only knew the way I feel,
Your skin, your hair, your smile, so fake, so dead.
You lie and lie and talk and talk, and nothing's really said.
I know I cannot get away; I'll stay and do my best to play along,
As if nothing ever happened, but we both know that is wrong.
My head aches at the thought of you. Everything is ruined at the thought
Of things you still might do.

You won't let me go now, but soon I'll leave and I'll show you how a real
person lives.
And when I finally get away, I know you'll worry about what I say.
But I won't tell cause I'm afraid.
Afraid of you and what you'll do.
But when I run and when I smile and finally feel right,
You won't be there to bring me down, to turn my smile to constant frown.
Be as mean as you can be, do all you can to threaten me.
I won't care because you see, someday, I'll make you crawl.

CHAPTER 4

Covered in Blood
and
Never Been Happier

"AND NOW I'D LIKE TO introduce our winner, Cindy Redick."

Well, this was a first. Everyone was applauding. Redicks never won anything, mostly because we never entered anything. A few months earlier, Mom had come home from RCA with coloring books. Her company was sponsoring a coloring contest, and it was her fantasy that I might win it. First prize was a new bicycle. I thought the coloring book was boring . . . what did I know about playing by the rules? I started adding to the pictures on the pages—creating mountains and birds where there weren't any—and colored those, too. I guess you could say I "colored outside the lines." What the hell—why not? I knew I wouldn't win anyway. After all, we weren't winners. I gave the coloring book back to my mother and forgot about it. But then, on a hot afternoon, with the stench of rubber from Cooper Tire hanging in the air, she came bolting through the front door, calling my name.

"Cindy!" Mom said, so excited she couldn't contain herself. "Cindy, you did it! You won the coloring contest!" It was as if she were telling me I got into a great college or something. "You won!" She stood back to watch my reaction. "You get a brand-new bicycle!"

I won? Me? No, that couldn't be right. Someone made a mistake. I wasn't any good at anything, certainly not coloring. And I specifically remembered coloring outside the lines. There was a life lesson in there for me, but of course I didn't see it until I got older. I still don't do well staying inside the lines, doing things by the book, or taking the path most chosen, doing what people "expect" me to do—at all. Truthfully, most of the things that have worked out best for me in my life, things that have brought me the most success, and yes, happiness, have been situations when I didn't stay within the lines.

A few weeks later, there I stood at an RCA awards luncheon, receiving my prize. It was a bicycle—and not just any bicycle—it was the most beautiful red bicycle I had ever seen. It was new and shiny and it wasn't a hand-me-down. It was the first thing I ever had that was mine, and mine before it was somebody else's.

It changed my life.

First, for the first time in my life, I felt like a "Somebody," not just dead-end trash. I won. I must have some type of talent; someone might see it someday. Maybe even I'll believe I have it.

Second, it was freedom—a way for me to escape from the dead-end street. That bicycle was my ticket to independence, a way to get away, pure and simple.

In the summers, I went and grabbed Darlene, and she'd jump on her sister's bike, and off we'd go. Destination: Riverside Park to hang out at the pool and listen to Stevie Wonder: *"My cherie amour, lovely as a summer day."* I had inherited my sister's old two-piece bathing suit; it was a worn-out light pink with little flowers, waist high and droopy on top. It was saggy on me—not only because I was stick thin but because the elastic was tired and stretched out. I stuffed toilet paper into the bra, since my boobs were nowhere on the horizon. I was in junior high so I was wearing a training bra, but there was nothing to train.

And I was afraid there never would be. No boobs. No period. Puberty was just not showing up for me, and I secretly knew why. I was certain that this was going to be God's punishment for being a *bad* girl, for the sin of having been molested and having participated.

Adolescence can be a particularly cruel time, and starting your period was a rite of passage that separated the teenagers from little girls. Everybody, even the boys, knew who had started and who had not. In gym class, when you had your period you could sit out. All the popular girls from Marathon Oil families would sit there on the bleachers, giggling into their ponytails about "that time of the month."

Not me. I never got to miss a gym class. My twelfth and thirteenth birthdays went by. Nothing. It seemed like everyone else had started but me.

When I went shopping with my mother at Kmart, we'd push the cart past the Kotex aisle and I'd wonder whether there would ever be a time when we'd need to buy them for me. I wanted to experience what one of those pads felt like between my legs. Even so, I was afraid to talk to her about it, because I figured I'd done this to myself. I was even kind of hoping she didn't notice. I'd been bad, and I didn't work right because of what I'd done. My female plumbing was broken, and it could never be fixed. God would see to that.

Then it happened. One night I slept over at Darlene's. When I woke up, I felt an unfamiliar stickiness between my legs. I reached down to see what was going on. My fingers came up red.

"*Dar-leeeeeeen!*" I yelled, waving my bloody fingers in the air. "What do I do?"

I hadn't started with a trickle but with a gush, as if a dam had broken. I was covered in blood and had never been happier.

"Finally!" she exclaimed. "It's about time. I'll get you a Kotex."

It was bulky and uncomfortable, but I wore it like the badge of honor that it was. Finally, I was a member of the club. It was a huge relief, a sign from the heavens that I wasn't doomed, that I was "normal."

Normal at least in that way. . . . And life, well, things seemed to be looking up a bit.

In 1969, Donna came home with big news. Bob the Motorcycle Man had proposed. My big sister was getting married. This was a huge deal—

she was marrying up, as they put it. Bob Wittenmyer was a high-class guy from the better part of town, a college graduate. The surprise wasn't that they were getting married, because they'd been dating for a while. The kicker was that she was not going to let her father give her away. Donna didn't even want him at the wedding.

She hated him, but she had her reasons. As Dad's drinking spiraled out of control, so did his infidelity. Unfortunately, Donna got a front-row seat.

When he didn't come home nights, Mom went out looking for him. She didn't want to go by herself, so she took Donna along with her. She dragged Donna into the houses of other women that Daddy was sleeping with, in effect rubbing her nose in her father's adultery. More than once, Donna had walked in on Dad while he was in bed with another woman.

They weren't sleeping.

She saw it all— not something any daughter should see—but that's the kind of thing that just gets burned into your brain. When you're engaged and about to commit your life to your fiancé "till death do you part," the graphic image of your father in the physical act of breaking that vow is tough to get over . . . or forgive.

The week before the ceremony, she and Mom were still fighting about it. "I hate him! He's not walking me down the aisle. He's not invited. I can't stand the sight of him. I've seen much too much of him already." Donna was standing in that tiny, gross bathroom, the only one in the house. It was hot, which made the smell of pee almost nauseating.

"He is your father. He is a good person. It's only when he drinks. . . ." Mom was defending him, or trying to, so that we could create the illusion that we were a normal family, at least for the wedding. She was attempting to shout, but she was no louder when she was shouting at Donna than she was when she was shouting at Dad.

Donna held her ground. "I hate him," she said with disgust. "I don't want him there. I'm ashamed of him. You know as well as I do *why* I'm ashamed of him. I don't want him shitfaced in front of Bob's family, and I don't want him anywhere near my wedding. I'm sorry that he's your husband. I'm even sorrier that he's my father."

A few weeks later, they were married. It was, like all of our family weddings, a simple ceremony in our church, with a reception in the basement. No food, no alcohol, no dancing. In fact, I didn't even know those types of elaborate weddings existed until I was much, much older. I was in the wedding—with *That Girl* hair, dark brown with bangs and a big flip at the end. Dad was not there. He was at the local bar down the street—probably his preference, actually.

Not long after they got married, Bob got a great job with Lockheed, and he and Donna moved to Sunnyvale, California, just south of San Francisco. Once they settled in, Donna bought Mom and me plane tickets to come visit. I was so excited to make the trip. I had never been on an airplane before, probably because I'd never been anywhere that was far enough away from Findlay that you'd have to fly to get there. Back then, flying wasn't as common as it is now. Only "people with money" enjoyed the luxury of flying.

Donna picked us up at the airport. She drove us around for a little while; I saw the Pacific for the first time and the Golden Gate Bridge, but neither of those attractions compared to seeing their beautiful little brand-new home. Donna pulled into the driveway of this tidy tract house in a planned community. No railroad tracks in sight. We got out of the car and went up the little walkway to the front door. It had an inset stained-glass window panel.

"I'm so glad you're here," Donna said as she threw her arms around us. "Please take off your shoes."

The idea was to keep from getting dirt from our shoes onto the carpeting. At home in Ohio, it was the other way around. We left our shoes on to keep anything in that filthy rug from getting on our feet.

When I stepped inside, I stepped into another world, a world that was clean and bright, a world where everything was new. The carpet was beige and plush—so plush that my footprints followed me and remained imprinted in the pile as I walked across the room. But then I saw it . . . I made a beeline for something I'd never seen before.

"Donna, what is this?"

"That's our sofa."

"It looks like leather."

"It is."

It was pale and buttery and soft, and it was a thrill just to run my hands over it. I flashed back to being a little kid in the A&P, running my hands over foods I could not have.

In that moment, the door of possibility cracked open just a little. "Gee," I thought to myself, "maybe Redicks *are* capable of having nice things."

Then Donna brought us into her gleaming kitchen, which was equipped with the latest appliances. I'm sure Mom was envious, but she tried not to show it. "How much do you pay in rent?" she asked.

"We're not renting, Mom," Donna replied with a certain amount of pride. "We bought it. We have a mortgage, but this is our house."

I'll never forget the smell of the California night air, and sitting out on their small patio, gazing up at the stars, dreaming of all the possibilities.

Donna drove us around sightseeing—Fisherman's Wharf, Sausalito, cable cars, all the great tourist spots. When she took us into Haight-Ashbury, I couldn't believe my eyes. There were no flower children in Findlay, Ohio, and the idea that not every place was like home hit me like a ton of bricks. This was 1969, and the Haight was all peace, love, feathers, incense, music, and hippies. Everyone had long hair, both men and women. Everyone had headbands on and beads. The opening lines from Scott McKenzie's song: *If you're going to San Francisco, be sure to wear some flowers in your hair*" blared out from the radio. It was the song of the times. I was in awe. I felt a little like Dorothy in Oz, except I wasn't all that anxious to go home—I liked what I was seeing. Donna bought me a pair of bell-bottom jeans, which were all the rage at the time. I think I was the first kid in Findlay to have a pair.

The trip to the West Coast changed my life and my perception of the possibilities of it. When I went back home, I was a different person. I was full of dreams of a bigger, better life. One thing was for sure: if I was going to have it, I would have to earn it myself. I wasn't really old enough to be working but I got a job at the Red Barn, flipping hamburgers. The pay wasn't much, but I had some money in my pocket and it was all mine. For some kids, working in a burger joint is a dead-end job, but never once did I think I was going to be stuck there.

My sister and her buttery sofa gave me an incredible gift—the gift of possibility thinking. For the first time, I had a real vision of what a better life looked like—and someone in my own family was actually living it. Donna had left the dead-end street behind forever. And because she'd done it on her own, I understood that making that vision happen was entirely up to me. My future was in my own hands. From that point on, I knew I was going to be a Somebody.

CHAPTER 5

On the Run

GOOD-BYE, TRAINING BRAS. After the arrival of my period, my boobs were not far behind. I used to run around the neighborhood with my new friend Carly, hanging our old training bras on doorknobs of boys we had crushes on, ringing the bell and running away. Carly and I became friends in junior high. We went to the same school, even though we lived in different parts of town. Glenwood Junior High was kind of in the middle. I walked; she got dropped off. Considering we came from different sides of the tracks, we got along really well. We filled in each other's empty spaces—the rocks in her head fit the holes in mine. She lived in the nice end of town, in a perfect house with a perfect family. Her dad worked at Marathon Oil, and her mother was the perfect, pretty mother. I was moving up in the world.

Turned out my vision of her "perfect" family was a little off—her dad was an alcoholic, just like mine—only hers was "functional," and only drank at night. How do children of alcoholics always manage to find each other? Is there some sort of Drunk Radar, a homing device that helps us zero in on the only other people who can really understand what we go through every day? Even though Carly knew all about my dad, through all our years of being best friends she never mentioned her own father's drinking to me until we were adults. Her family was into keeping up appearances—and they were masters at it.

My family had no appearances to keep up, especially not these days. Mom and Dad had split up, again. I remember exactly when it happened. It was a warm spring day. The grass was a dark, rich green, and my brother Mike was out behind the old push mower. The smell of freshly cut grass was in the air. I was fantasizing about Nick, a new boy I had met, as I was doing my Saturday chores: cleaning my room, dusting our rotten old furniture, and taking out the trash. I thought, foolishly, that things were temporarily safe. That Dad was somewhat stable. As the child of an alcoholic, I probably should have known better by then.

Dad started off his morning with several bottles of Rolling Rock, a few bites of smelly cheese, and a Valium. Typical. What wasn't typical was that Mom had already started crying. I knew it was much too early for that—usually the family melodrama didn't get going till after dark. She wandered out into the kitchen and started in on Dad. "Martha called me this morning. She saw you out last night with . . . with *her*. I told you to stay away from her. I am done with you and your womanizing. Get out!"

Bad timing.

"What the fuck are you talking about? With who?" Dad said with a sneer. He was trying to bluster his way out of it.

No dice.

"Teresa, that whore you have been sleeping with. Ikey, how could you do this to me and the kids?" Mom's voice was trembling, just like the rest of her, and the tears were really flowing. I don't know which was shaking more, her or her voice. "I can't do this anymore. I work so hard and you come home drunk, if you come home at all. I thought things were gonna be different here."

"It's all your fault, goddammit! You drive me away. You and your fucking perfect ways. You are such a fuckin' perfect goddamn angel, aren't you? You wonder why I sleep with other women? Because you don't know how to fuck. All you know how to do is put me down."

I winced. *That* was cruel, and not easy for me to hear. I remember hiding on the stairs, wishing she would smack the shit out of him. Instead, there were just more tears.

"I hate you," she said finally, between sobs. "I only put up with you for the kids!"

Right.

"I hate you too, you stupid bitch. You make me sick. I'm outta here."

With that he grabbed his keys to the latest Brougham LTD, the new dark green one borrowed like the others from the used-car lot, and swaggered out of the house, slamming the screen door so hard it broke in half.

That was the last we saw of him for a few months.

Good riddance?

Not exactly.

I should have been glad he was gone . . . but I wasn't. I hated him so much, but I missed him more. That's dysfunctional, but every child of an alcoholic knows the feeling. I hated that our house felt empty without him. I hated his easy chair sitting there, with no one in it. I missed his television shows, Art Linkletter, Jackie Gleason, and *The Ed Sullivan Show*. No one seemed to put them on now that he was gone. I missed the smell of his Swiss steak on Sunday and the smell of his cigarette wafting in from the front porch.

And most of all, I *hated* my mother's crying every night. If she hated him so much, why was she crying?

But then, why was I? Just his smell and his toxic personality were enough to make me cringe, but Dad being gone made me feel sad, confused, and angry at the same time. And of course, no one really talked about it.

Even though she had kicked him out, Mom spent a whole lot of time fretting and worrying about him. In spite of everything, she still clung to whatever was left of the grand romance that started their relationship. This pathetic wishful thinking was a bizarre fantasy—like somehow Dad was going to magically turn back into the man she fell in love with in high school.

Not gonna happen.

More than ever, my father was the town scandal, both as a disgusting drunk and as a man hanging out and now living openly with some bimbo who was not his wife. Maybe he loved her. But I doubted it. He had only one love, and it came in a bottle. *She* was the one he really couldn't live without.

It was just as well that he wasn't around to meet Nick, who by now had become my first boyfriend. Nick was a year older than me, which made him all of sixteen, and he was adorable. He had dark, thick curls and beautiful green eyes that sparkled when he smiled. I thought he kind of looked like an elf. We'd met at the local roller rink. He smoked, sometimes two cigarettes at the same time—I was young enough to think that was cool. He'd walk me home from school, but the most fun we had was at night in the summer, when I slept out in the side yard. My brother David had left behind an old tent that I pitched in the yard on warm nights. Outside, there was no getting away from the smell of Cooper Tire, but, pungent as it was, it was still better than the suffocating, lingering smell of pee inside the house. Nick used to sneak over and tiptoe into the tent. We got out flashlights and read magazines about faraway places under the holey sleeping bag. We'd make out a bit, but it was entirely innocent. Although I thought of myself as daring, I was extremely conservative sexually. I wouldn't let Nick "touch" me, which frustrated him as a horny teenager.

I've always had an edgy, fun side, and Nick appealed to my adventurous spirit. That worked for a while to keep me distracted and in denial about what was going on at home, but more than anything, the adventure I really wanted was to run away from my dead-end life in that dead-end house. And now, a fatherless family.

There was only so far that red bike could take me, and I was feeling like I wanted to run, to explore, to get a bit rowdy. I must have inherited this from my father, because it certainly wasn't a personality attribute I ever saw in Mom.

I needed to go find adventure, a feeling that has stuck with me my whole life. One summer night I was spending the night at my friend Tina's. I needed an accomplice, so I thought I'd give her a shot. "Whaddaya say we go to Florida?"

Tina was quiet, sweet, and well behaved, kind of like my mother. "Are you nuts?" she replied. "Besides, I thought you wanted to go back to California."

"I want to go lots of places," I said. "California's too far to hitchhike, but we could hitchhike to Florida in a couple of days."

"Hitchhike! Are you crazy? We'd get raped or killed!"

"Come on. Let's do it. It has an ocean. Tina, you gotta see the ocean. We'll hitchhike, then get a room. I have some money saved." She looked at me with a grin. We both giggled, and started plotting.

It was easier than we thought. We pulled off the double switcheroo, but on a grand scale. I told my mother that I was going with Tina to visit her grandmother in Lexington, Kentucky. Tina told her mom the same thing in reverse. We recruited a friend who had an "older" voice to play the part of the mother on the phone. She called each one, pretending to be the other. Our moms worked full time, had lots of kids, and had very little energy. They just went along with the plan, probably grateful that someone was taking one of us away for a while. One less kid to deal with. And times were simpler then. There were no cell phones or computers to call or send e-mails to confirm things. They simply believed everything we told them, and then fell for the fake calls.

Score.

It was a cool summer morning, and my mother left for work, believing that Tina's mom would be picking me up shortly for our drive to Lexington. Tina's mom dropped her off at my house on her way to work, thinking my mom was off getting gas and would be back any minute. The two of us quickly repacked our clothes into backpacks and jammed the old suitcases in with the dust and broken stuff under my bed.

We walked to I-75 and stuck out our thumbs, headed south. Tina was scared to death that we would be raped or killed by strangers. Stuff like that didn't happen in those days, or so I thought. Within fifteen minutes, a nice, middle-aged man in a nice, new car stopped.

"How old are you girls?" he asked.

Tina and I answered in unison, but we had a slight miscommunication. "Fifteen," she said.

"Eighteen," I said, at exactly the same time.

The driver looked at us closely. It was obvious which of us was telling the truth. "My name is Paul, and I have a daughter your age. You're lucky I'm the one who stopped for you," he said. "Don't you realize how dangerous it is to be hitchhiking?"

"Honestly," I told him, "it couldn't be any worse than what I just left."
I was nothing if not ornery, but I looked him straight in the eye as I said it,
so I think he knew I was telling the truth.

"Where are you going?'

"We're going to Florida, to see the ocean," Tina said.

"You're in luck. I'm headed to Fort Lauderdale for a golf tournament.
Hop in."

For doing something foolish, it turned out way better than we could
have hoped. Paul was a great guy. We told him our story, and he didn't
complain when I told him we had to stop in Lexington, Kentucky, which
was a bit out of the way. Paul even got us our own room at the Holiday
Inn—*and* he even paid for it! I wrote my mother a letter from "Tina's
grandmother's house," then made sure it had a Lexington postmark. Paul
took us all the way to Fort Lauderdale. When he dropped us off, he wrote
down his phone number. "Here's the hotel where I'm staying. Promise
you'll call me if you get into any trouble."

Tina and I thanked him and took off for the unknown. Our first destination? The ocean. The Atlantic Ocean was the most beautiful thing I
had ever seen. The sand was white and powdery and there was a strong,
warm smell of salt in the air; very different from the ocean or beaches of
California. We dropped our backpacks on the sand and went running into
the warm soothing water, kicking and laughing. I will never forget the
feeling of excitement and freedom of that moment.

We stayed in the dumpiest hotels. The cockroaches were the size of
lizards, but we were having so much fun we hardly noticed. We didn't have
much money, so we'd eat a doughnut for breakfast and lunch. Maybe if we
splurged we'd split a McDonald's cheeseburger for dinner. At night, we hit
the beach bars.

This was my first introduction to the three Ds: Denial, Distraction,
and Dancing. It worked. We met some amazing guys, including one Hamilton John Trent III. I'd never met anyone before whose last name could
be his first name, and vice versa, let alone anyone with a numeral after his
name! He was three years older than me and had long hair and an attitude. He was from New York City. I was enamored. He would walk with

me on the beach, holding my hand, telling me stories of the big city. He loved music and would recite words to songs by the Doors and the Rolling Stones. I was gone for him. Head over heels. Tina met a guy too, and we ended up hanging out with them most of the week.

After a week of eating cheap food, lying in the sun, and enjoying the guys, it was time to go home. We were almost out of money, but we were completely out of Coppertone. As we started packing up in the morning, Tina looked in the mirror and screamed. Her total face was beet red. Everything that wasn't red was already peeling.

"No way I'm hitchhiking with this face," she announced. With that thought in mind, we dug into our wallets. Pooling our resources, we scraped together just enough money for two bus tickets back to Findlay. Naturally, everyone else on that twenty-four-hour bus ride had brought plenty of food, but we were too proud to beg. When we got home, my mother wondered why we were so ravenous, but we chowed down and made up stories about Tina's grandmother and our trip to . . . Lexington.

That trip to Florida was the beginning of a new way of living and thinking for me. It was also the start of a very adventurous time in my life. I began making fake IDs for myself and another friend, Terri. We started hitchhiking to Bowling Green, Ohio, about a half hour up I-75 on the way to Toledo, to go dancing at college bars. It's a great college town, and the students from Bowling Green State University kept the bars in business.

Terri was much more adventurous and gutsy than Tina. I never would have done it by myself, but give me a wingwoman and I'm off to have a good time. True then. True now. And we did have great times—those were the days of live bands, platform shoes, cuffed straight-leg jeans, Boone's Farm, and 3.2 beer. Besides, after Hamilton Trent III, I had developed a thing for older guys and Rolling Stones music, both of which were to be found aplenty in the college bars of Bowling Green.

Terri and I never had any trouble getting in. We handed over our IDs with the dates changed to look like we were eighteen, even though we were just fifteen at the time. We did a crappy job of forging the changes with eyeliner. Back then, nobody looked too carefully, or if they did, they didn't care. I wasn't much into drinking but I loved dancing, and we danced all night with "the better sort of college man."

For me, the trips to Bowling Green were yet another manifestation of the three Ds. Dancing was a distraction mechanism, a way of denying how bad things really were. When I went dancing, I lost myself in the music and the movement. I was stepping into a fantasy life, anything to escape from the reality at home. I wouldn't have thought it was possible, but things had gotten worse. Mom had caved—again—and let Dad move back in. Dad, of course, was drinking more than ever.

And all too soon, there was a fourth D: Drugs. Not me, my brother Michael. I found out about it quite by accident. Mike had an old baby-blue Rambler that he was selling. It was parked out back on the gravel driveway. After he listed it in the local paper, someone came by to look at it on a hot summer day. Mike wasn't home, so I took the eager teenage boy back to see the car. He walked around the outside, kicked the tires, looked under the hood, and decided to take a look inside. He opened the driver's side door and lifted up the floor mat.

To his surprise—and mine—we saw a huge assortment of drugs under the mat. There were pills, pot, papers, white powder in bags, and things I couldn't even describe. In a rush I realized that Mike, who now had long hair, played in a rock band, and was never ever home, was into things that Mom probably didn't know about it. "Does this come with the car?" the guy asked with a chuckle.

"You'll have to talk to my brother," I replied as I quickly covered the stash back up with the floor mat. "I don't even know what that is."

As he drove away, I was panicked. I was scared that the police would come and take Mike away, take *me* away! Should I tell Mom? I certainly couldn't tell Dad. Should I tell Mike? I decided to pretend it didn't happen, and within a few weeks the car was sold.

No surprise.

CHAPTER 6

Good-bye, White Trash;
Hello, White Camaro

SCHOOL WAS OUT AND it was a warm summer night. Everyone was cruising up and down Main Street in Findlay, Ohio—everyone with a car, at least. Darlene and I were cruising with our feet, because Main Street was walking distance from home and besides, we weren't old enough to drive quite yet. The guys parked their cars and sat on the hoods, trying to be cool, smoking cigarettes, and blaring their car stereos. Led Zeppelin, the Stones, and the Doobie Brothers filled the air: *"Without love, where you would be now?"*

Main Street in Findlay was where it was at back then. Times were simple and people were, too. You simply . . . cruised. Up and down, around a few back streets by the old library, and then back up and down the main drag. Everyone knew everyone, pretty much—unless you had come in from "out of town."

That makes it sound much farther away than it was. I'm talking McComb or Van Buren, little towns close by that were even quieter than Findlay. Findlay was the "big" town of small towns, so it was the place to cruise, and often enough a new guy with an old, cool Chevy or an Oldsmobile full of crazy, giggly girls would come speeding into town on Friday night.

Eventually, later in the evening, everyone piled into Wilson's for cheeseburgers and malts. Wilson's is still there and is still my favorite hamburger joint. They made the best, real, old-fashioned "square" hamburgers, and some people believe Wendy's stole Wilson's recipe.

No contest. To this day, those salty, greasy, hand-cooked, loaded-up burgers are the most satisfying cheeseburgers I've ever had.

Wilson's is a small place on a corner with big glass windows. On Friday nights it was common to see the windows covered with colorful hand-painted banners supporting the local football team, full on with amateur pictures and exclamation points. GO, TROJANS!

It was a classic summer scene from small-town middle America. I loved it, but at the same time, in the back of my head, I knew that whatever was going on in San Francisco or Fort Lauderdale had to be a lot more exciting than Findlay on Friday night.

Darlene and I were right in front of Wilson's when I stopped and bent over to tie my shoe. When I stood up, five "older" guys wanting to know our names surrounded us. They were not locals. Turns out they were new in town and in their first year at some college a few towns away.

To me that was a good thing. After all my hitchhiking trips to Bowling Green to go dancing with the college guys in the college bars, I was spoiled. I found boys my own age boring by this point.

"Aw, c'mon, girls. Don't keep us in suspense. You got names, don't ya?"

I stood back and watched as Darlene giggled. She wasn't familiar with college guy bullshit, and acted very immature. It was funny and embarrassing at the same time. Now I knew why I didn't take her with me on my hitchhiking excursions to Bowling Green: she couldn't handle it. In fact, she didn't even know I did it. She would have shit her pants.

I didn't say anything as I watched her squirm. Clearly she was uncomfortable with older boys. After a few minutes with Darlene and her giggling, they started to walk away—all except one, who separated himself from the pack. He walked up to me with his hands in his pockets, eyes cast down. His hair was long and shaggy. He was cute.

"Hi. My name is Steve. What did you say your name was?" he asked me.

He had long brown hair and beautiful brown eyes. I was really taken by his look and his soft approach. He was adorable, older, and there was just something about him.

"I didn't," I responded, knowing how to play the game.

"Are you from around here?" he asked.

"Yeah. My family lives on Central Avenue, a few blocks away."

"Where's that?"

I explained where I lived, and that we were at the end of the street. Just enough information to let him know I was interested, but little enough to keep him curious.

At that moment, his friends teased him and pulled him away.

My heart was pounding. He was adorable. Oh my God. I was in love. Who was he?

Would I see him again? I wanted to run after him, screaming, "Come back! Kiss me, hold me, save me!" Could he be my dream guy? He was all I could think about.

And that was that, until one evening I was home watching TV in our ratty living room. The screen door was open to the warm night air, and I saw an old, beat-up Mustang come cruising down our dead-end street. Slowly it turned into our old gravel driveway. I stood up and peeked out the front-door screen. To my amazement, Steve was at the wheel.

I snuck out the front door.

He got out, stood beside the car, looked at me with the most beautiful smile, and handed me some simple flowers. "I found you," he said.

I was hooked. He melted me.

We started dating. He was tall, thin, and very good looking, and although he seemed a bit shy, he was also confident. I loved hanging out with him. It made me feel important. He took me to the local college bars. Steve drank beer and bought me my drink of choice, Boone's Farm Strawberry Hill. We had a great time.

When school started back up in the fall, I enrolled in the DECA work-study program. I didn't bother with college prep courses. After all, no Redick had ever gone to college. DECA was for kids who were on the work track, not the college track. While most of my friends were taking academic classes—English, history, biology, maybe a foreign language or two, I was taking "practical" courses like typing, marketing, and accounting—courses that would equip me to get a job in the "real world" right after high school graduation. I hated them. "Why am I doing this?" I thought to myself. "I am never going to be a secretary or an accountant! What a waste of my time." Who would have known I would end up as a writer and business owner, specializing in marketing.

Life.

High school classes took up my morning, but at lunchtime I headed for my "real world," which at this point consisted of working two jobs. In the afternoon I worked at an ad agency as a keyline artist, setting up graphics and illustrations. When I got off at four o'clock, I ran home, changed my clothes, and headed off to my second job. I had a coveted waitressing job at Bill Knapp's, one of the most prestigious restaurants in the area, and the fact that I was working there already made me a Somebody, at least in Findlay.

Working at Bill Knapp's had almost as much prestige as working at Marathon Oil. We Redicks never ate there, of course, but it was where all the "proper" families went after church or for a special occasion. The only time I got to taste the food was on break, or if I snuck a quick taste of one of their famous six-inch chocolate Celebration Cakes.

The restaurant put all of its new hires through a rigorous training program to make sure the waitstaff met their standards for cheerful, efficient service. I started there as soon as I turned sixteen; I was so proud when I put on my little yellow uniform—with matching hat—for the first time. And I was a great waitress, so the money was great, even though the restaurant didn't serve any alcohol. By being willing to smile and carry five plates up my arm, I was taking home $500 a week. I quickly saved enough money to buy myself a beautiful, almost-new white Camaro.

I floated into the school parking lot in style every morning. I looked good when I got out of the car, too. With the extra money I was making, I started buying my clothes at Paul Harris, a store in the local mall that catered to the daughters of Marathon Oil. Those Goodwill hand-me-downs were banished from my closet forever. Once I left the house in the morning I looked like I came from money, not like white trash from the wrong side of the tracks.

I left the house every morning as early as I could. Like my sister before me, I tried to spend as little time there as possible. Now that Dad was back, home was more of a nightmare than ever. And he was getting meaner and drinking even more.

Only a fool (or my mother) would have expected anything to be different with him—different as in better—once he came home. It was right before the holidays. Mom wanted him with us to play Santa Claus and pass out the presents on Christmas morning, just like he used to. For Mom, however, I think it was something more. She struggled to maintain whatever was left of her own little fantasy world, trying to keep up the pretense that we'd somehow always been this happy, complete family with warm holiday traditions. In essence she was inventing a rosy past that never was. I'm not sure whom she was trying to fool—us or herself.

For his part, I think Dad was happy to be back, not because of what he was coming home to but because of what he was running away from. There was a rumor flying around that Teresa, the woman he'd been living with—and supposedly a relative of some famous country singer— had come down with some sort of major female disease, like ovarian cancer or something, and he just couldn't or wouldn't deal with it. The bottom line was that he was just incapable of doing that. He was much too dependent on his Rolling Rock and his Valium to be supportive of anyone with a serious illness. On the contrary, he was now so into his own substance abuse that he himself needed support; there was no way he could be there for someone else. If it had been Mom who got sick, I am sure he would have still run the other way, away from her and back to Teresa.

The school year flew by; suddenly I was seventeen. I was still working two jobs, but on summer weekends I got into my Camaro and headed up to Bushy Quarry to swim and lie in the sun. The quarry was everyone's favorite daytime hangout; it was like a magnet, attracting teenagers from

Findlay to Toledo. In the parking lot, someone always had a van blasting music out the back. We'd float around on rafts, working on our tans and dreaming of being Somebody someday.

By this time, my adolescent angular gawkiness was gone. I was slender but no longer scrawny. I had curves in the right places. One day I was floating on one of the rafts at Bushy Quarry in my favorite bikini, and I was vaguely aware that there was someone taking pictures.

I didn't think anything of it until the next evening, when I got home from work and saw the *Republican-Courier* newspaper (now called the *Courier*) lying on the kitchen table. My picture was on the front page of the Lifestyles section. The caption read something like, "Cindy Redick, young beauty, out enjoying the day at Bushy Quarry."

I was blown away. "I can't believe it! They took my picture! Dad, look! I'm on the *front page!*" *I was a Somebody!* Just a year had passed since I was cruising Main Street on foot with Darlene. Now I was driving a white Camaro and my picture was in the paper.

One glance at my father was enough to kill my happiness. "Big deal," he said between swigs of Rolling Rock. "It could have been anybody. You just happened to be there at the right time." He threw the paper aside and went back to guzzling his beer.

My mother, my biggest fan, had the opposite reaction. She made a big deal of it, which helped compensate a little for my father's sarcastic response. "Cindy, that's wonderful! See, I told you how special you are! You are so pretty. You just wait. You are going to do something special someday. I just know it."

And then she told me the story.

"You know," she began in somewhat of a whisper, as if taking me back in time to some magical place, "when I was pregnant with your brother David, my mother took me with her to a psychic one day. Now, I've never told any of you kids this. But that psychic sat there and told me I was gonna have a boy, which I did. But here is something else she told me. She said I was gonna have five kids, which I did, and that one of the girls was going to be famous."

True story.

Then she got all emotional and wrapped her little arms around me. "I think it's you," she said through her tears, "I think it's going to be you." I loved my mom when she talked like this. She was the queen of magical thinking.

I'll never forget that moment and the power in her words, and especially in her belief in the magic of the moment—her belief in the magic in me.

It was my first taste of celebrity, and my second taste of success since winning the red bicycle. Little me. I was on the front page. Maybe, just maybe, dreams do come true. Maybe, just maybe, I could dream. Maybe, someday I would be famous or successful or talented. Maybe I could even live by the ocean, or out in California . . . maybe the psychic was right.

ALMOST FAMOUS. It was a little pin that I had purchased a few years before. I kept it on my dresser with secret hopes of making my little dreams my big reality. It was at about this time that I started practicing writing my signature. Looking back, I'm sure my subconscious put me up to it, because instead of writing "Cindy"—the name everyone called me—I practiced writing "Lucinda," my real first name. I wrote it with a large, flowing, powerful *L*. If I was ever going to be a Somebody, I'd have to be able to sign my name with flair. But I was about to find out that the road to becoming that Somebody was long and hard, and a lot more twisted than I ever could have imagined.

CHAPTER 7

Love Gone Wrong

IT WAS SEPTEMBER AND I was a senior at Findlay High, with bigger dreams than the town could hold. I continued in the DECA program, taking "practical" courses in the morning and working two jobs in the afternoon and evening, but I was already looking beyond school to life after graduation.

I dated a few guys off and on, but Steve was becoming my everything: my fantasy of a better life, my fantasy of a better me. He was from a "normal" family from Toledo, Ohio, with money. He was smart, cute, and full of edgy fun. And there was something familiar about him. I was getting to know the real him. As a result of working a summer job and getting money from his parents, he himself was moving up in the world. He bought a hot new Corvette and great new clothes, and was getting quite a reputation around town. He was good looking and kind of rock-star sexy, with that shaggy hair and those big brown eyes. Heads would turn wherever we went. He walked with a swagger and had attitude. He was charismatic, and playful—very much like my father. In fact, in the coming months I was going to find out just how much like my father he really was. When he was good, he was very good. But when he was bad . . .

The longer we dated, the worse he behaved. I began to see that he had a sarcastic and mean-spirited flip side. But, of course, I knew how to pick 'em.

One day we were roaring down a narrow country road in his new 'Vette. He liked to go top speed on country roads, just to see what the car could do. We'd been drinking a few beers—and we were fighting. It was around this time that I had begun to suspect he was going out on me. Steve was a flirt, and I'd been hearing rumors that he was with other girls at my school. I decided to confront him.

Not the time or the place.

As I questioned him about the rumors, he began to drive even faster. I knew these roads like the back of my hand, and I knew he was driving way too fast. "Steve, you should slow down," I said, growing anxious with every slight turn.

His mood turned on a dime. "Who's driving, you or me?" he responded nastily.

"You're scaring me. . . ." My heart stared to pound. Old familiar feelings of "nowhere to run" snuck in from somewhere.

"Look, just take me home," I said, trying to calm him down.

"Just shut the fuck up," he said. "You believe what these idiots are saying about me, Cindy? Why the fuck do you believe these fools? They are just fucking jealous." His face was beet red, and his voice was getting louder and louder. It was quite a transformation. Within moments, he looked over at me with an almost insane look in his eyes. Fearful and anxious, I begged him to slow down. Instead, he hit the gas pedal even harder.

"*Steve, you are scaring me!*" Which was the truth, and this time he *was* doing it on purpose. "STOP!" I screamed. "If you're gonna drive like this, I want to get out!"

"Fine by me."

And with that, he slammed on the brakes, jerked the wheel, and deliberately put the car into a spin. As we were spinning he reached over, threw the passenger door open, and started to shove me out. Hard. Then he stepped on the gas again. It reminded me of a daredevil stunt from some car chase movie.

I no longer thought he was trying to scare me. I thought he was trying to kill me, and I thought for sure I was dead, either in the car or out. I reached for the center column and held on for dear life. *"STEVE! STOP IT!"*

"Get the fuck out . . . like, NOW!"

Hellooooo, Daddy.

Somehow we made it home.

You'd think that this would have been the end of our relationship.

Wrong.

I'd grown up with this kind of Jekyll and Hyde behavior. I was used to it. In fact, in some sick way it was familiar.

Steve didn't talk to me for days. I remember lying upstairs in my little pink bedroom, moaning and crying . . . for him. I tried to blame myself for what happened. Did a pretty good job of it, too. I had these pitiful conversations with myself:

"What did I do? *I overreacted.* He doesn't really love me. *Why should he?* I must have really pissed him off. Now someone else will get him. *You don't deserve him.* I'll die without him. *I'll die with him!*"

I always found a way to look past whatever he'd done that was bad and ugly. I always found a way to make excuses for him, found a way to make it my fault. "It's nothing," I told myself. "He just lost his temper. I shouldn't have brought it up about his being unfaithful. I shouldn't have said what I said. Besides, he loves me."

Then I would go into denial. I'd call a girlfriend and we'd head out dancing. Steve didn't like to dance, and he didn't know I went. If he had, he would have really killed me—he also had a jealous streak.

Denial, Distraction, and Dancing—my three Ds: a way to push away all my fears and problems, at least for a little while, and be in a fantasy world of fun, flirtation, and being beautiful. Ever since I can remember, I've always loved to dance. Still do. So did my mother. While I was in high school getting into bars with a fake ID, it was never about the alcohol. The music and the dancing and the attention were always the big attraction for me.

Enter Good-Time Susan. Susan waitressed with me at Bill Knapp's. Her family had money—her dad had an executive position with, you guessed it . . . Marathon Oil. Susan was a true little party animal— Michelob, music, and marijuana were her party favors of choice, and I loved her. She was beautiful, fun, smart, and liked to live a bit on the edge.

My new wingwoman.

Susan loved getting stoned. Me, I was afraid to get high, but there was a good reason for it—I was already feeling weird enough. I had started having these bizarre sensations, separations from myself. Out of nowhere, I would become spacey, bewildered, disoriented. Who needed pot? Sometimes it seemed like I wasn't in my body at all. This was a feeling I later came to know as dissociation disorder, a common symptom of anxiety that has no real cure. You simply feel "out of it" and disconnected. It can be mild or severe. It can come and go, but it can last for what seems like forever. I hated the feeling. To this day, if I am in an extremely stressful situation, I still get that symptom.

The first time it happened, I'd gone out with three girlfriends on a Friday night. We went to Big Boy for some vegetable soup, then, as was typical in a small town in Ohio with nothing to do, we started driving around on country roads drinking a few beers. I'd probably had all of two beers when I got that eerie feeling that I wasn't really there. I was there and not there at the same time. I felt like I was watching myself, looking down on what I was doing like some kind of airborne spectator, and it freaked me out.

"Uh-oh. This is it," I told myself. "This is the beginning. I always knew I would lose my mind. And now it's starting. I'm going insane." I was scared, but I couldn't tell anyone. After all, they would think I was crazy and put me away.

Of all my fears, my number-one fear was always the fear of going crazy. What made it worse was my mother's voice in the back of my mind, assuring me over and over that thinking would make it so. I couldn't shake the memory of her telling me, "If you think you're going to go crazy, then that's what you'll do." And as frightened as I was of how I was feeling, I was even more scared to tell anybody about it. Why? Because I was afraid they'd lock me up in that old building in Toledo. Forever. In my head I kept seeing the image of my face looking out from behind the barred windows of that gloomy insane asylum, where it would be my destiny to stay till I died.

Good-Time Susan knew none of this, of course. The idea that I was going nuts was another dirty little secret that I could not share with anyone. My friendship with Susan was based on music and adventure. It was Susan who introduced me to the next phase of rock 'n' roll—innovative, out-there, and even a little bizarre—Queen, and David Bowie in his "Ziggy Stardust" incarnation. I loved it.

Sometimes, after she'd smoke a joint or a bowl, Susan and I would sit on her floor and listen to Bowie—couldn't get enough Bowie. She'd be rocking back and forth, eyes glazed over, really into the music. With the help of marijuana, she seemed to be having an out-of-body experience. I was having these experiences all by myself, "naturally," and they scared the shit out of me because I couldn't control them. They showed up uninvited and left when they felt like it.

Susan was my wingwoman on more than a few long-distance adventures. To slip out, we used the time-honored technique of lying to our mothers, saying we were staying at each other's houses. Sorry to say, but by this time I'd gotten really good at it. Either that, or my mother had decided she really didn't want to know. She was in denial about so much of the rest of her life, why not about me as well?

Once our alibis were in place, Susan and I set off. She had a brand-new car, and the two of us would head out of Findlay—*Rrrrroad Trrrip!*—for Cincinnati, or Detroit, or anywhere there was music and fun to be had. One night we went to Detroit for a David Bowie concert—about two hours up I-75—stayed till late, and then drove home. We pulled into a local church parking lot, barely before dawn, slept a little in the car, and then returned to our respective houses. No one had a clue.

In twelfth grade, I drove up to Ann Arbor on a rainy Saturday and became taken with how beautiful the University of Michigan campus was. Going there became my fantasy all through senior year. No Redick had ever gone to college—why couldn't I be the first? After graduating from Findlay High School, I moved to Ann Arbor, thinking I could eventually enroll, but I found out you had to live there for a year to establish residency. Without being a Michigan resident, college tuition was out of reach.

The ad agency where I'd been working as a keyline artist suggested

I give modeling school a try. My mom gave me $500 to enroll in the John Robert Powers modeling school in Detroit. There was another Bill Knapp's restaurant nearby, so I could make some money while John Robert Powers was teaching me to walk with a book balanced on my head. I got an apartment in Ann Arbor, which was close to Detroit, with a girl who was a science major at University of Michigan, and started living my life. For the first time, I was entirely on my own.

One night I was planning to drive back to Findlay to visit Steve, but I stopped at a local party before heading to his place. I ate a bite of a cheeseburger and a couple of brownies and left. It had started snowing, and I had the Doobie Brothers on the eight-track: *"Old black water, keep on rollin'; Mississippi moon, won't you keep on shinin' on me."*

Lost in the music, I started singing along. I was aware of the close harmonies and the complexity of the guitar riffs. Cruising down the interstate, all I could think was that this song had never sounded so good. Looking out through the windshield, the snowflakes looked as big as tennis balls. I was totally lost in the moment, floating along in my Camaro. Then I glanced down at the speedometer.

Big mistake. Holy shit! I was doing all of twenty miles per hour.

My heart started pounding as I pulled off the road. I felt spacey really spacey—and I didn't like it a bit. Panic set in. Somehow I mustered enough courage to get back on the interstate and make it to Findlay.

I rushed into Steve's apartment and collapsed in his arms. "Something is very, very wrong with me," I told him.

"What did you do before you left?" he asked.

"Nothing much. I just stopped in at a party. Didn't have any wine or beer, but I did eat a little."

"What did you eat?"

"I had a cheeseburger. Oh and then I grabbed some brownies. My head is spinning."

Steve's eyes narrowed. Then he started to laugh. "You're stoned!"

The brownies. Of course! No wonder the Doobie Brothers sounded so great—I had eaten the equivalent of a doobie or two in the brownies before I left Ann Arbor.

"Stoned is actually a good thing," Steve said. "You just didn't know what it was. Relax and go with it. Like the music, it makes everything more intense—*everything*. Here, come lie down with me—I'll show you." Steve pulled me down onto the bed next to him. For the first time, we made love. This was my first "real" sexual experience of going "all the way." Unfortunately, it wasn't great. He was not a giving lover. No surprise.

Of course, neither one of us had used any protection. Of course, two weeks later my period was late. And, of course, I freaked out. I was so afraid that I was pregnant. When I told Steve, he made it very clear that he didn't want a child. In fact, he made it even clearer that if I was pregnant it was over. I got down on my knees and prayed about it, because I wasn't ready for motherhood, especially single motherhood. When my period finally showed up, it was the second time in my life when I ended up ecstatic to be covered in blood.

It's no surprise, either, that Steve and I broke up shortly thereafter. I decided it was time to run away, again. I transferred to another branch of the John Robert Powers school in Washington, DC. They had branches everywhere—I could have gone to any one of them. I went to DC because I could; I'd never been there before in my life.

I answered a "roommate wanted" ad in the paper, and moved into a posh three-bedroom apartment with two slightly older girls—smart girls who worked on Capitol Hill. I landed a job as a waitress at the Twin Bridges Marriott in Arlington while I was going to modeling school. I loved it. For the first time in my life, I was thrown together with people from other countries. Everything in Findlay had been pretty much vanilla; now my friends were my coworkers at the restaurant—people from India, Venezuela, the Ivory Coast.

One drizzly day, in between the lunch and dinner shifts, I drove across the Key Bridge into Georgetown, just to look around. I looked in the windows of all the cool little shops and stumbled pretty much by accident upon the campus of Georgetown University. I thought the University of Michigan was beautiful, but Georgetown took my breath away. There was still this part of me that wanted to go to college—the same part that had taken the apartment in Ann Arbor. I sat in my car and stared enviously at the students walking around the campus. They all looked so perfect and preppy, like they came from perfect, healthy, rich families, even better than the Marathon Oil types. These were worldly, wealthy, smart people—they belonged there.

"Why can't I be one of these kids walking around with a backpack, instead of waiting tables at a hotel restaurant? What kind of people go here?" I wondered. "What kind of families do they come from? How smart must you have to be to get in here?"

"Better than you. And definitely smarter than you," I told myself quickly, answering my own question. A wave of trailer-trash insecurity washed over me. Once trailer trash in your heart, always trailer trash. "You're a DECA kid. Georgetown is way out of your league."

Today some might call it an inferiority complex, but for me back then, there wasn't anything complex about it. I just knew I didn't belong, because I knew I wasn't good enough. I drove back across the Key Bridge, still in my uniform, and clocked in for work.

A couple of months later, I had an unexpected visitor in DC. It was Steve. "Cindy, I've come to take you home. I've been such a jerk. I'm in love with you. Come back to Ohio and live with me."

I packed up my clothes in my little Triumph Spitfire—the successor to the white Camaro—and drove back to Findlay to be with Steve. I was waitressing again. So much for my modeling career.

I hadn't been back in Findlay long before I got a call from an old friend, Anthony Birelli. He went by Tony. He and I met for a drink to catch up. He had heard I was moving in with Steve and wanted to wish me well.

I flashed back to my history with Tony. I had dated him off and on while I was in high school, at different times when I had broken up with Steve. He was Italian, and he was gorgeous—big brown eyes and curly brown hair that you couldn't wait to run your fingers through. He was a regular at Bill Knapp's, and he was everyone's favorite customer. Good-Time Susan and the rest of the waitresses fell all over themselves to get his table. They all swooned over him.

Not me. I'm ornery that way—if everybody wants him, then I don't want the guy everybody wants. And of course, because I was the only one who didn't want *him*, I was the one he wanted. Whenever Tony came into the restaurant, he asked for a table in my section.

He was older than me, and I was just fifteen when I met him. Tony was originally from New York City but had moved to Findlay to manage the local cable station. He kept asking me out, but I always turned him down, because of the difference in our ages and because I was dating Steve. But one summer day, Tony asked me to go sailing with him at the reservoir. Steve and I were broken up, and he was gone for the summer, so I decided to take a chance. Besides, I had never been on a boat.

We had a great time. After sailing, he took me to his apartment and showed me how to dance reggae, and, yes, he was a perfect gentleman. It wasn't long before he swept me off my feet.

He invited me to go back to New York City with him for a weekend. We drove his minivan across the country to New York. We stayed with his parents in New Jersey and went into the city the next day.

Manhattan—wow! First stop: Macy's. I was petrified. I was overwhelmed by the size of the place and by the sheer volume of what was for sale.

No. That's a lie. I was overwhelmed by the fact that I knew I couldn't afford any of it. So overwhelmed that my first instinct was to hide. I took refuge somewhere in the forest of handbags. "Tony, take me out of here. I don't belong in Macy's," I told him.

"What do you mean?"

"My family doesn't shop in stores like this. Everyone's looking at me like I'm gonna steal something."

"Nonsense. Nobody's looking at you, and besides, you have as much right to be in here as anyone else. You're as good as anybody. Let's go to the top of the Empire State Building. Then we'll take a stroll up Fifth Avenue."

That night, he took me out to dinner. At first I thought there was something wrong with my menu, because it had no prices on it. Tony had to tell me that was the way the sophisticated places did it—back then, anyway. The lady wasn't supposed to know what her meal cost.

Just like the trip to San Francisco to visit my sister, the trip to New York changed me. Tony opened my eyes to a whole new world, a world I was determined to take part in.

But it didn't last long. When we got back to Ohio, my insecurities got the best of me. A guy like that would never get "serious" with a girl like me. And Tony wasn't consistent. He just seemed to disappear once we got back from New York.

Steve, on the other hand, had come back from a summer of working away, and he wanted to get back together. He wanted me to get an apartment with him. I said yes. My exit strategy from the house by the railroad tracks, for good. Besides, I had heard Tony had moved to New York.

Much of my ambivalence about moving in with Steve came from his nasty temper. But at least I believed he loved me and wanted to marry me someday. That was important. I pushed my fears about Steve's temper back into the dark corners of my mind—with all the other junk that was in there—and moved in with him. Living with someone back then was a big deal as well as a serious commitment. And to most of my friends, Steve was a good catch. He was good looking and going somewhere. He came from a good family.

I answered an ad in the local paper for a copywriter, writing commercials for a local radio station. To interview for the job, I had to write a few sample commercials. I was pretty creative and, to my surprise, I got the job. Little did I know, this was the beginning of my career as I know it today.

I sold advertising and wrote commercials—funny, creative radio ads—and then I would record them myself. Before long, I was being recognized around town by my voice on the ads. It was the beginning of my *ALMOST FAMOUS* life to come. And I liked it.

It wasn't too long after Steve and I had moved in together that I realized how much he was like my father—in more ways than one.

I was out to dinner with a girlfriend one night when a guy walked over to our table.

"Don't I usually see you with Steve Bennington—the guy with the red Corvette?" In a small town, a flashy car gets noticed—as do the people in it.

"Yes, he's my boyfriend," I said, wondering where he was taking the conversation.

"Did you know that your boyfriend has been fucking my girlfriend?" This really *was* a small town.

My jaw dropped. What are you supposed to say to that?

"If you don't believe me, here's her parents' home address. Go over there right now and see if his car's not out front." With that, he smiled and said sarcastically, "Have a great night," and walked out of the restaurant.

No chance of that now. I paid my check and got up and left the restaurant as fast as I could.

As much as I didn't want to do it, I drove to the address on the slip of paper he gave me. Sure enough, Steve's car was parked at the curb. I snuck up to the house and peered in the living room window. My heart was pounding. There he was with her, his lips pressed against hers. In her parents' house! Didn't they know he was living with someone?

To say I didn't take it well is an understatement. I'd watched my mother put up with a lifetime of it, and I'd seen how it had damaged her. I marched right up the front walk and rang the doorbell. She came to the door. It was obvious I'd interrupted something.

"Tell my boyfriend I'd like to talk to him at home . . . and by the way, your boyfriend knows everything."

I left her standing at the front door, with him staring on in shock, and drove home. The Corvette roared up to our apartment about ten minutes later. Steve all but tore the door off the hinges. "*Cindy! Where the fuck are you?*" he screamed as he burst into the room. Without saying another word, he grabbed my wrist, twisted it, and threw me down on the floor. He pinned me down and grabbed me by the head on both sides and started slamming my head against the floor.

"DON'T . . . YOU . . . EVER . . . DO . . . THAT . . . AGAIN!"

He punctuated each word in the sentence by pulling my head up and then slamming it down again. I thought I was going to die for sure. I reached up and scratched his face. He backed away. I jumped up in a panic and ran out the door.

I got in my car and drove to my mother's, shaking and crying—and, believe it or not, wondering what I did to make that happen, I also worried that I might not ever see him again. How sick. By the time I arrived at the brown-shingled house, my head had large bumps on the back, and the sides of my face were black and blue from his hands holding me and slamming me on the floor. One eye was swollen shut.

As I sat in the driveway crying, I cringed. I thought, "Was I back here for good? Was this my lot in life? Was this the best I would ever do?" My head hurt. I was heartsick.

When I walked in the door, my mother took one look at me and threatened to call the police. "*NO!*" I screamed.

"What if I want him back?" I thought. "He would never want me back if we called the police. Besides, you *don't tell*. Surely it must have been my fault."

Sins of the mother . . .

CHAPTER 8

Singer in the Band

I NEEDED TO RUN, to get away, from Steve, from Findlay, from the old brown-shingled house. Florida seemed like a safe bet because my sister, Donna, was living there now with her family, and I loved the ocean. Florida held the promise of warm breezes and a calmer life, along with the excitement of a new beginning. New adventures. I was a rebel after all, and running away was a familiar pattern of behavior for me. In 1978, at the age of twenty-two, I chose to walk away—or should I say run away—to Jacksonville, Florida. Some time in the sun with my sister nearby was a chance to heal, a chance to start over. Unfortunately, it meant starting over with nothing.

I didn't care. With my orneriness and independence, I had this "fuck it, I don't need anyone" attitude by now anyway. Frankly, I didn't want to get anything out of Steve. I just wanted out. I piled everything I owned into my Triumph Spitfire—"everything" consisting of my guitar and my favorite clothes. That left plenty of room in the car for all my anxieties. They made the trip with me as well—no way could I leave them behind. These were the days of no cell phones. I had balls. I drove through the night from Ohio, straight through to Florida along I-75. Semi trucks and beat-up cars passed me throughout the night. Who else drove at four in the morning?

Me and my psychological baggage drove south and arrived in Jacksonville, Florida. It was so great to be back, smelling the salt air and feeling the humidity against my skin. There was something calming and healing about it for me. And it was great because Donna was now living there in a beautiful house by the ocean with her husband, Bob, and their little girls Jennifer, who was six, and Lori, who was just one year old. Bob had taken a new job there with an insurance firm a few years before. They were really moving up in the world.

I got a job selling advertising with a local radio station, and then I found an apartment in a big complex that looked somewhat safe and fun, with a great pool area. I sold the Spitfire and upgraded, or so I thought, to a Datsun 280Z. In theory, this should have been a step up, but in truth it was a mistake. The guy who sold me the Datsun lied about what kind of shape it was in. The car had nothing but problems—problems I couldn't afford to fix on a modest salary of $200 a week. One of the things that didn't work was the air-conditioning . . . which meant I was cruising around Jacksonville in 100-degree weather sitting on lambskin seat covers and sweating like a pig—trying to sell radio time while looking like I'd been boiled to death.

Pretty soon this became a problem, and not just because I was trying to sell advertising while dripping with sweat. In addition to the fear that had never left me—the fear of going crazy—I started to become scared of driving. There were times I'd get on the highway and start to get panicky. I began avoiding the main highways completely, which of course made doing my job a lot harder. But I kept my fears to myself and managed to work in spite of it.

I was living alone, and that $200 a week didn't go far. By the time I paid my rent, utilities, and gas, there wasn't much left for food. I lived on a diet that consisted of two basic food groups—hot dogs and microwave popcorn. Made staying thin pretty easy. Healthy? Not so much.

After a couple of months selling advertising, the radio station manager approached me with a question. "Ever done a radio show?" he asked.

"Sure," I lied, giving myself credit for the radio commercials I'd voiced back in Ohio.

"Know anything about jazz?"

"Absolutely," I lied again. Again, coloring outside the lines. "What I don't know I'll learn," I thought to myself. What I *did* know about jazz could be summed up in two words: Al Jarreau.

That was the beginning of *Sundays with Cindy*, a weekly jazz program I hosted on Sunday afternoons. I added some blues to the mix—Keith Jarrett, Carlos Santana, and Herbie Hancock—but I still played a whole lot of Al Jarreau. The gig brought in a few extra dollars—enough to buy a better brand of hot dogs.

One Sunday at the station, all alone, I heard this scratching at the door. I opened the door and looked down to see an adorable German shepherd puppy with huge brown eyes, just sitting there on the front sidewalk, looking up at me. I scooped him up and later smuggled him into my "no pets" apartment complex. I named him Max. I kept him for three months before he got too big to hide. When management found out, he had to go. It broke my heart to give him away.

Perfect. Now I was broke, heartbroken, and really lonely.

I didn't have enough money to go out very often, so at night I'd sit in my apartment, playing guitar, drinking wine, and feeling sorry for myself. It was the ideal set up to give my phobias license to roam free off the leash. By now, there were not just the old ones but some new ones as well. The fear of flying made its appearance on the heels of my fear of driving. I didn't fly much, but when I did, I had a hard time getting on the plane, and I was a white-knuckle flyer until we landed. It was more than just being afraid of flying. I felt trapped inside, knowing I couldn't just get up and run out. I chose to stay home most of the time.

My apartment complex had a great pool, and the pool was the social scene. I loved to lie out there, especially on weekends—it got me out of the apartment, and it was something I could do for free. One guy, Stanley, who hung out by the pool every weekend, was clearly interested in me. I didn't know much about him, but you could tell he had money by the way he dressed and the car he drove. Had a brand-new 280Z and parked it next to mine. He was a tall, skinny guy with a large nose and weird lips. He also had shark eyes, kind of beady and intense. He was somewhat sophisticated, but there was still something about him that I didn't quite trust. "You know, I'm an attorney," he told me as he draped his towel over the chair next to mine. "I'm also a stamp collector. I just got the most amazing collection –it was a gift from my father. The stamps are beautiful—all foreign. I'd really like to show them to you."

Spider, meet fly.

Stanley was so persistent. After a while, it was easier to say I'd come see his stamp collection than it was to keep saying no. Besides, maybe he was someone who I could . . . maybe date. After all, he was successful and seemed to be really smart. But he wasn't particularly attractive. In fact, there were things about him that really turned me off. But he seemed nice enough. I tried to keep an open mind.

I threw on some shorts and a top, and we went up to his apartment to see his stamp collection. As soon as we walked in the door, he locked it behind us. I tried not to panic—I got that same trapped, claustrophobic feeling I got on planes –and I was instantly uneasy. Was he trying to keep someone out—or me in?

"Come and sit over here on the couch, Cindy, and I'll get the stamps. Would you like something to drink?"

"Ah, no thanks. I just want to take a quick look at your stamps. Then I've gotta go."

"Not before you tell me why you won't go out with me. I've been asking you out for two months. Why haven't you said yes?" he asked as he rummaged through a desk in the corner.

My mind raced ahead of my mouth. "I'll tell you why," I thought to myself. "Your hair is kind of greasy. Your nose is kind of out-there, and there appears to be dark hair growing out of it. . . . What am I doing here? . . . I need to GET OUT OF HERE!" I said to myself in the beginning stages of panic.

I didn't tell Stanley any of that, of course. "I'm going through a divorce," I lied, as if that somehow would deter him.

Wrong. He came over with his stamp collection, sat beside me, and turned to face me on the couch. "You know you're the hottest girl by the pool. You know I am attracted to you." Then he threw the stamp collection on the table and jumped me—literally. He grabbed me in a clumsy embrace and attempted to kiss me as he held me aggressively. My skin crawled. In addition to everything else, his hands were sweaty and he smelled like body odor from sitting in the sun. Almost immediately he pushed me down onto the sofa cushions and starting grabbing at my shirt, rubbing his sweaty hands against my skin.

I couldn't breathe. I felt trapped, scared to death. Somewhere deep inside I remembered this feeling of being physically overwhelmed and forced into sexual activity. I was *not* going to let it happen again. Ever!

I jammed my knee up between his legs so hard all the wind went out of him. "*Fuck! You bitch! What the fuck!*" Then he grabbed for his soon-to-be black-and-blue nuts, gasping in pain.

"Get off me, you creep!" I screamed. My fingernails gouged deep into his thighs. It would be a while before sleazy Stanley would be out by the pool in his Speedo.

While he was writhing, I jumped up and ran for the door. He was still moaning as my fingers fumbled to open the lock. I threw the door open and fled. As I ran down the hall to my own apartment, I thought to myself, "What did I do? Did I lead him on? Was he a rapist?"

I should have told someone at the apartment complex, but I wasn't good at "telling." After all, I must have done something to lead him on. It must have been my fault, somehow.

Old guilt trips are hard to break.

As soon as I was safe in my own apartment, I caught my breath and called Donna to tell her about the close call with Stanley. "You need to get out of there. And *I* need to go out," she said. "Let's go out for a while. You'll feel better."

Donna loved to dance as much as I did. We headed out in our tightest jeans and our platform shoes for the top of the Holiday Inn at Jack's Beach. Donna was married, but she still loved to go out and have fun. She and Bob had a good marriage and a great life together. They had two beautiful daughters, Jenny and Lori. He had changed jobs, and now had a great job in hospital management. They lived in a beautiful home within walking distance of the beach. Bob worshipped her, and both of them were devoted to the girls. Donna didn't work—all her energy went into her family. She was really involved at school and in the PTA. She took the girls to ballet lessons and swim lessons, and made killer Halloween outfits from scratch. Donna was the perfect mom; it was as if she was trying to give them all the attention she never got as a child.

We got to the club—two sisters out for a night on the town. The weird part was that we looked nothing alike. I was tall with olive skin, almost Italian-looking, and of course I was now golden brown with a Florida tan. Donna was petite, blonde, and green eyed—with a perfect body. She attracted men like flies.

After the two of us got separated, I went looking for her. I found her surrounded by an admiring fan club as she flirted and teased. As I tried to elbow my way into the circle, someone bumped into me. "I'm so sorry," he said. "Are you okay?"

"OMG," I thought to myself. I was at a loss for words. My jaw was moving, but nothing intelligible was coming out. Standing in front of me was six feet two inches of gorgeous, the most stunningly good-looking guy I'd ever seen. Daniel was built like a trainer, muscular but not overly bulky, with a handsome, chiseled face. He had beautiful green eyes, thick brown hair that was the perfect long-but-coiffed look, a bit preppy. He had a kind of John F. Kennedy Jr. appeal. He smiled with soft full lips and perfect white teeth as he introduced himself, and asked if I danced.

Did I ever.

As the music began to play, I walked out onto the floor and stood back for a moment to look at him. He was an amazing dancer and had a really gentle way about him. By the end of the evening, I had given him my phone number.

The following day, the phone rang at the radio station while I was doing the show. It was him. "Hey, why don't you come over when you get off the air?" I played my last Al Jarreau and jumped in my 280Z.

As it turned out, the radio station wasn't far from where he lived. I followed his directions and pulled into the driveway of a fabulous house that was right on the ocean. How was this possible? I was about to find out.

Daniel had put those handsome looks to good use as a Calvin Klein model and was paid accordingly. He was also a bartender—in a beach town like Jacksonville, bartenders are true celebrities. And Daniel was not just any bartender—he was the head bartender at Smuggler's Inn, at the time the hottest place in town.

For me, things were definitely looking up. Daniel broadened my horizons about what the good life could be like. We started to hang out and make the rounds of various exclusive clubs. I was arm candy—on a *really* good arm.

What I started to realize, however, was that being arm candy wasn't enough for me. No matter what the arm looked like, I needed affection. Daniel was a perfectionist, not keen on commitment, and not the best in bed. Not that I was an expert, but over time as we experimented, I found he just wasn't well . . . "good." He was a bit lazy, not at all romantic, and a horrible kisser.

What *was* appealing was that Daniel had managed to create this elegant lifestyle for himself. Why couldn't I do the same thing? I thought I was talented. I knew I had big ideas. Daniel was living the life I wanted to live, but I wanted to achieve it on my own. I sat and stared at my *ALMOST FAMOUS* button. You didn't have to be a genius to figure out that $200 a week and *Sundays with Cindy* wasn't going to get me there.

As if on cue, I got a call from my brother Michael. "What would you think about coming back to Ohio?" he asked.

"To do what?"

"To be the lead singer in our band."

"Are you serious?"

Michael had been touring the Midwest with his band since my last years in high school . . . since the days of drugs under the floorboards.

Before I graduated, it got pretty bad. Mike was not only dealing, he was using as well. Not sure what, but I know he drank too much and smoked pot. When Mom found out, she freaked. Instead of dragging Donna out in the middle of the night to look for Dad, she dragged me out in the middle of the night to look for Michael. Once, we found him in an old dumpy room above a local nightclub, stoned out of his mind. It was obvious that he was on something. She made him come back home to live, but it was only temporary. Michael had his own demons from growing up with our alcoholic father. Not only did he inherit Dad's love of music and entertaining, he also inherited Dad's love of alcohol.

During that wild period of his life, he had not been exactly responsible about using protection, which is to say that he knocked up his then-girlfriend—twice. By the time he was twenty, he was the father of two little boys. He and the girlfriend split up, and he was left to raise Andy and Benjamin on his own. And he shouldered that responsibility amazingly well, with Mom's help.

The miracle was that fatherhood straightened Michael out. He was making pretty decent money with the band. Mom watched the kids while he was performing. And he gave up drugs—all except alcohol. Like father, like son. But he started dating a wild, smart, and confident little thing named Mary, and she fell in love with Michael and his boys.

His band was called the Together Band. They were good, but this was the era of the chick singer out front—powerful, edgy vocalists like Chrissie Hynde, Joan Jett, Stevie Nicks, and Pat Benatar were at the top of the charts. Together Band was getting good bookings, but Michael thought they'd do even better with a lead female vocalist.

I'd always loved to sing, and through the years I had learned to play some simple guitar. But I liked a softer, more acoustic sound than Michael was looking for. Carly Simon was pretty much my speed, but my brother wanted me to learn electric guitar and turn into Ohio's answer to Pat Benatar.

I thought about it for a couple of days, took another look at my *ALMOST FAMOUS* button, and told Michael I'd be home soon.

I was a bit sorry to leave Daniel, even though the sex wasn't good, because everything else about him was. But I thought this was a shot I had to take. My brother David, bless his heart, came down to Florida pulling a small U-Haul, packed up all my belongings, and drove back to Ohio with me. Just being with David made me feel good about my decision. Besides, by this time my driving phobia was so bad I might not have made it otherwise.

I moved in with Michael's girlfriend, Mary. Mary was a pretty girl with shoulder-length blonde hair and soft brown eyes. She was fun and liked to have a good time, but more important, she was loving and nurturing and immediately took to taking care of Michael and his boys. Michael had told me I'd like her a lot, and he was right. And she was head-over-heels crazy about my brother. It was so good to see him and his kids happy.

I went out and bought a guitar, a Fender Stratocaster. Since I was already pretty good on acoustic, it didn't take long to get up to speed. After a couple of weeks of rehearsal, we took our show on the road. I was good to go.

All except for my anxieties, which had now grown to include panic attacks on stage. For me, that manifested itself as irritable bowel syndrome, accompanied by stealth attacks of diarrhea. It was awful. I would strut onto the stage with my stomach churning. Michael and the other guys in the band got used to me leaving suddenly in the middle of a set and making a beeline for the bathroom. Pepto-Bismol became my drink of choice.

Despite the stomach problems and panic feelings, I was having a great time. I loved the music, and I loved the attention: being the lead singer in a rock 'n' roll band makes you own the room. I met a handsome attorney from Toledo and a gorgeous builder from Chicago. This was going to be fun, I thought. Meanwhile, Daniel kept calling, begging me to come back to Jacksonville. I was feeling a lot better about myself, even with all the anxieties. I had options, and good-looking, interesting men were coming out of the woodwork.

We booked a great gig—two weeks at the Holiday Inn in Fremont, Ohio, just off Lake Erie, not far from my old fake-ID stomping grounds in Bowling Green. Fremont was also not far from Findlay, and Michael and I invited Mom to come hear us play on opening night.

Mary told me that she would also have someone there that night—one of her best friends—a guy named David. "You've got to meet him," she told me. "He's perfect for you."

"What's he like?" I asked.

"He looks kind of like Cat Stevens. He's wild and really fun, and owns a little landscaping business in Oak Harbor, just a few miles from here."

I loved Mary, so I didn't tell her that there was nothing appealing in what she'd just told me. I'd been to New York with Anthony Birelli. I'd made the rounds of the best clubs in Jacksonville with Daniel, the most handsome man in the universe. And now she wanted to fix me up with some redneck hick gardener from . . . where, Oak Harbor, Ohio? You've got to be kidding.

Right before our first set, the unusually big crowd buzzed with anticipation. I was feeling every bit the lead singer—powerful, sexy, and even a little bit dangerous. I was the Somebody everyone was waiting for.

It felt so good when I strutted onto the stage with my Stratocaster, wearing black spandex pants, stilettos, and a whole lot of attitude. I tossed my waist-length curly hair as I started belting out Pat Benatar: "*We are young; Heartache to heartache; We stand; No promises; No demands; Love is a battlefield.*"

Own it. Work it.

I put my heart and soul into it—God knows that had been the anthem of my love life so far. I looked out into the crowd and located my mother, right in front. But who was that strange little guy sitting next to her? The guy with the dark curly hair and a beard . . . the guy who looked like . . . well, Cat Stevens?

And what was he saying to her? He was leaning in, smiling and talking in her ear, and pointing at me.

"Is that your daughter up there?" he asked her.

"Yes, it is," she responded guardedly.

"Well, my name is David Bassett, and I'm going to marry her someday."

CHAPTER 9

Lightning Bolts

DAVID ALWAYS TOLD people that the minute he saw me, it was lightning bolts. From that moment forward, he was madly in love with me and knew he was going to marry me, just like he told my mother.

When my mother told me what he had said, I had the opposite reaction. "Are you kidding me?" I responded.

"Cindy, who is that guy, anyway? Who does he think he is?" my mother asked. "He told me he is going to marry you someday. Why, he doesn't even know you. He's weird," she said, shaking her head and watching him dance.

Some guy I hadn't even met had just told her that he was going to marry me. That was kind of funny. Especially coming from someone like him. I didn't even really like him.

It didn't sound like such a great idea to her, either, as she continued with a suspicious tone. "You stay away from him. He's horny," she warned.

With all my mother's hang-ups about sex—the ones my father had bellowed about since my childhood—she said *that* like it was a bad thing.

Physically, he did nothing for me: not nearly tall enough, sooooo not my type.

Worse yet, he was now making a total ass of himself on the dance floor. David Bassett, the man who had already declared that he was my husband-to-be—*to my mother*, no less—was rolling around on the floor doing the Alligator with every woman in sight.

Oh. God. Spare me.

And while he was doing that, he was looking up at me and grinning like a lobotomized fool. Who is this guy, and how unhinged was Mary that she'd think he'd be a good match for me?

At the break, Mary introduced me to him. After watching his dance moves, however, I decided I really wasn't interested. That said, he was kind of interesting looking. He was shorter, five foot nine, stocky build, and a bit wild looking. He had long, curly black hair, and big, beautiful, kind, and happy green eyes. His eyes actually sparkled when he smiled, and he smiled a lot, especially when he was looking at me. It was almost too obvious. He was love struck. He had a prominent nose, but it was kind of cute, in a way. And he had a closely shaved beard. David was looking at me with these puppy-dog eyes, grinning from ear to ear. In my stilettos, I towered over him. I wanted nothing to do with him. Especially when Mr. Chicago Builder and Mr. Toledo Attorney were lurking in the back of the room. They both seemed so promising. They were both quite good looking and . . . tall.

That night rolled on, and so did his funny behavior. I remember him dancing right in front of me, as if wanting me to look at him, watch him. He would do this weird thing where he would squat down, legs spread, and open his arms wide, moving them back and forth as if he was wading through a large pond of water. Then he would turn his head from side to side, all the while smiling and looking at me, hoping I was watching. Then he would laugh and smile. If he was anything, he was certainly entertaining. He was a character. He looked way too happy and stable for me.

The next morning, the phone at Mary's started ringing and wouldn't stop. It was David. I refused to take the call—the first time, the second time . . . and the fifteenth time. "Tell him anything you want to, Mary, I don't want to talk to him. He's just not my type."

"Look . . . would you please just say hello or something?" Mary pleaded.

"How many times do I have to say it? No, no, no, and NO!"

"You don't get it," she declared. "He's such a great guy."

"You saw what was going on!" I argued. "He was rolling all over the floor with those women."

"I think he was just trying to impress you. He's funny and a little crazy," Mary replied.

"He impressed me all right, as some kind of weirdo."

"Please," Mary begged. "Talk to him . . . just once."

As if on cue, the phone rang again. Mary looked at me. I shrugged. She handed me the phone. David started talking rapid-fire, as if I might hang up on him at any moment—which was a definite possibility. "I know I'm really bothering you," he said, "but please, please come over to my house. Can I just make you dinner?"

Free food.

If I was financially strapped in Jacksonville, I was damned near broke now. I'd gone from making $200 a week in Florida to making $75 a week singing with the band. Michael's promise of good money and the potential for fame had lured me back to Ohio, but it had yet to materialize. For now, it was all I could do to put gas in my car.

As annoyed as I was, I heard myself agreeing to go to David's house for dinner. Mary smiled and gave me a thumbs-up.

Next day, as I drove my Datsun 280Z out over country roads from Fremont to his house in Oak Harbor, I was sure I'd made a huge mistake. "Over the river and through the woods . . . it's a long way to go for an over-done hamburger," I thought cynically. I didn't have low expectations. I had no expectations. "I'm doing this for Mary," I said to myself, "to get her off my case and to make this guy stop calling all the time."

I pulled into the driveway, and there was the first surprise. His house was a converted garage/barn, beautifully landscaped, with all kinds of trees and flowers out front, very charming. David answered the door in designer sweatpants and a polo shirt. Second surprise—he cleaned up well. He was flanked by the rest of the welcoming committee: Mercy, a Doberman, and Sheaton the Wonder Hound, a golden-brown Chesapeake Bay retriever—two of the sweetest, most affectionate dogs I'd ever met.

A fire crackled in the fireplace. The sounds of a Mozart concerto serenaded us from the stereo. The walls of the living room were covered in small but well-chosen Ansel Adams prints. Pictures of European ski destinations were hung in the dining room, and the smells wafting out of the kitchen were delicious. David had draped a cloth napkin over his forearm like a professional waiter. He immediately offered me a glass of excellent wine.

The food he prepared tasted as amazing as it smelled. Third surprise: David was an accomplished cook. That night he served me a salad that we ended up calling "David's Salad," filled with fresh tomatoes, hunks of cucumber, onions, chunks of blue cheese, Italian dressing, and some delicious barbecued chicken breast. And when I say "served," I mean it literally. He hand-fed me dinner, bite by bite. "Do you ski?" he asked me as he gently fed me the fabulous food on a well-chosen fork.

"Never could afford it," I thought. "Never got the chance," I replied.

"These photos come from places where I went helicopter skiing," he said. "We'll go back there—together."

"I'd like that," I found myself saying.

"What the hell? Who said that?" I asked myself. These were words I'd had no intention of saying. I was amazed at him. Even more, I was amazed at myself. Why was I responding this way? I didn't know what to make of this guy, except that I'd badly underestimated him. David told me about places he'd been, places he wanted to take me. By the end of dinner, my head was spinning.

He excused himself briefly to go back into the kitchen, and then returned. "What do you do with all of them?" he asked me after he had cleared the plates.

"All of who?"

"All of the men who fall madly in love with you?"

I was still smiling at the idea that I might have lovers stashed in cold storage all over the country when he pulled my chair away from the table and gently led me back into the living room. After quickly changing the music, he bowed somewhat formally and asked, "May I have this dance?"

He took me into his arms, smiled, and looked into my eyes as if he were in a daze. He led me around the living room expertly, romantically. We were light-years beyond the Alligator now.

"What is your real name?" he asked with a whisper. His breath against my ear gave me chills. Hmm. That was different.

"Lucinda," I replied, surprised by the question, and even more surprised by my reaction to his breath in my ear.

He pulled back long enough to look me deeply in the eyes and smile. Then he drew me close to him once more. "Then that's what I'll call you," he declared.

"I've never really liked my full name," I admitted.

"But you're not a Cindy," he said firmly. "Lucinda is so much more sophisticated, more beautiful, more music to the ear. Maybe it just took you a while to grow into your name, but it really fits who you are.

"And you *will* fall in love with me someday, Lucinda," he promised. "You just wait and see."

At that moment, the clock on the mantel chimed. I looked at my watch and freaked. The time with David had flown by, and now Lucinda/Cindy was about to turn into Cinderella—me and my Stratocaster were due onstage belting out Pat Benatar in just a few hours.

"I have to go, David," I said. "I'm late. If I leave now, I'll barely make it."

As I looked for my purse, my eyes landed on what was sitting beside it. On the counter was a small bottle. For some reason it intrigued me, and I picked it up. "What is this?" I asked.

"That's Kama Sutra Oil of Love," he replied. "It's sort of like a flavored massage oil."

I took off the little cork and put some on my lips. It was warm and tasted like spice. Then I walked over, lifted his chin, and gave him this really long, passionate kiss. By the end, both our lips were on fire.

I left David standing in stunned silence. He looked at me dazed, with his lips still in kiss formation. I ran for the door.

"Wait!" he called as I jumped into my car. "What's your favorite flower?"

"Lilacs!" I shouted out the car window as I took off for Mary's at top speed. I needed to get back and get ready to go onstage.

About a half hour later, there was a furious pounding on Mary's door. "Mary! It's David. Let me in!"

Mary opened the door and he stormed inside. "Where is she?" he asked. His voice sounded urgent, desperate almost.

"Back there," Mary answered. "But she's got to go play, like now!"

I was in the bathroom, putting the finishing touches on my stage makeup. In the mirror on the door to the medicine cabinet I saw David barreling down the hallway. Actually, all I could see was David's face. I almost stabbed myself in the eye with my mascara wand—the rest of him was hidden behind a Volkswagen-size bouquet.

Lilacs. Armloads of them.

There were literally too many for him to carry, and they were dropping all over the floor as he walked toward me. Mary didn't know what to make of it, except that it was making a mess. "David! What the—" she shouted.

"She told me she likes lilacs," he yelled back as he swept past her.

"Here," he said, as he arrived at the bathroom door. "These are for you, Lucinda."

"Oh my God, they're beautiful!" I exclaimed. They smelled amazing, but there was no time to even put them in water. I was already late. "I'm sorry," I said as I edged my way toward the door.

"I want to take you to Lake Erie and Put-in-Bay! I want to take you skiing," he yelled after me. "And . . ." He paused. "I want to have babies with you!"

"What?"

"I want to marry you!" he screamed after me.

That was the beginning of Us.

Dammit!

This was not what I'd planned. It was good-bye, handsome Toledo attorney, and good-bye to the builder from Chicago. I had all these plans to be the hot lead singer, with my choice of handsome guys, but it all got blown out of the water, because David Bassett had entered into my life.

Not just entered in, but rushed in like a tidal wave, and swept me off my feet. What I didn't know was that he would actually become my life raft. And this was only the beginning.

David followed me to the club to hear me sing that night, and every night after that, no matter where we were playing. He sat through all the sets. And every night he brought me flowers. At first, more lilacs, then roses, and then love poems.

We were inseparable. From that moment on, we went everywhere together. When I got sick and went home to my mom's in Findlay for a couple of days, he drove there and made me chicken soup. But not just any chicken soup. This was made with cinnamon and lemon, a recipe that came from his Lebanese/Syrian grandmother.

As winter turned to spring, one day he pulled up at Mary's. "Come with me. I want to show you something," he said. He took me to Catawba Island to a little bar. "Sailing," Christopher Cross's hit song, was booming out from the sound system. "I promised I'd take you on Lake Erie," he said. "But first, dance with me. This is going to be our song."

We headed for Put-in-Bay, on South Bass Island, via the local ferry. We rode bicycles out to Commodore Perry's monument and then spread a blanket on the grass. David had packed this great lunch, with fancy sandwiches and a bottle of wine. "I'm so in love with you," he told me.

"You don't even know me," I replied.

"Has this ever happened to you before?" he asked. "I feel like we're the stars of some great romantic movie. I want to spend the rest of my life with you." He picked me up in his arms and swung me around as we fell to the ground laughing and kissing. It was magical.

We went back to his house in Oak Harbor and danced some more. We kissed, and David started leading me toward the bedroom.

I put on the brakes. "We can't do this," I said.

"Why not? You're an adult woman."

"I haven't known you that long," I countered. By this time we'd been dating about two months, but we still hadn't slept together.

"Lucinda. It's okay. Trust me."

Trust. Oh, that. Trust was a problem.

Even though I knew how David felt about me, trusting was hard to do. My previous romantic relationships hadn't exactly gone well, not that I had much experience. First, there was Steve, who was as self-absorbed in bed as he was about everything else, and then there was Daniel in Florida, who just wasn't, well, passionate. I hadn't had an orgasm with either one of them. And then, of course, there was all the sexual baggage I was still carrying from being "sinful" as a child. I had not yet grasped the concept that I'd been abused—that I was a victim. I really knew nothing about "making love."

Despite everything, David's passion and his tenderness won me over. "Okay," I said, "but I'm not going to spend the night."

He was an amazing, tender, gentle lover. I was so overwhelmed with how loving he was, I cried. So that's what sex is all about. I got it—finally.

He was such an incredible lover—thoughtful, sensitive, and attentive. That first night I stayed till three o'clock in the morning, then snuck out like a thief in the night, doing the walk of shame, scared to death that someone might have seen me leave. After all, I was a "good" girl and didn't do things like this.

One Saturday afternoon, he picked me up at Mary's. "Let's go. There's something you have to see." He pulled up to a boat store and proudly announced that he had just bought a small catamaran. It was sitting on a trailer, waiting to be put in the water. That day, we sailed out from Port Clinton toward Put-in-Bay, right past a group of small cottages. They were rustic A-frames, pretty basic—okay, they were dumpy—but David said they belonged to a friend of his. And one of them was available for the summer, if he would clean up the property in trade for rent.

A few weeks later, we moved in. This time in our relationship was so romantic, as if we were living in a dream. I finally felt safe. We'd come back from me singing with the band at about two o'clock in the morning, and David would build a bonfire on the beach. We'd lie next to it and make out, drink wine, and talk for hours—about life, our dreams, the future.

We spent our days sailing on Lake Erie and our nights in bed, wrapped around each other. He always woke up before me. I know this because whenever I opened my eyes, he was the first thing I saw, sitting on the floor of our little cottage, just staring at me. And every morning, there would be a new love poem tacked on the wall. David wrote the poems on paper plates—there must have been a hundred of them, one for each day of that amazing summer. He surrounded me with fresh flowers and repeated in so many different ways how beautiful he thought I was. More than feeling loved, I knew I was worshipped and adored.

By now, the Together Band was getting better gigs all over northern Ohio and southern Michigan. No matter where we played, David would be there—proud and adoring with poems and flowers. I was up to earning $100 a week—better, but still not enough to keep me going without David's support.

David did what no other man had ever done for me—he took care of me. He nurtured me—body and soul. He cooked for me. He doted on me. He bought me a little puppy. We named her Mercedes, because I'd told him that someday I was going to drive one. Meanwhile, however, David kept my Datsun from falling completely apart, something it threatened to do almost daily. He replaced the bumper and kept it filled with gas. One night we were driving home and the car right behind us was tailgating really bad. David slammed on the brakes, jumped out of the car, and ran back to challenge the other driver. "What the fuck are you doing?" he said.

"Uh, I'm sorry," he said sheepishly. "I thought you were somebody I knew."

"I don't care!" David said. "Following that close is really dangerous."

"And so is confronting some unknown crazy person face-to-face," I thought. It turned out okay, but the guy behind the wheel could have been drunk, or crazy, or both. That's when I realized that David was the kind of person who would jump in front of a train for someone. He wouldn't think twice, even in a situation where he should have been cautious. "This guy has my back like no one in my life ever has," I thought. And that was David his whole life.

Labor Day came and went. The winds were blowing hard off Lake Erie, and there was no heat in the cottage. It would soon be time to leave the beach and move back in with Mary. David didn't understand why I wouldn't move in with him in his house back in Oak Harbor, but that was a commitment I was not ready to make. I was never one to leap into relationships to begin with, and lately Daniel, Mr. Gorgeous from Jacksonville, had been calling, begging me to come back to Florida.

"Maybe you should come down and visit me, and see this Daniel guy again," Donna counseled. "The girls miss you. I miss you. I know you've had fun with David, but is he really your type? He is moving so fast. Maybe you need a little perspective."

Maybe she was right. I decided to book a flight, even though I hated to fly. I needed to get away for a bit. I needed to try and figure out what I really wanted.

Telling David I was going was painful—for both of us. "We've had a great summer together," I began, "but before I left for Florida I ended a very bad relationship. I don't want to make any more mistakes. While I was in Jacksonville, there was this guy I was dating. It was never really resolved—I just left. When I got back to Ohio, you pretty much overwhelmed me. I need to go back to Florida; I want to see my sister, Donna. I also need to see Daniel and just see what I feel for him."

"Of course," David said, fighting back tears. "I understand. Do what you have to do." Then he sat down on the floor, surrounded by all three dogs, and gently cried. "Please God, let Lucinda come back to me," he said, looking up at the ceiling and petting the dogs. They knew he was upset. "She'll come back, guys, you'll see." I don't know if he was reassuring them or himself.

I felt so awful. But somehow I managed to get on the plane.

It was eighty-five and sunny in Jacksonville when Daniel picked me up at the airport in his new Jaguar. "Drive my car while you're here," he offered.

"Okay, but at some point we need to talk," I said.

"About us?" he said.

"About whether there *is* an us," I replied.

"I've been an idiot, Cindy," he confessed. "I couldn't tell you how I felt about you. You never said it in so many words, but I know that you left partly because you wanted more from me than I was able to give. I wasn't ready for a committed relationship then, but I am now."

There it was, the words I'd been hoping to hear, or at least so I thought. Daniel had everything I was convinced I wanted—the house on the ocean, the glamorous, exciting life—and he was offering to share it with me. If he'd said that a year earlier, I probably never would have left. Now, just hearing someone call me Cindy was jarring—that seemed like a lifetime ago.

I was tempted at first. For starters, I'd forgotten how good-looking he was. All too soon, however, I was reminded of all the little things about him that bothered me. Daniel was a bit narcissistic—if you looked like that, why wouldn't you be? He was as neat as David was sloppy. David was ADHD; he was also a pack rat. He had shit spread out everywhere in a jumble—books, socks, papers, car keys, underwear, unopened mail—with no sense of organization whatsoever. Everything was chaos and disorder. It seemed to me that he lost everything he touched. He also paid absolutely no attention to how he dressed, and I'd been honest enough to tell him that bothered me. Most of the time, David went through life looking like he needed a haircut and a steam iron—and a pair of long pants.

Daniel was the exact opposite. He was a model. He was meticulous and well dressed— really put together, to the point of being a little prissy and compulsive about it. His shirts were folded and neatly stacked in his closet. His closet was bigger than the entire A-frame at Put-in-Bay, and his impeccable array of suits and sport coats was lined up with military precision. All his hangers matched—I suppose I shouldn't have been surprised when he got pissed because I got sand in his Jag.

His irritability about the sand did it, actually—the universe has a way of telling you where you belong. I'd just spent a magical summer on the beach. Sand was inevitable. So was dog hair. Daniel had no room in his well-ordered life for anything messy or untidy. How would he deal with my dog? Or children, for that matter, which was something I knew I wanted, someday. And when he kissed me, well, there was just nothing there. Daniel just didn't do it for me physically. All I wanted to do was run back to David.

I was so excited to see and hold David that I could have flown back without a plane.

When I landed he was waiting for me, holding a bouquet of lilacs, wearing new cashmere pants and a new pair of leather wingtip shoes. He was stylin', but more than that, he looked cuddly and inviting. It was obvious that David had made an effort to look more polished, but it wouldn't have mattered if he'd been wearing his worst moth-eaten sweatshirt, his oldest pair of shorts, and his holiest sneakers. As soon as I walked off that plane and saw him, I knew I was home.

I also knew it was time to end my singing career. I got tired of late nights and life on the road. I got tired of poverty. I took a job at a radio station in Toledo, selling radio advertising. It was the end of David's life as a landscaper as well—he sold his business and got a position with a software company in Toledo. David and I were officially a couple. He took me to good restaurants and introduced me to escargot, wines, and the finer things in life. That winter he taught me how to ski.

The fact that I was now safe and secure in my relationship with David, however, brought my other insecurities roaring back as never before. In short, they took over my life. My anxiety and panic attacks were in full force and becoming a daily occurrence. David loved to travel, and he booked this really adventurous trip for us—three destinations over a month's time. It should have been a great experience, but I was having panic attacks the whole way, except that I didn't know that's what they were. In the car, in the plane, everywhere. I couldn't get out of my own head.

In retrospect, I believe that for the first time in my life I felt somewhat "safe." That someone was there to catch me, take care of me. On a subconscious level I think I allowed myself to face my fears and insecurities for the first time, and it manifested as anxiety and panic attacks. Unfortunately, it surfaced on this wonderful trip.

Our first city was Acapulco, and by the time we got there, I was a wreck. Our room was on the twenty-fourth floor. It had a great view, but the window was broken, and I started obsessing that I was going to jump out the window and kill myself. At David's insistence, the hotel moved us into a different room. This one had a balcony, which only meant that now I was sure I was going to jump off the balcony instead of out the window.

I was no fun. David wanted to go out on the balcony, be carefree, listen to Rick James, eat fruit, and dance naked. David *loved* to dance naked. Whenever we went sailing, as soon as we got out into the middle of Lake Erie, he'd take off all his clothes and dance on our little boat. Now, however, he was stuck being in love with a lunatic—a head case who wouldn't set foot on the balcony and couldn't say why.

It wasn't that I didn't want to dance with him on the balcony—I did— it was just that I was absolutely certain that when I got out there, I was going to go crazy and jump off. I was still afraid of losing my mind, just like I had been since I was little, except now I was worried that when I went insane in Mexico, nobody would be able to speak my language.

It got worse when we got to Utah. We went skiing in Park City, where the chairlift carries you high above the slopes and canyons to the top of the mountain. The two-person chairs were open—like on a Ferris wheel, but in a straight line. Wouldn't you know we got stopped halfway from the base—David and I were suspended out there in midair. The ground was hundreds of feet below. The wind was whipping, and the chair was swaying crazily back and forth.

I started having the biggest panic attack of my life. All I wanted to do was to get out of there, any way I could. I quickly sized up the situation: the fastest way out was straight down. Panicked as I was, the idea that the plunge would probably kill me didn't seem like that much of a drawback.

"If this chair doesn't move soon," I told David, "I'm going to jump." I heard my mother's voice from long ago echo inside my head: "If you think it, you'll make it happen," her voice promised. *"I've got to get off this chair!"* I said in a panic.

He could see that I was freaked out. "Don't look down." He took my hand. "Focus forward. Breathe." They got the chairlift restarted just in time. After that, we rode the gondola—or tried to. That wasn't much better, because I got antsy about being closed in.

The last destination on our trip took us back to Jacksonville. David got a chance to meet Donna. He also met Daniel when we were out one night. "So you're the guy she ended up with," Daniel said when I introduced them.

Daniel was gracious and confident, but clearly he was sizing David up. David was totally intimidated, and not just because the top of his head was level with Daniel's nostrils. I could see the wheels turning inside David's head—he was running down the checklist comparison between himself and Daniel. I could also see that by his calculations, he was coming up short, both literally and figuratively. He looked at me with fear in those puppy-dog eyes. He was terrified that I might leave him for Daniel after all.

Not going to happen.

I took him down to the ocean, lay down beside him on the beach, and kissed him. "You blow him away, as a man, as a person," I assured him. "You blow him away, and I am so in love with you." Then I stood up, grabbed a long piece of driftwood, and drew a huge heart in the sand. "Lucinda loves David," I wrote in the middle.

David was so in love with me. He loved me unconditionally, but I had never been more unlovable than during that time. "Neurotic" didn't begin to explain it. I came back from that month-long trip more agoraphobic than ever. I was having more and more spacey, out-of-body experiences—dissociative experiences—like I'd had with Good-Time Susan on the way to Bowie concerts. I had irritable bowel syndrome—lovely. I couldn't go to the bathroom unless I was all by myself—literally. David had to leave the house or hotel room. I couldn't be in a car unless I was driving. I wouldn't ride in the backseat of anybody else's car. I didn't want to get on a plane. I didn't want to get in an elevator. I didn't want to socialize with people unless I could drive, and even then I had to say where we went, how long we stayed, and when we left. By now, this was who I was. I had turned into the world's worst anxious person. I needed to control every moment and everything we did in an attempt to avoid or control my anxiety and fear. It was as if, now that I was safe and had someone to "save" me, I was releasing all my fears and anxieties full on.

Nobody had put a name on what was wrong with me. David could see that I got really anxious, but since I didn't know what was wrong, my anxiety manifested as anger. I would just get pissed off and invent justifications for every frickin' thing. I'd say no to whatever I couldn't or wouldn't do. I would make excuses for not wanting to go places and do things.

Nevertheless, David kept asking me to marry him. I kept turning him down. I don't know why he stayed with me. I knew I loved him and I knew I needed him, but I was scared—scared I was going crazy, scared I was going to die of some horrible disease, scared I was going to lose control, lose my mind, just scared of everything. I was so obsessed with being scared I couldn't even enjoy the moment anymore.

Why didn't I want to get married? I kept making excuses, but the truth was I was scared of marriage, too. My parents' marriage sucked. I'd been in a committed relationship with Steve. That sucked, too. There was also a part of me that knew (or hoped) I was going to be Somebody—the *ALMOST FAMOUS* somebody who had practiced her signature as a teenager. I didn't like the idea that someone like a husband might get in the way.

Well, that, and the fact that I was sure I was going to go nuts. It's not like there was any "maybe" here. I had no doubt that there was a room with my name on it in that old Gothic loony bin in Toledo—the same one with the bars on the windows that had scared the shit out of me when we drove by it as a girl. I was just waiting for the men in the white coats to throw me into a straitjacket and take me away.

While we were in Mexico, we had met a fabulous couple from New York. We really hit it off, and Jamie and Charles invited us to come visit them in Manhattan. By this time I was refusing to fly at all, but I was willing to drive, and I'd just bought a new Honda Prelude—candy apple red—and off we went.

Somehow, Interstate 80 near Morristown, New Jersey, struck David as a good place to try to propose—again. "Why don't I just get you a ring?" he asked.

"What for?"

"An engagement ring. You know, a diamond," he replied.

"If and when we get married, all I would want is a big fat band, no diamond. But I'm not ready for that anyway. We've been all through this."

"What if I told you that I had an engagement ring in the trunk?" he asked. David had an ornery side. Ordinarily, his orneriness was sort of charming, but this wasn't funny. Besides, I was sure this was a bluff.

"Yeah, right," I said. "I don't believe you."

"What if I told you it had a diamond in it?"

"I told you I don't want diamonds, and I've already told you—I don't want to get engaged. Tell you what—just pull over and you can show it to me." Bluff and call.

"No," he said with a laugh. "I don't have a ring in the trunk. Just wanted to get your reaction," he said, patting my leg and grinning. I drove the rest of the way into New York, thinking the issue had been put to rest.

On our first night in the city, Jamie and Charles took us to a comedy club. There were about four hundred people there, and a guy was onstage telling jokes. He was a little outrageous, even a little raunchy—a Don Rickles kind of guy, a bit heavyset with a sly laugh and sarcastic tone—and everyone was having a good time. Our table was right next to the stage, and before long the comic pulled David up next to him onstage and asked his name and where he was from.

"I'm David Bassett, and I'm from Toledo, Ohio."

Right away, people were laughing, just at the name Toledo. Now, Toledo has been a punch line ever since Corporal Max Klinger wore a dress in *M*A*S*H*, maybe before. And then of course there was John Denver's ditty: "*Saturday night in Toledo, Ohio, is like being nowhere at all.*" So already this was a golden set up.

"And what are you doing in the Big Apple, Mr. Toledo? If you want to watch our grass die, you'll have to go to Central Park."

David laughed. Then he stepped back and took a deep breath, looked down at me, smiled, and said, "I came to ask her to marry me."

I died.

"You did?" Comedian as straight man.

"I did." David was Costello to his Abbott.

"And when do you plan on doing that?"

"Well . . ."

"Well . . . why don't you do it right now? Come now, little lady," the comic said, pulling me up onstage next to David.

Little lady, my ass. I was pulled up on stage, despite my pulling back.

"Oh my God!" I thought to myself as my heart pounded. "David, don't do this to me. Not up here. Not in front of all these people."

"I really didn't plan on doing this right here," David began, "but . . ."

He reached into his pocket and pulled out a wide band with a three-quarter-carat marquise diamond. My mind flashed back to our car ride and his teasing. So there *was* a ring in the trunk!

In that moment, panic set in like you wouldn't believe, and I knew what was coming next. *Oh no. Oh God no.* At that moment, if you'd given me the chance to go back to being stranded two hundred feet above Park City in a chairlift, I'd have taken it.

"Lucinda, will you marry me?" It was all I could do not to bolt from the room. While I was still in shock, he slipped the ring on my finger.

I couldn't breathe, let alone respond.

David was still grinning as I leaned over to whisper in his ear—it was the only way to be heard in the pandemonium of the club. "I need to get out of here. *Now!*" I think everyone thought I whispered "yes" into his ear.

The room erupted in applause. The comedian offered his congratulations, as did Jamie and Charles. From all over the club, bottles of celebratory champagne started arriving at our table, sent by people we didn't know.

We excused ourselves through the crowd. People grabbed at us and congratulated us as we headed for the door. "There they go, folks," the comedian called after us. "What a great couple. Mr. and Mrs. David Bassett. . . . Probably headed back to the hotel for a quickie."

David didn't realize that I was monumentally pissed off till we got out to the street. "How could you do this to me?" I cried.

"But, Lucinda . . ."

"And in front of everybody!" I was livid.

"But . . . but I'm so in love with you. . . ."

I yelled, "I did *not* say yes!"

With that, I took off the ring and handed it back to him. "You keep it," I said. "I can't handle all of this right now."

It was a diva performance worthy of the scared, angry, agoraphobic, afraid-of-going-crazy batshit bitch I'd become. David wilted before my eyes. He was devastated.

When we got back to Toledo, our engagement was touch and go. And I still wouldn't wear the ring. After a few months, I think David had given up, because he stopped asking. I spent many nights sitting by myself in our little home, wondering what life would be like without him, or more important, with him, as the wonderful husband and loving father I knew he would be. Finally it was just after Thanksgiving and we were putting up Christmas decorations, including stockings by the fireplace.

I slipped a small box into his stocking and then suggested he look inside. "That's not cool," he said. "I'm not supposed to look in my stocking till Christmas morning."

"I think Santa left you something in there a little early," I said.

David's arm disappeared into his stocking up to the elbow, and I could see the outline of his fingers grasping the box I had stuffed way down at the toe. He pulled it out and opened it. In it was a ring I'd bought for him, engraved with our initials, and a note:

Will You Marry Me?

Love, Lucinda

We both cried, and he ran upstairs to get the engagement ring he had so desperately wanted me to wear. As he slipped the ring on my finger, we both whispered loving words to each other. "I love you so much, David. I am so sorry for hurting you. I was just scared. But you are such an amazing man. You are so good to me, and so loving. It's just that marriage doesn't always work. But I want us to be together, to build our lives together. I want to have babies with you." As I said this, warm tears slipped out of the corners of my eyes and slid down to my lips. I could taste the salt in our kisses.

"Lucinda," he whispered as he kissed me, "you are life to me. Please never leave me. I want to spend forever with you." With that we kissed and made beautiful, precious love as if to consummate our promise of life together, forever.

(top left) The trip to visit Donna and Bob in San Francisco.

(top right) The big hitchhiking trip to Florida and my first time touching the ocean.

(middle) Singing with the Together Band.

(bottom left) My brother Michael and his then-girlfriend and eventual wife, Mary.

(bottom right) Lightening bolts; kissing on the beach near the cottage.

CHAPTER 10

Fixing People

WE GOT MARRIED SO FAST after that, you might have thought I was pregnant. I wasn't, but that's another story. Just ten days later we said our vows—it was December 8, 1982. What should have been—and ultimately was—one of the best days of my life started out as anything but. I woke up on my wedding day with a fever and laryngitis. On any other day, I would have stayed in bed. I was deathly pale and had zero energy—the beginning of a really bad cold or the flu. Whatever it was, I felt horrible. The big problem was not just getting through the ceremony itself. David and I were going on a simple honeymoon ski trip to Michigan right after the reception. It would be windy and bitterly cold out there on the slopes. Nothing like newlywed pneumonia to start a marriage off on the right foot.

We were getting married at 7:00 p.m., so my plan was to see a doctor and get something to jumpstart the beginning of a recovery—or at least make me feel a little less like I'd been freshly exhumed to walk down the aisle.

Dr. Philip Fisher was the new doctor on my health plan. Luckily for me, that day he was in and seeing new patients. I had no idea who this guy was, but he got high marks from my colleagues at the radio station. The even better news was that he could see me right away.

I checked in at his office at 1:00 p.m., and he walked into the examination room shortly thereafter. He was conservative-looking, smart, and very focused, with short brown hair and glasses. Interestingly, I noticed he was wearing jeans and Earth shoes underneath his lab coat. Not typical for those times. He spoke in direct, short sentences. I could tell he was all business and didn't want to waste time. But still, there was something about him that made me trust him. "I'm sick," I croaked weakly.

"Tell me about it," he replied.

I'm sure I gave him more than he really needed to know. I started telling him about the chills and fever, but then something led me into talking about my history of panic attacks and agoraphobia. I think I was anxious about the wedding and getting married (although I didn't tell him about that, at least not right away), and he seemed to be someone I could talk to. The part about anxiety got his attention.

"Have you been doing anything about it? Are you on medication?" he asked.

I told him that a few months back I picked up several books written by Claire Weekes, an Australian physician, including *Hope and Help for Your Nerves*, *Peace from Nervous Suffering*, and *Simple, Effective Treatment of Agoraphobia*, and that her advice in the books was really helping me. "I'm not all the way better yet, but I'm much better than I was. And no, no drugs. I think it is just so helpful to know you are not going crazy. And that you are not alone."

"So . . . you've basically started to cure yourself?" he asked.

"Pretty much. I had to do something, because I was a basket case," I admitted. "And I couldn't function anymore the way I wanted to. I went on a trip this past summer with my boyfriend—well, my fiancé—and I ruined it for both of us with my anxiety. I decided to do some research, and I found these books. I also found some tapes on anxiety. All of it together has really helped me."

"Did you ever see a doctor?"

"For a short period of time, I went to a psychiatrist, because I was afraid that I was going crazy. He gave me some kind of pill, and then I drove home. I felt zonked and more than a little weird, so I turned on the TV. On the Discovery Channel there was this program about someone who had gotten a partial frontal lobotomy or something, like McMurphy,

Jack Nicholson's character in *One Flew Over the Cuckoo's Nest*. I went into a full-blown panic attack and called my fiancé and told him—I was sure someone was going to do a frontal lobotomy on me."

"What did he say when you told him that?"

"He said, 'It's about time.'"

"Really!" Dr. Fisher smiled and began to laugh.

"David is always trying to help me not take life so seriously," I explained.

"Ah. Good for him. . . ." Dr. Fisher replied.

"Anyway, this psychiatrist put me into one of his therapy groups," I continued, "except that it was all different kinds of people with all kinds of weird problems. One guy kept shaking his head, and I finally asked him what was wrong. 'I got spiders running through my ears,' he told me. And, of course, after that I was checking my earlobes every five minutes for black widows. I was convinced I was going to get everything that the rest of the members of the group had."

"Didn't this psychiatrist make you feel any better at all?"

"Nope. I finally stopped going after he assured me that panic attacks were something I was stuck with for the rest of my life—that this was something I would struggle with forever."

"Well, unfortunately that's what a lot of doctors believe," said Dr. Fisher.

"Not Claire Weekes, and not me, either. After reading her books, I started realizing that I was scaring myself. I also realized that I could talk myself out of it and think different thoughts. Now I'm learning to manage my scary thoughts. And when I feel like I'm working myself into a panic attack, I say different things to myself and talk myself out of it. I can actually get into an elevator now. I can ride in a car if someone else is driving. I can get on a plane and almost enjoy it."

I also told Dr. Fisher about my history of irritable bowel syndrome. When I confessed that recently I'd noticed some rectal bleeding, I saw him reaching for rubber gloves and nonchalantly placing them on his hands, ending with a theatrically loud *snap*!

"We don't need to go there," I said firmly. "I am not prepared to do that."

"Would it make you feel better if I took off my pants, too?" he said with a grin.

I laughed in spite of myself. Doctors can be cold and impersonal, but he was none of that. He was trying to make light of the situation.

"Listen," he said. "It's probably nothing, but rectal bleeding is not something to ignore. Let me just do a quick exam and get a sample. It *is* necessary."

I took a deep breath and he took his sample. Done. Ugh. What an introduction.

And that's how we met.

"You know," he said, removing his gloves and washing his hands, "my patients come to see me with all kinds of symptoms—stomachaches, headaches, muscle spasms, sleeplessness—and for about 85 percent of them, what's wrong with them is rooted in feelings of anxiety and depression. I put them on antidepressants or antianxiety medication, but that's anything but a permanent solution and can lead to a whole different set of problems."

I glanced at my watch. It was nearly 2:00 p.m. I had to run . .

"What's the matter?" he asked. "Got a hot date?"

"Actually, yes, I do. I'm getting married in about five hours."

"Are you serious? You've got to be kidding me!"

"No, I'm dead serious."

He examined me a bit further and decided to put me on an antibiotic for my sore throat and sinus issues. Then he continued, "I'm fascinated by what you're telling me about helping yourself get over your anxiety and panic attacks. Can you call me when you get back from your honeymoon? I want to hear more about what you did to help yourself. Meanwhile, get outta here. Go get married."

I rushed from his office to transform myself into a bride. I quickly did my own hair and makeup, put on the seventy-five-dollar off-the-shoulder dress I'd bought at the Lyons store, and headed for the glassed-in conservatory in the park, where the wedding would be held. By this time, I had also taken some cold and flu medicine and was feeling a bit better. It had started snowing, and the falling snowflakes added to the fairy-tale, romantic feeling of the evening.

It was a small, simple wedding—about fifty friends and family would be there. I put one long-stemmed red rose on each table as David went off to pick up the long tin trays of food from Beirut, the local Lebanese restaurant. He also picked up my dad from the local bar. He was still sober enough, more or less, to give me away. We said our vows as the snow fell all around us. We had written them ourselves. It was a beautiful, magical evening as we stood in front of the large live Christmas tree that filled the room.

My joy was tempered by what I saw happening to my brother David. Sadly, he was following in our father's footsteps and becoming a severe alcoholic. It had been coming on for a while, but now it was worse—much worse. His wife had left him because of his drinking. He could no longer hold down a job. He came to my wedding, but this was an exception he made just for me. Otherwise, he didn't go out much at all—he'd become a recluse. He spent all day inside his house, blinds drawn against the sun, drinking peppermint schnapps.

Between untreated post-traumatic stress disorder stemming from his time in Vietnam and the lingering emotional scars from having grown up in our ever-so-dysfunctional family, I knew that my brother really needed to get help. My father's legacy had struck again. I went to see him after I had finally put a name on my problems and was starting to see some improvement. "I know what's wrong with me," I told him, "and I think it's the same thing that might be wrong with you. I have anxiety and panic attacks. I think maybe you have anxiety and depression, and drinking is your way of dealing with it."

"Yeah, well, you may be right, Sis," he said, fondling his glass of peppermint schnapps. "If that's what I've got, this is how I deal with it," he added, rattling the glass.

"No, no!" I exclaimed. "You don't understand. This is going to kill you."

"It's possible," he replied flatly. With that, he lifted his glass, shook it at me defiantly, and chug-a-lugged the contents. "Cheers."

The almost violent clink of the ice cubes scared the crap out of me. It sounded like a death rattle. David Redick didn't want my help or anyone else's. He had given up on himself. Sins of the father. I wanted desperately to help him, but at the time I didn't yet have enough skill or knowledge about what he was dealing with.

By now David and I were living in Toledo. I was still selling radio adver-tising. I was okay with it for the time being, but it was just a job, certain-ly not anything I wanted to call my life's work. I still had my *ALMOST FAMOUS* button, and I knew that nobody gets famous—or even almost famous—for selling radio time in Toledo.

What I wanted more than anything else, however, had nothing to do with fame or career. What I wanted was a baby. I ditched my birth control pills. David and I tried and tried to get pregnant. We tried for about a year and a half—the "clinical scientific" method—taking my temperature and all that. Nothing doing. He went to the doctor; he wasn't wearing the wrong jockey shorts, and there was nothing wrong with his sperm count. That meant that *I* was the problem.

Oh, shit.

I knew exactly why it was my fault. My head went straight back to my childhood— straight back to my overwhelming sense of guilt over the role I played in what I still did not understand had been sexual abuse. Forget the idea that I was a victim—that was just not on my radar. Forget the idea that as a child, I'd been powerless to prevent what happened. I still thought it was something done *by* me, not *to* me, and I was sure I was being punished by God for being sinful, dirty.

Guilt. Blame. Anger. Shame.

I blamed myself for having broken God's laws. Now I had to pay the price. God's punishment would be to deny me the thing I wanted most of all—a baby.

Heavenly payback.

I felt . . . doomed. I didn't say anything about it to my husband. I was too afraid. I didn't want to confess that I'd never be able to give him a child. I did think about telling my ob-gyn, because I suspected that the sexual "games" I had played had somehow ruined my plumbing, but I was too ashamed.

Guilt. Blame. Anger. Shame. A vicious cycle from which there would be no escape, at least not for me. You see, bad things do happen. Things you worry about do come true. I knew I was going to be punished, and this was the worst punishment of all.

Miracles happen, too.

Turned out that all it took was a business trip to Chicago and a whole bunch of bad weather. It rained for four days straight. We spent most of our time in bed.

About two weeks after we got home, my period was supposed to show up. It didn't. A week later, it still hadn't. David was in New York on business, and I called to tell him.

"I think you're pregnant," he said.

"I don't think so." I figured it was proof that my uterus, my ovaries, *something* in my system was damaged, and damaged in a way that could never be fixed. I didn't dare tell David that I knew I'd never get pregnant, and I certainly could never tell him the reason why.

"Lucinda—go get a pregnancy test," he said, "just to be sure."

I went out and bought a pregnancy test at the store. I got home, went into the bathroom, and said a little prayer to God. "Please, please let me be pregnant. I am so sorry for what I did. Please, God. I want this baby for me, for David." A few minutes later I was stunned and shocked when the test turned up positive. I had just seen the results when my friend Rachel knocked on the door. I was still screaming with joy when I let her in.

"Rachel! Raaaachel!" I was dancing and leaping around like a lunatic and screaming at the top of my lungs. "The rabbit died! The rabbit died!"

"What?" Rachel peered over her glasses at me in disapproval. She was a rather staid—okay, stuffy—intellectual with a PhD in something off the wall, like medieval German literature. Whooping and hollering and dancing around—like I was doing—was simply not done.

"The rabbit died! I'm PREGNANT!"

I felt like I'd won the lottery. Maybe God wasn't out to get me after all. I called David back. After I told him the news, we cried with each other over the phone.

"You know what, Lucinda Bassett?" he said between his tears. "It's all going to be okay, just like I told you. You're going to live your life. You're going to be married to me, and you're going to have our beautiful babies, and your life is going to be amazing and normal. You just wait and see."

I was so ecstatic that I was in the clouds for several days. It took a dreadful phone call from my brother Gary to bring me down—way down. "Get in the car and get to the hospital as fast as you can," he told me. "David's here. I went to see him at his house 'cause I couldn't get hold of him. When I got there, I found him half-dead. Acute alcohol poisoning."

"How is he?" I asked.

"I've already called Donna and told her to get on a plane," Gary replied.

"I'll call Donna, too. She hates to fly almost as much as I used to."

"She'll have to get over it if she wants to say good-bye. Sis, the doctors don't think he's gonna make it."

"Oh my God. Are you sure?"

"He doesn't look good."

That was a grotesque understatement. When I got there, the person in the bed was unrecognizable as my brother David. The only way I knew it was him was that Gary, Michael, Mom, and even Dad were all there beside him. Dad was bloated and fat and smelly, but he was just as overcome as the rest of us as he watched his son being tortured by a disease that was knowingly passed down by him. David was all yellow, including his eyes, and he was swollen up so bad he looked inflated. He had monitors beeping by his bedside and tubes running in and out of him, including ones that were pumping blood out from his nose and mouth. It was horrid.

At first I was afraid to go in the room. I didn't want to expose my baby to whatever he had. His doctor gently told me that the yellow was a sign of severe jaundice brought on by the cirrhosis. It wasn't contagious. I went into the room, crying, and held him. We all stayed there for several hours, devastated.

And then the monitors stopped beeping. There was just one solid tone. Flatline. David Redick was dead. He was only forty years old. My mother began rocking back and forth—I don't even think she knew she was doing it. Then she turned and looked at my dad with complete and total disgust. He was looking away from the bed. She was in shock.

"NO!" she shouted as she grabbed my father by the shoulders and violently spun him back around to face the lifeless body in the bed. "How dare you look away! Take a good look, Ikey! This is the way you're going to die, too! I hate you. I HATE YOU!"

Donna's flight had been delayed by bad weather. She never arrived in time to see David alive, and it was something that affected her terribly through the years to come. Guilt. Blame. Anger. Shame.

Donna was devastated and furious with my father. She hated him before, but now she hated him even more. It was his fault David was dead. It was his fault she struggled with her own demons, and his fault our family was fucked up.

But Donna's wrath, as intense as it was, was nothing compared to my mother's. I had no doubt that she held my father responsible. She believed he had killed David as surely as if he'd plunged a dagger into his heart.

All her life, Mom had had this teeny, mousy voice. Not now. Now she was as angry as she was anguished. The expression of her grief started in her throat as an almost otherworldly keening wail, but soon rose to a mighty roar, which she directed at my father. "*You!*" she growled. Fueled by a lifetime of pent-up rage, it was a voice I'd never heard from her before. If I hadn't been looking straight at her, I'd have never believed that sound was coming out of her body. "Look at your son, Ikey," she continued, her eyes boring into him. "Look at what you've done! I hate you. I want you out of my house. I WANT YOU OUT OF MY LIFE!"

After David's funeral, my mother made my father move out. I knew this time it was for good, because she got rid of the easy chair in the living room. I helped her take it out. She also ripped out the dingy gold carpet that had been there since we moved in. There were maggots under it, right where Dad's chair had been. Right where he had spent many nights sitting on the floor peeing himself, propped up against that chair. It was disgusting, nauseating, and enough to make her never, ever want him back.

I don't really remember much after that, except that I was pregnant and sad. I had something I wanted so badly, a baby growing inside me, but I was so deeply mourning the death of my brother.

David had been our gentle giant, the loving, sensitive one of the family. He played guitar; he didn't have a temper. When David died, a little piece of each of us died with him.

Then, one day when I was grieving for my brother, I felt a flutter, something that made me rub my belly involuntarily. I wasn't far enough along for my baby to be stirring inside me, but I was sure something had moved. I wondered if it was the transfer of David Redick's beautiful and gentle spirit into the child growing in my womb. "Doesn't God recycle?" I thought to myself.

With a baby on the way, David and I wanted to buy a house. Although I liked our house in Toledo, we were just renting. We started looking in Oak Harbor, where David's family ran a small supermarket. The Bassetts owned a few IGA markets in the vicinity, and they had invited him into the family business.

The Bassetts were known for their local grocery stores, especially their wonderful family-style customer service. The Bassett family was a far cry from mine. David's was a perfect family, and I was proud to be part of it. Richard and Dorothy Bassett had three children, David, Mike, and Jody. David's dad was full-blooded Lebanese and had taken over the grocery store from his mother, who had started it many years ago. Richard was funny, charming, a bit sarcastic, and a great businessman. He came from a long history of great authentic Lebanese cooking, which his wife, Dorothy, learned to embrace. I would always search through their refrigerator in hopes of finding leftover kibbe or tabbouleh. We had wonderful dinners full of family at Grandma Bassett's home in Oak Harbor. She was a wonderful cook.

Dorothy Bassett was a positive force in the family. Always upbeat and full of fun, she loved to have all the kids for a meal or a holiday. She was funny, loving, and very proud of her family. She sold real state in the area and enjoyed her and Richard's social life.

Mike was David's older brother by two years. He graduated from college and immediately stepped in to help his father expand the grocery stores, opening more stores in the area within a few years of his join-ing the family business. Mike was outgoing and social, and brought a lot of personality and much-needed business skills to the family grocery store business.

Jody, the baby of the family, was a few years younger than David. She was a little ball of fire and one of the most confident women I had ever met. She was very pretty, with dark eyes; long, dark, full hair; and a beau-tiful smile. She inherited her mom's wonderful positive attitude and her dad's head for business. She eventually became one of the top cell-phone salespeople in Canada. Unfortunately, she died of oral cancer in her late thirties. Some wondered if there was any correlation between her con-stant use of her cell phone at that time and the oral cancer. The Bassetts mourned her death as deeply as I mourned the death of my brother.

Even though I missed him greatly, I now tried to look ahead to the birth of our baby. That included finding a home. Oak Harbor is a small town—a village, almost—about thirty miles outside of Toledo, right on the Portage River. I'd always wanted to live on the river; I'd even picked out which house I wanted. It was an old white farmhouse, and it was owned by the Kebergs, an elderly couple who had lived there forever. Just on a hunch, David and I went to visit them. Over tea we offered them a $10,000 check as a good-faith retainer, securing us the first option on the house if they ever decided to move. Mrs. Keberg was reluctant, but her husband was unwell. About a month and a $95,000 mortgage later, the house and its fifty acres were ours.

At the time I was still working at the radio station, and when I was newly pregnant I'd lined up a guest for the noon news—someone to come talk about phobias and panic attacks. The woman was a no-show. As it got close to noon, Kevin, the disc jockey, asked, "Lucinda, where's my guest?"

"Maybe she had a panic attack and bailed," I said, smiling. I meant it as a joke, but he didn't think it was funny. He still needed a guest for the noon news show.

"Then I guess you'll have to come on yourself and talk about your own panic attacks and how you've overcome them," Kevin said. "You're just going to have to take her place, Lucinda."

We had a slot for a guest, an empty chair, and no time to get a replacement. From his point of view, what he was saying made a lot of sense. From my point of view, no way. Even though I was pretty much over the anxiety, I really didn't want to talk about how messed up I'd been, certainly not on local radio.

"But . . ." I was still insisting that I wasn't going to do it as Kevin hustled me into the studio and put my mic on.

"Our guest today is Lucinda Bassett," he began. "Lucinda, tell me about your experience with anxiety and panic attacks. What is anxiety, and what is a panic attack, exactly?"

"Well, anxiety is worry. You worry that you might lose control, or you feel panicky in certain situations, like driving or flying. Your heart starts to pound; you feel like you can't breathe. And for me, I felt like I was going crazy. But I wasn't. I was just having something called a panic attack."

As I talked, the phones lit up. People were asking me questions. And I had answers.

"Why do I feel so anxious when someone else is driving or when I am flying?" one lady asked.

"Because you are not in control. People who are anxious need to feel like they can come and go as they please, or they will feel trapped," I replied.

"What do I do when I start to feel anxious while I am speaking in a meeting?" a male caller asked.

"Plan an ending to your presentation that lets you stop sooner. You will just feel better and more in control, and you will probably run longer as a result. And imagine your audience sitting in their underwear. It will make you smile and relax. But most important, avoid caffeine and sugar before you speak, or even fly, for that matter, because they are stimulants and can create feelings of nervousness and anxiety," I said confidently.

I made them feel better. I gave them hope. I reassured them. The five-minute interview turned into a half hour. When I got off the show, the phone lines lit up like firecrackers. We were overwhelmed.

"See all those calls on hold?" Kevin asked. "They're all waiting to talk to you." It was my first clue that I was onto something. People were desperate for help.

Meanwhile, I was enjoying being pregnant, even though I got gestational diabetes, a temporary condition that happens during pregnancy when the body can't make enough insulin. I went to see Phil Fisher about it. After he and I had bonded over rubber gloves on my wedding day, he'd become my regular doctor. He'd also become my good friend. As soon as I told him that the home pregnancy test was positive, he took me right away to the hospital to confirm it. Phil was almost as excited and happy about my pregnancy as David and I were.

"How are you doing with the anxiety?" he asked during my checkup.

"It's almost gone," I replied. By this time, my agoraphobia and panic attacks had all but disappeared. I was using the skills I had learned from Claire Weekes's books to conquer my fears, and one by one they were falling away. I was feeling, well, normal. No, *better* than normal. I was married to a man who adored me. I was joyously expecting the birth of my first child—I had that pregnancy glow. And even though my brother had died, life was looking better.

Except for the death of my brother and my concern for my father, things were okay. In addition to being happily pregnant, I was really pleased by the positive response to my radio interview. I wasn't the only one. "I heard about what happened at the radio station," Phil Fisher told me. "We should do something together to help people with anxiety and depression. Not everyone is a self-starter like you. I'd like to help more people do what you've done. What do you think about doing outpatient groups on anxiety and depression here in my office? We can teach them what you've learned. Together, I think we can really help people."

"I'm in," I said. Didn't think twice. Didn't have to. Why wouldn't I jump at the chance to work with this man? Phil Fisher is one of the most brilliant, confident, assertive men I've ever met. Besides, I was still something of a hypochondriac (a common symptom of anxiety disorder), and the idea that I could have a doctor in my pocket sounded too good to be true.

"How do we get the word out?" he asked.

"Leave that to me," I replied with a smile. I'd spent several years writing and selling advertising, and I thought that some of what I'd done had been pretty creative. I knew how to get people's attention—and it all began with offering them free group sessions.

I placed an ad in the *Toledo Blade* with a personal quiz that listed some of the major symptoms of anxiety and panic disorder. I went right to the symptoms that had affected me personally. Do you worry about losing your mind? Do you have panic attacks? Do you worry about death and dying? Do you have a hard time sleeping? Are you afraid of losing control? Are you afraid that you'll embarrass yourself in public? If you experience any of these, come to a free seminar.

There was no way to know how many people would show up. As it turned out, about fifty men and women responded to the ad—all ages, sizes, shapes, and colors. We jammed them into the waiting room of Dr. Fisher's office.

For the first half hour or so, I just told everyone what happened to me. "Hi. My name is Lucinda Bassett, and my anxieties were so bad that I couldn't ride in an elevator or fly in a plane. I went to a psychiatrist for help, but he put me in a group of people who had spiders crawling in their ears and doorknobs to polish. He told me that my mother and father were all messed up. He told me that I should be mad at my whole family and assured me that I'd be having panic attacks for the rest of my life. Meanwhile, I was beginning to find my own road map for overcoming anxiety and stress. You don't have to live with this. You can overcome it. Dr. Fisher and I will show you how."

Then I invited others to stand up and share their stories. Our initial group of fifty became a group of twelve who signed up for a group treatment program. This was the start of the Midwest Center for Stress and Anxiety. Little did I know how big this little engine would become, and that it would help millions overcome problems with anxiety and depression.

For fifteen weeks in a group format, Phil Fisher and I talked to them about everything—how to work through a panic attack, how to deal with obsessive scary thoughts, how to deal with out-of-control anger, how to use diaphragmatic breathing to bring your fears under control, to name just a few. I kept rerunning the ad for the free seminar, so that we started a new small group of twelve every few weeks. We also benefited from tremendous word of mouth. Soon we were running three groups of twelve each week. It wasn't long before people were driving for hours on end to participate in our programs. They were changing their lives; they were losing weight, quitting smoking, getting off alcohol and medications for anxiety and depression, and getting their lives back. By the end of the fifteen weeks, they knew how to manage their time, they knew the importance of exercise, and they knew how to control worry. They were getting better, they were flushing their meds down the toilet, and they were going back to their doctors and beaming about their miracle recoveries.

This was not supposed to happen—what we were doing flew in the face of the conventional psychiatric wisdom of the day. At the time, the standard treatment for people with anxiety and depression was much like what I had experienced at the shrink's—sign up for Freudian therapy, spend a fortune, and waste a lot of time talking about your mother twice a week, then join a group with people who had symptoms that were completely different from your own.

Prescription drugs often were part of the therapy. The situation is much better today, but at the time there were only so many meds that were available and a lot of them were bad—like the one that had me convinced I was a lobotomy candidate. Many of them had terrible side effects—increased depression, lack of sex drive, inability to have an orgasm, weight gain, sleeping issues. So not only are you anxious but you can't sleep, can't get a hard-on, can't have an orgasm, and you're twenty pounds heavier.

And you wonder why you're depressed.

Although I had started from the basis of Claire Weekes's program, I had also done a lot more research on my own. Through what I learned and through dealing with the many individuals in our groups, I came to realize that people with anxiety were not only not crazy, but were extraordinarily gifted. They were very intelligent and also highly creative. They had vivid imaginations. They were futuristic, outside-the-box thinkers. This was something to be celebrated.

At the first meeting of every group, I began by saying, "You are amazing. There's nothing wrong with you. In fact, you are chock-full of potential for greatness if you can take those personality traits, those ways of thinking that are destroying you because you're turning them inward, and start focusing them *outward*, where they belong. You can transform that energy of anxiety and the personality traits that are associated with it into something positive that can help you build a great life for yourself."

This was the premise that made us unique. There is nothing wrong with you if you are anxious. In fact, you are unique and full of potential! Truth.

The program continued to grow. We fielded phone calls from people saying, "My aunt in Texas wants you to come help her," or "I have a cousin in Florida who really needs this program. . . ."

I could see the lightbulb go on in Phil Fisher's wonderful brain. "You know," he said, "we should really put this on tape. If we did, we could help people all over the world."

I bought a little tape recorder and started recording our sessions. Participants in the program received the tapes, together with a little workbook I created to go along with them. People loved them, because they gave them a way to keep in touch with the principles we were teaching.

David was incredibly supportive. He went out and bought me my first computer—an Apple IIc, which seems almost like a dinosaur today. I said a little prayer of gratitude for those typing classes I'd suffered through in the DECA program at Findlay High, because the materials I developed became the first *Attacking Anxiety and Depression* program.

At the time, however, it didn't really register that that's what I was doing. I just knew that I had found what I was good at—fixing people. It was too late to fix my brother David, but I was helping hundreds, and eventually thousands, of others. Once again, I was coloring outside the lines. And once again, it was working. It didn't bother me in the slightest that I had no fancy college degree, no medical training. Dr. Fisher had that covered—as a physician with training in psychology, he had all the credentials and licenses we needed. Me? I was the walking success story—the living proof that this approach worked. I was the peer-support person and the one who walked the walk. I was what recovery looked like. But more important, I was divinely driven. Finally I had found my mission in life. I was writing and creating the product with Dr. Fisher's input, and we ran the groups together.

Meanwhile, the baby was large enough to push on my diaphragm. I could actually hear my voice change on the various tapes we made for the very first version of the *Attacking Anxiety and Depression* program.

My due date came and went, but this baby showed no sign of coming out. By now it was February 1986, and I felt as big as a house. I couldn't even tie my own shoes. I went out to take a walk and slipped and fell on my ass. That night, my water broke. Finally. Whoever was in there was coming out. David bundled me into the car and we headed for Toledo Hospital. I always knew David loved me, but I was about to find out just how much.

CHAPTER 11

Motherhood and Miscarriage

I'VE ALWAYS BEEN on the slim side, but now I was a blimp. My weight was all out front, and frankly, it was kind of frightening at this point to think something that big was actually going to come out of me. Lurking in the back of my mind was the ominous fact that big babies run in our family.

David wanted this baby as much as I did. In bed he used to lie there with his head up against my tummy, waiting for the excitement of a kick or a push, and talking to his unborn child. As I got bigger and bigger, I could feel the little feet pushing on my diaphragm. Even though it was uncomfortable, back then I thought that was cute. Now, however, I was so done. I just wanted to get this baby out of me. I wanted to sleep on my stomach, tie my own shoes, and feel sexy again. It was time—in fact, way past time.

The baby had other ideas. I was over two weeks past my due date, so she must have liked it in there. But finally, on that fateful night at two o'clock in the morning, I was lying in bed and my water broke. When we arrived at the hospital, I was only two centimeters dilated and stayed that way for what seemed like forever. I was in agony with each contraction, but nothing was happening. In hospital language, the labor was not "progressing." No kidding—it was as if this baby was holding onto my innards for dear life.

David stayed glued to my side. He was feeling my pain. He was so loving and concerned. He stood beside me, helped me practice my breathing, and reassured me that things were going to be okay. But I was concerned about him. We were now going on about fifteen hours of labor here, and I still wasn't dilating.

"Go get something to eat," I told him finally.

David shook his head adamantly. "No, I'm not leaving you," he said.

I squeezed his hand and moaned for the nine zillionth time. The contractions were horrible. I was scared, exhausted, and overwhelmed, like most women in labor. But mine went on for forty hours, and David was beside me every minute. Eventually the doctor came in, checked me again, and said I was at eight centimeters. Then, it seemed out of nowhere, a nurse wheeled in a bassinet with a little baby gown and beanie and little blankets.

"Lucinda, look!" David whispered to the side of my cheek with tears in his eyes. "See, there's the crib! And there are little baby clothes. Lucinda, everything's going to be okay. You're going to have this baby. Your life's going to be normal, and we're going to be happy. It's going to be all right. *You're* going to be all right."

"No, I'm not," I replied with anxiety. Despite his constant reassurances, I was sure something was very wrong. And the fact that the baby was still refusing to come out was all the proof I needed.

As if on cue, the nurse came running back into the room. "You've been in labor for a very long time, Mrs. Bassett," she said. "We're going to put in a fetal monitor. We're afraid the baby's heart is starting to become stressed. We're concerned that the baby might be at risk."

"David, I'm scared." I started to panic more. "What if the baby is damaged? What if I can't get it out? What if I can't do this?" I started to cry.

David went running out into the hall. At that point I think he was afraid of losing me. "Hey, someone, where's the damn *DOCTOR!*" he bellowed. "We need a doctor in here *NOW*! *Where is the fucking doctor?*"

The obstetrician appeared, looked at the monitor and at David's and my scared, anxious faces, and announced that we were out of time. The anesthesiologist came in and explained the process of giving me a spinal through a needle in the lower back. After the procedure, I lay there waiting and praying for the pain to diminish. "We're taking you down into the OR, Mrs. Bassett, for a C-section. Mr. Bassett, you can come along. You need to get scrubbed up now."

Once in the operating room, everything seemed surreal. I had that horrible feeling of bewilderment and panic. I couldn't breathe. I saw everyone running in green scrubs around me, but I couldn't quite take it all in. All I did know was that whatever was in that spinal wasn't strong enough. Once they give you a spinal, you're not supposed to feel a thing. My labor pains were gone, but to their surprise and my horror, I felt exactly when the doctor started cutting. "Stop!" I screamed. "I can feel it!"

"You're hurting her! You're hurting her!" David shouted.

I started flailing my arms around. "Oh my God!" I thought to myself. "They are ripping through my stomach and I can feel the whole thing!" I was in full panic mode. "David, stop them. I can feel it! Someone help me, please!"

Next thing I knew they were tying my hands down to the table. That was it. Trapped. I felt David grab one of my restricted hands, trying to reassure me. As he looked into my eyes he was crying. "Lucinda, I am so sorry. God, this is so awful."

He looked at the obstetrician. *"DO SOMETHING!"* he cried. "She is *FEELING* it!"

He looked back at me. "When we get through this," he said, "I'll take you anywhere you want to go. Tell me where."

"Florida," I whispered through tears of my own. "Florida."

All of a sudden there was a gas mask being applied to my face and an IV being placed in my arm, and I was in twilight.

At that moment the doctor started pulling out the baby. "Oh, my," he said, "you have a very big baby boy here."

Wrong. I knew that was wrong. "No," I said in a daze. "It's a girl."

"Well, young lady, you are right . . . it is," he said, correcting himself with some surprise as he kept pulling. "You have a big, beautiful, baby girl, and she has a lot of hair."

There she was, shaking and crying. Beautiful little "big" Brittany had come into the world. They cleaned her up and handed her to David. God, was he proud! He came strutting over to me with her in his arms and held her up beside me. "Look, Lucinda. Look how beautiful she is!"

He laid her beside me. She was healthy, ten pounds, two ounces, and none the worse for the forty-hour ordeal. Me, not so much. I was not doing well. I'd never been fully anesthetized. Once they'd pulled her out, the doctor started sewing me back up. I could feel that, too. Layer by layer, I felt every stitch. I was numbed by the extra anesthesia, but still, I felt the tugging. It was a very strange sensation. Why wasn't it like in the movies, where the woman pushes the baby out, sits up, and holds her, smiling lovingly with her husband? Not in the cards for me.

After checking her out and cleaning her up a bit more, they brought our daughter back into the OR. I was still tied down, so David scooped her up and went to show her off to my mother, who was waiting out in the hallway. "Isn't she beautiful!" he exclaimed to anyone who would listen. "Isn't she the most beautiful thing you've ever seen?"

I had no idea he would be that happy or proud.

As they were wheeling me out of surgery, David stuck her on my boob—she just latched onto that thing and started sucking like crazy. Up until then, I hadn't even known whether or not I was going to breastfeed, but I quickly understood that the choice was no longer up to me.

They put me in a room with another new mom, who had just given birth vaginally. She was doing great, one of those sit-up-and-enjoy experiences that I fantasized about. An endless parade of noisy visitors filed in to see her. Unfortunately, they had to pass right by me. I was still moaning. I felt awful. David set up camp in a little corner of the room in a green vinyl chair, right by my bedside, holding Brittany.

The hospital staff tried to encourage him to go home, or at least to go get something to eat. "Your wife is fine. The baby's fine," they told him. "Go home and get some rest. Take care of yourself." With their reassurance, he left to go home and get some much-needed sleep.

He wasn't gone an hour, though, when the phone rang on the table beside me. "Lucinda, are you okay?" he asked softly, almost in tears from exhaustion. "Is the baby okay?"

"Yes," I said, "we're okay."

"Lucinda, I just want to come back and be with you."

As soon as David walked in, he made his way through my tiny little space in the room, moved the hospital table aside, wrapped himself around me, and kissed me gently. "I can't be home right now without you," he said. "I was so scared I was going to lose you. I had to come back." Then he asked the nurse to bring in the baby so he could hold her. As he wrapped her up in his arms, David settled into the chair beside my bed, cuddling her and looking at me. "I love you, Lucinda. I love you so much."

And there he sat with his head on my bed, smashed up against me, holding her, and pretty much didn't move until I was discharged. And if you ask me about the most memorable, loving times in my life, this truly is one, if not *the* one.

For all the agony of her arrival, Brittany's birth was the beginning of a happy time for us. Little by little, we renovated our farmhouse, making it our own and doing a lot of the work ourselves. On weekends we'd put Brittany on the floor in the living room in her baby seat, while we used vinegar to sponge off layers and layers of old wallpaper. Step by step, it became our amazing little piece of heaven in Oak Harbor, Ohio. We had it all: a wonderful marriage, a beautiful, healthy new baby, a fabulous home, and David had the offer of a promising new job.

David's family offered him a job in their grocery business—again—and this time he accepted it. This was a position he had initially rejected when he first graduated from Ohio State. Rather than getting "tied down" working in a supermarket, he had taken Mercy the Doberman and Sheaton the Wonder Hound and headed out west to Jackson Hole, Wyoming, to start his own landscaping business. The idea was to establish his company in a place he loved, where he could ski, hike, and mountain bike. After some start-up issues and financial challenges in the first year, however, he decided it wasn't going so well, so he came back to Ohio and opened his landscaping business there.

David was always such a free spirit—an adventurer—and I loved that about him. But now that we were a family, we had to have our adventures closer to home. We bought an old boat and went waterskiing on the river. Sometimes we'd venture out onto Lake Erie and cruise around Port Clinton. We even went back out to our old favorite romantic spot, Put-in-Bay.

It was a great life. Oak Harbor was a wonderful place to raise children—a farming community of about three thousand people near Lake Erie. Everybody knew each other. It's a beautiful Midwestern town with gorgeous old Victorian houses, brick streets, and oak trees with lots of shade. The Portage River was our back door. It was such a beautiful little scenic property. We even had ducks and chickens and at one point, two goats.

The local farmers grew corn, tomatoes, strawberries, and peaches, and driving down country roads in summer you could actually smell their sweet ripeness in the air. We had a big apple tree in the backyard, and every year we went to the Oak Harbor Apple Festival. The weather changed dramatically from one season to the next, and each season brought its own delights. We had fabulous snowfalls, and at Christmastime there would be deer in our backyard. We told Brittany that they were Santa's reindeer.

The holidays there were wonderful "family" time. We often split our holidays between David's family and mine, which meant two Thanksgiving dinners. David's aunt Nancy invited the whole clan. Sometimes there were twenty-five people or more. All the kids played while the women cooked and the men watched TV and chatted it up. We all sat down at a long table to a fabulous meal.

There were memorable Thanksgivings at our house, too. By now, Donna and Bob and their two girls had moved from Jacksonville, Florida, to Louisville, Kentucky, where Bob had landed a major job as a hospital honcho. Because they were so much closer, we got together more often, especially for the holidays. On Thanksgiving morning, the huge country kitchen in our farmhouse was filled with the smell of sage and onion and sausage as we made the stuffing. It was also filled with laughter. Since childhood, Donna and I had always been extremely close. We had so much fun together. Sometimes we would laugh so hard we thought we were going to pee our pants.

One Thanksgiving I had bought a gigantic twenty-four-pound turkey. Donna and I got it all prepped and ready to put into the oven, but after we put butter on it, it got too slippery to carry. We dropped it. The bird went power-gliding thirty feet across the kitchen floor like it was jet-propelled. That set off a round of pee-in-your-pants laughter that left Donna and me doubled over, helpless and gasping for breath. We broke out in sporadic giggles all through dinner, just at the thought of it.

We loved watching *White Christmas* together. I was Vera Ellen to her Rosie Clooney (or was it vice versa?): "*Sisters, Sisters; There were never such devoted sisters.*"

My mother would come over from Findlay to be with us, and not just during the holidays. Without Dad, Mom was now doing much better. She had stayed with him through all those very bad years because she somehow still really loved him (or at least she still loved the romantic idea of the man she had married), but on a deeper level I think she was also afraid of ending up alone. I have recognized this fear in myself off and on throughout my life, and that's probably where I got it from.

Although my mother lacked confidence and strength, she was such a wonderful mom and always put her children first. When my brother David died, Mom blamed Dad for what happened, and it was something she knew she could never forgive. She not only kicked Dad out but also found the guts to stick to her guns and not let him return, as she had done so often in the past.

Then she reclaimed her life. No longer a doormat, she put her own stamp on that house on the dead-end street. After tossing Dad's chair—that chair had such a presence, such power, such symbolism—and the disgusting gold rug, she put in the prettiest soft blue carpet and fresh white curtains. As soon as I saw that, I knew she was really done with him.

All those years when my father was going out on her, she worked; she came home; she ironed clothes; she put food on the table; she took care of her five kids. I don't know that I could have done what she did. Her life had always been all about her children. And when we had kids of our own, it became all about her grandchildren as well. I learned how to be a mom from watching my mother be a grandma. Now that the drama and trauma of Dad and alcoholism was out of her life, she seemed to be calmer, happier, and really enjoying her later years.

The beauty of my mother was that she saw beauty in the simplest things. She had a way of making everything special. She and I would drive down to visit Donna and Bob and their girls in Louisville. She sat in the back with Brittany, pointing out cows and wildlife, and telling her stories. My mom was just a simple, lovely person. With Dad out of the picture, she was pleasant, living in the moment, enjoying her life and her grandchildren.

As Brittany, David, and I settled into life as a family, David dove wholeheartedly into working in the family supermarkets. He did everything he could to learn the business inside and out. He stocked shelves; he cut meat; he worked in the offices; he even opened up pharmacies in the stores. I was still doing groups with Phil Fisher. Not only were we seeing a lot of people face-to-face, we were also selling a lot of *Attacking Anxiety and Depression* cassette programs. Each cassette had a written workbook segment that went with it. There were fifteen cassettes and fifteen workbook "chapters"; I mailed them out, one lesson at a time, as people progressed through the program. For convenience, I rented a tiny office across the street from the Bassett grocery store in Oak Harbor. It was right next door to a beauty salon. As I sat there, the sharp ammonia smell of perm solution would waft in and sting my nostrils. That storefront became the first official home of the Midwest Center for Stress and Anxiety.

Brittany was still in diapers when I decided to start speaking out on anxiety and depression. I joined the National Speakers Association. After an amazing, inspiring, highly motivational weekend retreat, I came home thinking that just maybe I could do it. After all, I was entertaining, and I had skills to teach. I started locally. I approached Owens Corning in Toledo and pitched them on doing a one-hour stress management keynote speech, dealing with stress and anxiety and its role in the workplace. My asking price: $500.

They bought it, which produced a real "Oh-my-God!" moment on my part. What had I done? Who did I think I was? What could I possibly have to say that was worth $500 an hour? At the time, $500 for an hour sounded like a lot of money, but I didn't factor in the week I needed ahead of time to prepare content. By the time I walked into the auditorium, I was overprepared—that is my nature—but I walked in with confidence and that entertainer swagger. At the end, I got a standing ovation, plus a request from Owens Corning to do ten more sessions.

That was the beginning. I went on to do seminars for other corporations in the Toledo area, including McDonald's, Chrysler, and AT&T. Then I branched out, going to cities like Buffalo, Pittsburgh, Louisville, and Cleveland—even Toronto. We put an ad in the paper, held a free seminar, and sold *Attacking Anxiety and Depression* programs in the back of the room. The response was overwhelming. People would come from miles away. Sometimes we'd get crowds of up to two thousand people.

As the program grew in popularity, it became harder and harder for me to send out the cassettes singlehanded. To keep up with the mailings, I hired a woman named Carolyn Dickman. Carolyn was a "graduate" who had gone through one of our earliest group sessions with Phil Fisher and had successfully overcome her own anxiety and depression. She was a warm and kind person with an Erma Bombeck sense of humor. She was also a mom with six kids. I was really happy when she agreed to work with me. "It'll probably be only a couple of hours a week," I told her apologetically. "I'm just sorry that I can't promise you more than that."

At this point the Midwest Center for Stress and Anxiety consisted of her desk and my desk in our little office beside the beauty salon, and a small back room. Carolyn and I took the cassettes that were being dubbed off for us in Toledo, paired them with the proper Xeroxed content I had created, made copies for that week (run off on our overworked copy machine), and popped them into the mail. We also answered the phones, talking people through panic attacks or other anxiety-based crises. By this time we were getting calls from all over the country.

It was around 1989 when I got it into my head to get on *Oprah!*. When I announced that I was going to try to be a guest on her show, I'd say there were roughly zero people who thought I'd be able to pull that off—well, except for David, who was convinced I could do anything. I paid no attention to all that negativity—once again, I was coloring outside the lines. And once again, it worked.

Amazingly, it was easier than I thought. I picked up the phone, called the show's producer, and told my own story: how I'd had panic attacks that were so bad I couldn't even travel, and how I recovered and was now helping thousands of people with the same problem. She had only one question: "Can you be here next week?"

I called my mother with a question: "How'd you like to come with me to Chicago?" My mom loved Oprah. She also loved Chicago, and she hadn't been there in years. A dream come true.

Oprah treated guests on her program extremely well. Mom and I were picked up from the airport in a limousine, and they put us up in a great hotel. The night before I did the show, my mother and I walked around downtown Chicago. When we wandered into an art gallery, they handed us each a glass of champagne. My eyes went immediately to two beautiful pieces of art—musicians with violins and cellos. To me, those paintings represented a level of life I aspired to. They were expensive, $1,500 apiece. That was a lot of money to me at the time; still is. Maybe it was the champagne, maybe it was the limo, maybe it was the anticipation of success from doing the *Oprah!* show, but I bought them on the spot. They're hanging in my dining room to this day.

The next morning, as Mom and I got into the limousine to go to the studio, I flashed on my *ALMOST FAMOUS* button. I still had it; it was on my desk in Oak Harbor. "Cindy Redick from Findlay, Ohio: you've come a long way," I told myself as I settled into the leather seats in the back of the limo. "You've *arrived*."

The show went extremely well. I sat on that stage sharing my personal experience with anxiety and panic attacks, as Oprah stood in the audience throwing questions my way. I was in awe of how comfortable she was with herself on camera. But I was also amazed at how comfortable I felt. We worked together well. I seemed to have a knack for entertaining while educating and motivating, all at the same time. And Oprah could feel it, too. My mom was in the audience beaming when Oprah told me, "Girl, I've got to have you back!" Now *that* was a moment. Oprah was as good as her word; a couple of months later, I was on again, this time talking about women and stress. And this time, I had the entire hour.

There is always a lag time of several weeks between when a show is taped and when it airs. I knew that appearing on *Oprah!* would give us a boost—I just underestimated how much.

Carolyn and I were totally unprepared for the deluge that hit us once my segment aired. We were swamped by callers wanting to buy the program. The phones never stopped ringing. We were answering calls and shoving tapes out the door as fast as we could, and it wasn't nearly fast enough. Clearly it was time to get more help. "David, we're overwhelmed," I said. "Isn't there anyone at the grocery store who needs a job?"

David sent over a woman named Barb. She was tall and busty, and decked out in cowboy boots and a fancy white dress. Her husband was a truck driver, and she was funny and sassy and seemed competent enough. I threw her into the back room with minimal instructions: just start mailing out cassettes and workbook chapters as fast you can.

Talk about trial by fire. Barb emerged at the end of the day, all disheveled, her white dress crumpled, her perfect little ponytail askew. "Did I get the job?" she asked.

I did a double take. "Didn't my husband interview you before he sent you over?"

"Nope."

We both laughed. "Job's yours if you want it," I said with a grin. After a first day like that, I was amazed that she didn't go running off in the opposite direction, but Barb had an incredible work ethic and was completely dedicated to what we were trying to accomplish. She eventually became our order-processing manager for the entire company. Carolyn Dickman went on to become one of the Midwest Center's most effective speakers, the Educational Director, and one of my best and dearest friends. And she now has about nine million grandchildren.

When Brittany was not quite three, I got the happy news that I was pregnant again. She was overjoyed at the idea of becoming a big sister.

She'd put her head on my belly and talk to the baby, just like her father had with her before she was born. I was about two and a half months along when I went in for a checkup—routine, or so I thought. Dr. Alberts, my OB, did an ultrasound, then told me, "Well, I've got some bad news. I'm ninety-five percent sure your baby is dead."

Shock.

"Excuse me?" I said in total and complete disbelief.

He went on as if it was no big deal that he just hit me over the head with a sledgehammer. "Now, I can go in and do a D&C—dilation and curettage—we'll schedule it for tomorrow. If tomorrow's not good for you, it'll have to wait till next week, because I've got to go to a conference."

Dr. Alberts was unbelievably detached and unaffected. He looked at it as "removing retained tissue," but I was losing a baby, a child. I was speechless, just sitting there in shock, trying to take it all in—and failing. There was nothing I could say.

"You said ninety-five percent," I said, finally able to get some words— any words—out. "If there's even a five percent chance that you're wrong, then we're not doing anything."

"All right then," he continued, just as detached as ever. "We'll wait till next week. In the meantime, maybe you'll get rid of it on your own." He stood up and walked out of the room.

I sat there in disbelief with his choice of words. How coldhearted. I was also scared and heartbroken. Devastated, I decided I would go home and take my chances.

Over the weekend I did indeed have the miscarriage. The worst of it was that David was traveling on business; I was all by myself. I remember sitting on the toilet, bawling my eyes out, as all this stuff—what had once been a baby—was coming out.

As much as Brittany's birth was the beginning of a good time, the loss of that child was the beginning of a bad one, and not only the miscarriage. A lot of the bad had to do with my father. After Mom kicked him out, Dad pretty much had nowhere to go. He started living in cheap rooms in "safe" houses for destitute people and alcoholics. He was a step away from being homeless. Make that half a step.

I would drive up to Toledo and find him—sometimes that wasn't easy—and take him out to dinner. It was a continuation of the role I'd played since childhood. I was still the caregiver, the one who tried to rescue him, even long after the rest of the family had given up on him. I did this even though he represented everything that scared me: instability, addiction, alcoholism, and, of course, guilt, blame, anger, shame—that whole broken-family dynamic where life in the home revolves around the dysfunctional person.

I ran *from* him because he was violent and scary and unpredictable, even as I wanted to run *to* him, trying to save him. (That was always me, the one who would run into the burning building. And that simultaneous attraction-repulsion contradiction has been with me my entire life.) Yes, he was repulsive, but I took care of him anyway, or tried to. He was my father, and despite everything, I loved him. Maybe, just maybe, I could rescue him. And if I could, maybe, just maybe, he would finally love me.

Then one night the phone rang. "I'm trying to reach Cindy Redick, the daughter of Roy Redick. I believe they call him Ikey."

"I go by Lucinda Bassett now, but yes, that's me."

"I'm Dr. Hugo Bolton. I'm the attending physician in the emergency department at Mercy Saint Vincent Medical Center. Your father was assaulted—mugged—and beaten in the safe house where he was living."

How ironic.

(top left) Our wedding night.

(top right) David Bassett, aka "Cat Stevens with an edge."

(middle) Lucinda Bassett, changing lives.

(bottom left) A tender, timeless moment of David and Sammy.

(bottom right) Brittany with David, the love of her life.

CHAPTER 12

Death, Speaking, and Success

I WENT TO THE HOSPITAL every day to see him. I washed and brushed his hair. I massaged his hands and feet. Loving gesture that it was, it was unpleasant—in fact, gross. His legs were swollen and ulcerated. They were also numb from the alcoholism—the clinical term is peripheral neuropathy. His toenails were discolored, and the toes themselves were a bit bent under, almost like claws.

Sometimes I took Brittany with me to visit him. She was about four years old, so cute, with big curly locks. She didn't seem to want to go, but I thought it might be a good idea. Somewhere in the back of my head I wondered if he would make it through this. She was apprehensive when we entered the room. I wondered if the contrast between Grandpa Redick, the three-hundred-pound homeless alcoholic in the hospital, and Grandpa Bassett, David's father, the prosperous, well-groomed man who owned a chain of supermarkets and played golf, struck her the same way it struck me.

My father was diagnosed with a cerebral aneurysm—when he was kicked or punched in the head, some of the blood vessels in his brain had been weakened and had ballooned out. It was a result of the mugging, but his alcohol abuse made it worse than it otherwise would have been. No surprise there. What is *good* about alcoholism?

Dr. Bolton and the other physicians taking care of my father told me that they expected him to recover—but just from the mugging, of course. Not from the cirrhosis, not from the peripheral neuropathy, not from the diabetes, not from the hypertension, not from the heart disease . . . and not from the rest of his serious health problems, all of which sprang directly from his love affair with the bottle. They told us that his aneurysm would resolve gradually, given bed rest and medication to prevent seizures. Then he'd be discharged to go home.

Now where was that, exactly? After what happened, we felt we couldn't let him go back to the shelter. But where else could he go? My mother was distraught at the possibility that he might have to come back to live with her, which was yet another irony. For most of her life she'd been afraid that he'd leave her and she'd end up alone, without her husband. Now she feared ending up *with* him—with him as in, stuck with him. That's how far she'd come since David died. They'd never actually divorced, and the idea that he might come back into her new life—her white curtains, soft blue carpeting, and doting grandma life—was upsetting, if not downright frightening.

"What are we going to do with him?" she asked me with concern.

"I don't know, Mom. I wish I did." I didn't have an answer, but I knew I'd have to come up with one soon. None of the other kids were going to do it. Gary was living in Kentucky, David was gone, Donna hated him, and Michael had his own issues to deal with by this time.

Meanwhile, the doctors thought they'd release him in a week or so.

The next time I went to see him, it was evening and I was alone. The remnants of his dinner were still on the tray. Hospital food may not be the greatest, but other than when I came to Toledo to take him out for a meal, this was the longest stint of decent nutrition he'd had since Mom kicked him out.

I rolled the tray table off to the side. "Hey, Dad," I said as I sat down on the edge of the bed. I took his hand. He looked tired and old. As I looked at him, though, I was amazed that at seventy-two, he still had dark hair, most of it anyway, and great skin. As I looked at him, I also thought about how much I looked like him. I had his full lips and his eyes, for sure. I also shared his olive skin and height. I sat there, holding his hand, waiting for him to wake up a bit.

"Do you know how much I love you?" he said in a soft whisper.

"What the hell did he just say?" I thought to myself.

I shook my head, wondering whether I'd heard him right. In my entire life I'd never heard him say that before, not to me, not to my mother, not to any one of us. As kids, we all craved it, but it always seemed that the more we wanted, needed, and even asked for it, the more he withheld it.

So where was this coming from? I reached what I thought was the only logical explanation: either because of the brain injury or because of the meds, he'd become deranged, delusional. "Do you know who I am?" I asked him, still holding his hand.

"Sure. You're Windy Cindy."

Time warp. In an instant, I was seven years old again. That's what he always called me—when he was sober, anyway. Whenever we went out for sticky buns, he'd sing this song: "Cinderella's got a fella . . ."

"It's Daddy!" I'd squeal in delight. I always thought I was his favorite. Striving to earn his love and affection—and never getting it—was for me one of the most painful, most pathetic things about growing up in that dysfunctional house.

I sat on the side of the hospital bed as my eyes welled up with tears.

"You still here?" he whispered gently.

"Yes, I'm here," I said.

"I love you, and I'm so proud of you," he said, looking straight into my eyes. His eyes were yellow and a bit swollen.

"Who is in there?" I wondered.

I took a deep breath. . . . "I love you, too," I said. Then I patted him on the hand, stood up, and walked over to the window with tears rolling down my cheeks. It was dark out, and the parking lot of the hospital looked empty, lonely. I felt so sad. Where had he been all our lives?

That night as I drove home, all I could think about was what he had said. To everyone's surprise, he died hours later, that very same night. The doctors told me that when he got out of bed to go to the bathroom, the aneurysm ruptured and triggered a massive stroke.

We had a simple funeral for him. I don't remember much about it, other than that I had to go pick out the casket and make the arrangements. Me, who hated funerals, death, and dying. Me, who at one time couldn't even talk about death and dying; but someone had to do it. I don't remember whether Donna came for it or not; she hated him so much. What I do remember is how bizarre it was. As horrific as the whole experience had been, I think we all felt a sense of relief that it was finally over—even my mother, perhaps especially my mother.

How sad that at the end of someone's life, people are glad you are dead. Especially when that someone is your father. Ever since I was a little girl, running in my frozen bare feet after the police car that was taking him off to jail, I'd been sure I could fix him or rescue him. As he got older, even I had to admit that he was way beyond fixing. We'd put him into rehab at one of the VA hospitals a couple of times, but it didn't work for him any better than it had worked for my brother David. To be successful, you actually have to want to stop drinking. Dad wouldn't even admit he was an alcoholic.

Toward the end he was such a mess, with a bunch of medical problems that no one could even begin to address unless he stopped drinking. And that was never going to happen. Figuring out what to do with him when he got out of the hospital was going to be a huge problem.

This made grieving odd. Still, I was sad when he died, because I did love him—or at least the idea of him. In a way, I guess I was just like Mom—I loved the man he was when he was younger, the man he was when he was sober. I loved the man he had not been for a very long time. It meant a lot to me that I got to have that moment with him—the man I remembered, the man who remembered me—in the hospital, right before he died. Even so, I never told anyone except David what he said. I guess I felt guilty that I got those words and no one else did.

Shortly after he died, I was in Cleveland getting ready to speak to a sold-out auditorium packed with 1,200 people. Before it started, I was out front helping my staff put the final touches on the front table and greeting people as they entered. I was feeling a bit antsy before going onstage, which was not unusual for me. Then, seemingly from out of nowhere, a man came shuffling toward me. He was large, maybe three hundred pounds, and he walked with a limp—like my dad. He reached into his pocket, pulled out this rumpled piece of newspaper, and held it out toward me. His hand was shaking—like my dad's. "This you?" he asked.

I nodded. I could see my picture in the ad he was holding: LUCINDA BASSETT, APPEARING SATURDAY.

"Do they call you Cindy?" he asked.

"My family does," I said.

"Then I'm going to call you Cindy, too," he said. "I came a long way to see you."

We stood there chatting for a few minutes, and as he talked, I had the strangest feeling about him. Finally one of my assistants interrupted me. "Lucinda, it's time to get started."

"Well, it's been a pleasure talking to you, but I've got to get up there," I said, gesturing toward the stage.

As I turned to leave, he grabbed my arm. "Hey, can you get me a chair?"

Every hair on my body stood on end. "What did you say?" I asked, turning back toward him.

"Can you get me a chair?"

This was an eerie blast from the past, an echo from childhood, a request from beyond the grave. Because he had a bad leg, my father often asked me to get him a chair, and he said it just like this man did. Hearing it again now, so soon after he died, was so disconcerting that it gave me chills. I asked one of my assistants to put a folding chair at the back of the auditorium and escort him to it. Then I ran up the side of the auditorium toward the stage. I felt anxious and weird and almost like I wanted to cry, but, as they say, the show must go on.

At that time in my speaking career, I started my presentation with a lot of my dad's jokes. I guess it was sort of a tribute to him, a way to remind myself that despite everything there were some good things about my father's legacy—especially my entertaining personality, my knack for telling jokes, and my ability to connect with people. As I began talking about my dad and what a jokester he was, the old man who had come up to me was now directly in my line of sight. I could see him at the back of the room, shaking his head and nodding and laughing as I was talking. I liked it that he was enjoying what I had to say. I had to force myself to forget about him, though, and focus on my audience. About twenty minutes later, I looked back to where he was sitting, and the chair was empty. He was gone.

When Dad died, I felt bad that he never got to hear me speak. In a way, maybe he finally did. I'll never know what that was about, but me and my magical thinking would like to believe it was him, finally coming to see me shine.

After Dad's death, life was getting back to normal. Living in Oak Harbor was still like living in a Norman Rockwell painting. It was a real community. David was working in the Bassett's Market. Everyone in town knew him and loved him. He would go to the county fair every year. Once, I came home from Chicago after doing a segment on *Oprah!* and two goats came trotting up the long driveway to greet me We had goats, chickens, ducks—I'd open the door and they'd go running through the house. Brittany was now about five, and thriving. We had some great friends. Family was close by, and we were happy.

We saw David's family all the time. David came from a big family—in addition to his parents, there were aunts, uncles, and cousins, and they all loved Brittany. We also had a group of close friends, including Bruce Winters and his wife, Pat, and Allen McKean and his wife, Pam, and their families. David had grown up in Oak Harbor, and he went way back with these guys. I felt surrounded and protected by this loving circle of people who were connected to one another, and to David and me. And of course that circle included my own family, especially my mother and Donna.

Donna came to visit often, bringing Jenny and Lori with her. Brittany loved Jenny and Lori so much, and we had great fun with each other and our kids. The summer after Dad died, we rented a hotel room on the lake, just the two of us, with our girls. I looked over at her lying next to me on the beach blanket. I had always envied her figure—five feet four and curvy. As we lay there in our bikinis laughing, watching the girls swim and talking about life, she motioned to me to look at her groin. "Look at this," she said, pointing to some large lumps in her groin area. "What do you think these are?"

CHAPTER 13

Another Death,
Another Life

DONNA CALLED ME a couple of days later. "The doctor thinks it's an infection I got from shaving. He put me on antibiotics."

We were both relieved, and I had some exciting news to share with her. My period was late, and I really hoped that I was pregnant. David and I still wanted another child, but my miscarriage was so overwhelming and it was such a bad experience that there was no way I was going through another pregnancy with that doctor. In early spring of 1991, I went looking for a new ob-gyn and found Dr. Stapleman, a smart, young, hip female obstetrician—a doctor who got it, in part because she was a woman. I had taken a pregnancy test and it came out positive, but I wanted to be sure.

"Yep, you're pregnant all right," she confirmed.

I was so excited. After losing the other baby, I was afraid I'd never be able to have another. My old scary thoughts came back. "That was luck. You know what you did. You know you don't deserve another child. You are doomed to a life of strife and unhappiness." This was my subconscious mantra, except that I didn't realize it at the time.

For now, I was in the moment and once again grateful and excited about the baby. On the way home from the doctor's office in Toledo, I called my sister to share the news with her. It was pouring down rain as I headed home down Route 163 toward Oak Harbor. "Donna! Guess what! I am pregnant again!"

"See, I told you! I'm so happy for you." That was Donna, always supportive, always there for me. "I knew you were pregnant!"

I loved her so much. Then my mind immediately went to her and the lumps in her groin.

"Hey! By the way . . . ," I said, "those lumps in your groin. The antibiotics took care of them? They're gone, right?"

"No, actually. They're still there. What do you think I should do?"

It started to rain even harder as a dreadful feeling of foreboding came over me. "Listen. I don't want to scare you, and I'm not a doctor. But I am afraid those could be, well, something else. I think you need to do something right now that you're not gonna wanna do." I knew she was a bit of a hypochondriac. "You need to stick your fingers in your armpits and see if there are lumps there, too."

"I don't want to do that right now," she said defensively. "I'll just wait till I go back to the doctor."

I was worried about lymphoma, and she knew it. "Just do it right now."

I waited.

"Oh my God, there *are*! There are lumps under my arms!" She was panicked.

God, I hated that moment. I wanted to be there, to hold her, to reassure her. She started to cry. "It's cancer, isn't it? I always knew I was going to die young."

"Donna, listen to me. Don't talk like that." I was holding back my own tears. "Call the doctor and get back in right away. Get to a specialist. It could all be from an infection, I guess, but I am concerned."

As we talked, I could tell that her panic was increasing. And frankly, so was mine.

"Listen to me. Where is Bob? Call him now. Call the doctor right now and ask to see a specialist." I tried to give her specific advice and console her at the same time.

The next couple of days were spent worrying with her until finally she saw the specialist. Donna called me back in a real panic. "They think I have cancer," she said through her tears. "The doctor says they are pretty sure I have non-Hodgkin's lymphoma. I don't have all the details yet, but it doesn't sound good. I'm scared."

I was angry. Shaving infection, my ass. This was not good. I knew we were all in for a rough ride, especially her.

All of a sudden, it seemed like there was bad news everywhere. David was as happy as I was that we were having another baby, but four days later he came home with bad news of his own. I could tell as soon as he walked in the door that something was wrong. "I'm out," he said.

"What do you mean 'out'?" I asked.

"Out as in 'let go.' Out of the stores. Out of a job," he replied.

"But how is that even possible? It's your family's business!" I said. "My father came to me and said that the stores are struggling," he began. "That they need to cut back on people with larger salaries. Between me and Mike, I had to be let go. After all, Mike came into the stores years before and helped build them into what they are now. He had put his life into it for many years before me."

"That's it?"

David nodded glumly. "That's it."

When his dad and brother had asked him to come back into the family business, David had jumped in with his enthusiasm. We'd thought this was going to be his lifetime career. But now, he was out.

I could tell David was heartsick. He enjoyed working with his family and enjoyed the grocery store business. His warm personality made him a real asset, and all the customers loved him.

We were both distraught with the news. What would this mean to us financially? David had been the major breadwinner for our family. I barely made enough money to pay the babysitter. I was overwhelmed, knowing we had another baby on the way.

So . . . my sister's got cancer. David's out of a job. What else could possibly go wrong?

I was about to find out.

A few days after all that bad news, I started spotting. Another miscarriage seemed to be looming. This is never a good sign early in a pregnancy, especially given my history, and Dr. Stapleman was concerned that I might lose this baby, too.

At this point, I got incredibly pissed off—at God. I was overwhelmed and anxious. Life wasn't fair. Where was the peace of mind and security thing? When were things ever going to calm down for me, for all of us Redicks? Were we doomed or cursed? One night in particular I was really struggling with all the bad news. I went into the living room of our little farmhouse—the farmhouse I was afraid we'd lose because we couldn't make the mortgage on my income alone—and got down on my knees.

This "prayer" was almost a full-on rant.

"God, I'm pretty discouraged right now," I began. "I lost my brother David. I lost my father. My sister has cancer. My husband is losing his job. I had a miscarriage. I'm pregnant again, but now I'm spotting and the doctor says I might lose this baby, too. I've had enough. I get the feeling you've abandoned me—are you even up there? When I'm helping people, I talk about you all the time. I give you a lot of credit for my recovery, but with all that's happening, I'm about to give up on you. If you want me to keep believing in you, you have to give me something to believe in. I need a few miracles here. You need to heal my sister. And then you need to let me have this baby. Bring this little soul to me. If you do, I promise you that I will never doubt that you exist ever again."

Who the hell did I think I was to bargain with God like that? But there I was, on the floor, praying, bargaining, and crying. Then, I got up off my knees, went upstairs to our bedroom, and started rummaging through a dresser drawer. I found what I was looking for—a simple little gold cross on a thin gold chain, a gift from one of the women who had successfully completed the fifteen-week program with Phil Fisher and me. "God," I continued as I put it around my neck, "I am not taking off this cross until this baby comes out alive and healthy, and until my sister is healed."

I went to see Dr. Stapleman the next day. She knew how devastated I would be if I lost a second child. "We're going to try something new," she told me, handing me a prescription. "This is for progesterone suppositories, a treatment that is supposed to help stop spotting and save pregnan cies like yours. Let's see how you're doing in a few days."

They worked, and the bleeding stopped.

We needed money now more than ever, and since the pregnancy seemed to stabilize, I went back to speaking again. My next engagement was in Buffalo, New York. I decided to take my mom and Brittany with me. I would do that sometimes. It made the trip more fun, and we all enjoyed a stay at a decent hotel for a few days.

We were overwhelmed by the turnout. We were set up for 400 peo- ple, but about 1,500 showed up. We were not prepared; since I thought it was going to be a small group, it was just one assistant and my mom to help out. The Holiday Inn, where the event was being held, wasn't prepared, either. I was running back from meeting with the banquet manager to request more chairs and stopped to make sure things were in control out front. People were swarming in from all sides. "Mom, you stand out here and help hand people brochures as they come in. I'm going to get some more pencils and help them set up more chairs," I said hurriedly. "Most important, be sure to keep Brittany with you at all times."

She stared at me, first blankly, then instantly terrified. "She's not with you?" she asked.

Talk about panic! OH MY GOD!

"NO!" I screamed. "Where is she?? I left her with *you*!"

Not this. God, not this. I started running through the crowds of people, pushing them away. All I could think about was her beautiful little face and those curls. How sweet and outgoing and "friendly" she was. NO! I was sweating and tripping as I ran through the crowd screaming her name. "BRITTANY!... *BRITTANY!*"

I was afraid someone had taken her, and every nightmare scenario imaginable went zooming through my mind. I went screaming frantically down the center aisle toward the stage. I don't know why, but something told me she might be there. She was a bit of a showman herself these days, and sometimes on trips she'd get up there before my presentation, grab the mic, and pretend to be me. Brittany! BRITTANY! *BRITTANY!*"

As I pushed through the dense crowd, there she was, on stage, this adorable little thing, holding the mic in her hand, trying to figure out how to turn it on. God, she never looked so adorable, so beautiful, so mine. "Brittany!" I cried as I picked her up and hugged her tight. Then I sat her down on the stool that was put on the stage for me. Especially since I'd been spotting during this pregnancy, there were times when I felt like I needed to sit for a minute. "Now, don't you move," I said. Then I gave her the mic and she started saying hello to everyone. It was really cute, but it also gave me the time I needed to put my head back together before beginning my presentation.

Later that night I was lying in bed, eyes wide open, going over the events of the day in my mind. I knew how close I'd come to losing her in the crowd. But I hadn't. Suddenly I was overcome with gratitude—it washed over me like a wave. "Thank you, God, for not taking Brittany from me," I prayed. It was a very powerful moment, a reminder to me to stay focused on the positive and precious in life, instead of getting dragged down by all the problems.

Yes, David lost his job, and even worse, my sister was battling cancer. But she had a chance to survive it, and I was pregnant, and Brittany was lying beside me, safe. Life was a gift.

When I got home, it was becoming apparent that David Bassett was now a man with time on his hands. Finally loose from his obligations to the grocery stores, he walked across the street to our tiny little office, put his notebook down on my big old wooden desk, and said, "I guess I'm going to have to come and work with you." Then he sat down.

In my chair, at my desk.

He looked at me, discouraged and almost deflated. He was teary eyed—but I wasn't sure if it was emotion or the smell from the perm solution from the beauty parlor next door. David wasn't nearly as used to the ammonia smell as I was.

I felt bad for both of us. I was sad for him and scared for us. How were we going to make it? As we sat there, overcome and uncertain about our future, Allen McKean walked in.

David had known him forever. Allen showed up with a bottle of champagne, as if this were a huge celebration, not a wake. It was quite an entrance, and he laughed as he slammed it down on the desk and said, "David, I have a feeling this is going to be the best thing that ever happened to you."

Little did he know that he would turn out to be right. It was certainly the farthest thing from my mind at the moment. David had done some accounting for the Midwest Center, but I had no idea what more he could do for us—we just weren't big enough to need much of anything else.

But then it happened. The brainstorm struck him one night as we were in bed watching TV. This was the beginning of the era of the infomercial. Channel-surfing around the dial, it was hard to avoid seeing John Gray talking about *Men Are from Mars, Women Are from Venus*, or Tony Robbins hawking *Personal Power*, or Victoria Principal selling her line of beauty products, Principal Secret.

"Hey! We could do this," David said. Robbins and Principal were hugely successful, in part because of the marketing firm Guthy-Renker, which had produced their infomercials. "You have all these people who have gone through your program who love the program and love you. We could do one of these infomercial things. You would be great on it. We have great people who have successfully used the product. They could give testimonials."

I was smiling and thinking, "What a great fantasy."

No fantasy. David was now on board, and his persistence helped us grow far beyond what I'd ever thought possible. Next thing I knew, he pulled together two plane tickets to Los Angeles. Even more unbelievably, he got us a meeting with Guthy-Renker. It was so exciting for both of us. We stayed at a local Marriott in Studio City and looked forward to our meeting with Bill Guthy and Greg Renker about the possibility of making an infomercial for *Attacking Anxiety and Depression*.

ALMOST FAMOUS, I thought to myself as we looked out of our room over the city.

The next day we headed to the meeting with high hopes and a well-prepared presentation (a change for me, and one of the benefits of adding David). It was a bit intimidating at first, because Bill Guthy and Greg Renker are very smart, powerful men. Bill Guthy is tall and handsome with a gentle demeanor, but don't underestimate his business sense and ability to negotiate. Greg Renker, also handsome, is very sophisticated, and the quieter of the two. He seemed to want to sit and listen to us sell him as Bill asked most of the questions.

The meeting went well, or so we thought. David and I were a great team. I did the song and dance about the product and the wonderful way it helped people. I shared my personal story of recovery, and David talked numbers. They seemed intrigued. We were so excited when we left that we cruised into Hollywood, sat at an outdoor café on Sunset Boulevard, and drank a bottle of champagne in celebration.

We were a bit ahead of ourselves. They turned us down. The product's appeal was too narrow, they said, and besides, at $400, it was too expensive. You'll never be able to sell it on an infomercial, we were told. It can't be done.

It was a bit discouraging, of course, but that's when Cindy Redick stepped back into the picture. "Don't tell me it can't be done. People have been telling me that all my life. We'll just do it ourselves." It was time to get busy coloring outside the lines.

I called my brother Michael and we sat and talked for hours about how we could put a show together. He came on board to do the sound and music, producing and editing. By this time he had a recording studio in his house—and, of course, he'd married Mary. His sons Andy and Benjamin now had a younger brother, Ryan.

We hired a local camera crew. I brought in people from our groups and sat them in front of the camera. I sat in front of them and interviewed them about their life with anxiety and depression before the program, and then asked them to describe how the program had changed their lives. "Tell me, what was your life like when you had anxiety disorder? Can you describe a panic attack to me? How did it affect your family? How did your life change after going through the program?"

We just sat and talked, one-on-one. None of it was scripted. I asked questions, and these people who had been helped by the program answered from the heart. The stories they told were amazing—both the negative and then the positive. Their genuineness and sincerity really came through, and that made it both moving and extremely powerful.

Michael had to edit fifty hours of footage down to twenty-eight minutes, thirty seconds. He had to underscore it with the appropriate music at the appropriate times, and figure out what to do for the "Call to Actions." These are the two-minute slots that make people want to pick up the phone and order the product. He did an incredible job, especially considering he had never done it before.

It was time to see what kind of response it would get. We started small, buying local airtime around Toledo. *Attacking Anxiety and Depression:* three installments of $129.95, plus shipping and handling. Operators are standing by"—which meant that David brought in half a dozen cashiers from the grocery store to answer the calls and take credit card numbers over the phone. The first time it was broadcast, we waited nervously to see what would happen. Suddenly, at the first Call to Action, the phones started ringing off the wall.

People were calling in to give us their credit card numbers! It worked! The phone lines were jammed. As orders for the program kept coming in, we bought more airtime and slowly expanded into more cities. Eventually we bought time on larger stations. The infomercial helped us reach a much wider audience. Using it to sell the program as a complete unit in a single box also made shipping cheaper and easier. Instead of mailing audiotapes and workbook chapters one segment at a time, we were able to send them out as a well-designed, complete package. We started working with a local company based in Oak Harbor called Riverview Industries—they made, assembled, and shipped the product for us. I was very proud to be associated with them; Riverview specializes in providing work for adults with disabilities.

With the success of the infomercial, the Midwest Center quickly outgrew the little office next door to the beauty parlor. Both Carolyn Dickman and Barb came on full time, as did David and my brother Mike. Even then, we still had to hire ten more people to keep pace with new orders. Eventually we hired an amazing group of people to help us build the Midwest Center staff, like James Dickman and Monica Deck (Carolyn Dickman's son and daughter), Darla Van Horn, Scott Sprouse, and Dawn, Pat, and many others who ended up being with us for years. I stopped worrying about losing the farmhouse.

It was also during this time that Donna's prognosis started getting worse. Doctors had initially given her hope of possible recovery, but now they were suggesting five years. It was horrific. She was trying very hard to stay positive, but she had lost a lot of weight and all of her hair. She was on chemo and struggling to keep her energy and her attitude up. I was spending a great deal of time in Louisville with Mom and Brittany, trying to keep her and her family together.

It was also during this time that my second child was born.

After the initial spotting stopped, the pregnancy had gone along pretty smoothly, which was a huge relief to all of us—even to Brittany. Now she was six years old and really looking forward to being the big sister. Each time we went past a fountain she threw coins into the water, making a wish for the baby to come out healthy.

I was now far enough along to start getting serious about figuring out a name for our second child, a child I'd convinced myself would be another daughter. On my way into Toledo for an ultrasound, I tried out various girls' names, saying them aloud: Ashley, Chelsea, Hannah, Lauren, Nicole. . . .

Not so fast. "Take a look at the monitor, Mrs. Bassett," the technician said as she moved the wand over my belly during the ultrasound. "Based on what I'm seeing, I'd suggest that you might want to come up with a boy's name instead."

I couldn't make out much in that grainy gray and white image, but the key moving part I could see clearly was unmistakably male. Brittany wasn't going to have a sister, but a brother!

I gave away her pink Onesies and receiving blankets and started hunting through the other half of the baby name books. I liked the name Oliver, but Brittany kept writing "Samy" all over everything—I don't know why, except she just liked that name. David liked it, too. When I looked it up to see what the name meant, I found that Samuel meant "asked of God." As soon as I read that, my fingers went straight to the gold cross that was still around my neck—wasn't that exactly what I'd done in that prayer not so long ago?

I had tried so hard throughout my pregnancy to avoid having another C-section—I ate right, exercised right. It didn't help, at least not enough. After forty hours of labor, it was the same problem: I still hadn't dilated enough. Sammy, like Brittany, was a big baby with a big head, but Dr. Stapleman's anesthesiologist gave me an epidural, which made labor and delivery a much better experience. During the delivery, I didn't feel a thing. Samuele Bassett was born December 7, 1991, Pearl Harbor Day, weighing in at ten pounds, two ounces.

When he was about three months old, I was asked to speak at an anxiety conference in San Francisco. I almost didn't go because I was one of the few presenters who wasn't a doctor. But I was so honored to have been asked that I decided to do it.

As we were flying over Denver, the pilot came on to warn about severe upcoming turbulence.

How severe? "Flight attendants, please be seated."

Suddenly I couldn't breathe. "OhmyGod ohmyGod ohmyGod," I said to myself as I gripped the armrest, clenched my teeth, and shut my eyes as tight as I could. I panicked, just like I used to. All my worst white-knuckle fears about flying came roaring back. "Why did I agree to do this? The plane's going to crash. I'm gonna die. I won't be around for my kids, for my sister." I sat there terrified, overwhelmed by scary thoughts, waiting for the horrifying turbulence to begin.

Twenty minutes passed, but it seemed like an hour.

Finally the flight attendants came calmly walking through the cabin, serving drinks. "What happened to that turbulence we were supposed to go through?" I asked.

"Oh, we passed that area ten minutes ago. There wasn't any."

"What?" I thought to myself. "I sat here for twenty minutes scared to death, anticipating the worst, and there wasn't any?" There was nothing to do but laugh at myself. How many times had I done that? How many times had I worked myself into a panic over something that turned out to be nothing? What a great story for my presentation.

I got up the next morning and gave my talk. After I was finished, someone threw a big stack of papers at me. Evaluations. Audiences rated each speaker on his or her performance.

I riffled through them quickly. They were all 5s—5 on a scale of 1 to 5. No way these were mine, I thought. There were some really distinguished doctors who were also speaking at the conference. "These must be someone else's," I said to the woman who handed them to me.

"Nope. They're yours, Lucinda. You're one of our highest-ranked presenters."

Wow! I was so happy I could have flown home without a plane. I came back feeling really proud of myself, and confident in my ability to not only really help people but to put myself out there. I could be a Somebody.

Sammy was an easygoing baby. My mother loved them both, as she loved all her grandchildren, and we made frequent trips to see her in Findlay. I relived part of my childhood—the good part—watching my Brittany put pennies on the railroad tracks and waiting for the trains to flatten them, like I did. And catching lightning bugs, like I did. Whenever we went there, we revisited many of the places I'd loved growing up, including Wilson's for hamburgers and Dietsch's for ice cream. Sometimes we'd stop at the A&W near Fostoria, where carhops still delivered your order on a tray that hooked onto the window, outside the car. We'd have root beer, shredded chicken sandwiches, and sloppy joes hanging off the door. The kids love to stop there to this day.

Mom was an amazing grandma. She'd sit on the floor for hours, playing with Brittany and Sammy and their small plastic Little People, making beds for them out of tissues, then building make-believe tents out of sheets and forts out of sofa cushions. It was a peek into what my own childhood might have been, if she hadn't had to work all the time and been so overwhelmed by Dad and his drinking.

We'd all go together on trips to visit Donna in Louisville. Donna's daughter Lori loved Brittany. She'd buzz around in anticipation of our

·

arrival. She'd get so excited when she knew we were coming that she'd throw up. As soon as we got there, she and Brittany would put on these pink tutus and go twirling around the house on their tippy-toes. Typical girl-cousin stuff, but then again, Donna tried for as long as she could to carry on as if everything was normal. Even though she'd lost all of her hair because of the chemo, she started working with me, running groups for anxiety in Louisville. Within a couple of months, however, Bob asked for a transfer and moved the family back to Jacksonville. Donna really loved Florida, and Jacksonville had a big Mayo Clinic. He thought she'd get better treatment there.

I flew down to see her as often as I could. Sometimes we'd rent a small condo on the beach in Sarasota and take little trips—Mom, Donna with her girls, and me with Sammy and Brittany. Sammy was about seven months old at the time. Donna would hold him in her arms and walk him around the warm pool.

One night Donna and I were sitting on the balcony at the condo when everyone else was asleep. We were talking about the future and her illness.

"Cindy, I need to talk to you. Honestly, I don't think I am going to make it."

I sat quietly, giving her my full attention, trying not to cry.

"It's not going well. I don't know how much longer I can take these aggressive treatments, and I'm not in remission," she said. "I'm Stage Four. At first they gave me five years. But now they are saying it could be less than a year." She started to cry. "When I'm gone, you're going to have to be their second mom, you know. Promise me that you'll always be there for my girls."

I reached over and wrapped my arms around her. I wanted to tell her not to give up, to keep fighting. I wanted to use my magical thinking on her. I wanted her to believe that she was absolutely going to make it. But I knew she knew. "When do you let people 'give up'?" I thought to myself. "And is it giving up, or is it growing up and facing the truth so you can deal with it?" I wondered.

"I promise," I said, crying with her. "I love you. I am here for you, and I will always be here for them."

It's awful to see what cancer does to a person. The hair loss was just the first indignity. As her treatments continued, Donna kept losing weight. Soon Mom moved down to Florida to help Bob, who had pretty much stopped working at his job so he could devote himself to taking care of Donna. Donna had always been the ultimate mother, the glue that held that family together, and Bob and Lori and Jenny were really struggling without her. Bob was a wonderful husband and father, but he knew nothing about running a household. At that time, he didn't even cook. He was so dedicated to her and the children. At first he tried to keep up with his job, but finally he took a complete leave of absence to take care of Donna. After that, he never left her side.

The last time we went to the hospital, the doctors told us that there was nothing more they could do for her. As we sat in his office, the doctor looked at her, took a deep breath, and said, "Donna, the treatments aren't helping. They are actually making you quite sick. There is really nothing more to do."

Even though she knew that truth herself, she panicked. "Can't I keep taking the chemo? I want to live as long as possible."

The doctor looked at Bob. "I wouldn't suggest it. It is a quality-of-life issue now. These trips to the hospital are hard on you, and the treatments won't prolong your life. I am sorry, but I think you have less than a month."

Torture.

Bob started to cry. Donna was crying. I was stunned, scared, and in shock. How does a person accept his or her own death? Not knowing how soon it will come, what it is, or how it will happen? How would she handle it? How would we all handle it? How could they just "leave" us with this type of news? The doctor put his hand on her shoulder, suggested hospice, and walked out.

Hospice.

Donna hung on for a few weeks after they sent her home, but it was brutal. Her legs swelled up to the size of tree trunks; she sweated uncontrollably. She was sedated most of the time on morphine. It deadened the pain, but when she was awake she was groggy and went in and out of reality. When she slept, she had dreams of scary things. It was awful for her, for Bob, and for the girls. I remember going into the bathroom and finding little Lori, eleven years old, on the floor, with a towel wrapped around her, shivering and crying. She had just gotten out of the shower and she wanted her mommy. I sat holding her while she cried. All I could think about was what Donna had said on the balcony that night.

Donna Redick Wittenmyer died on February 10, 1993. She was forty-four years old. I had just flown down to see her and had taken Brittany with me. We had been there over a week, and I needed to go home and spend time with David and with Sammy, who was now just over a year old. The doctors said they thought Donna had a few more weeks to live. Unfortunately, they were wrong. She died two days after I left; I hadn't even unpacked before I hopped on a plane to go back. This time I took Sammy with me. Somewhere over Georgia, we hit terrible turbulence. The aircraft was shaking so violently that I thought we weren't going to make it. I was petrified. Unlike the episode on the way to San Francisco, I couldn't laugh my way out of it. We landed in Atlanta before going on to Jacksonville, and the flight was delayed.

While we were on the ground in the airport in Atlanta waiting for the connecting flight, I called Bob. "I don't think I can make myself get back on a plane," I told him.

"You have to. You'll be okay," he said reassuringly.

I boarded the connecting flight with Sammy and started to cry. I sat there looking out into the darkness as the plane lifted off the ground, moving slowly through the bumpy sky. "Donna, how I am ever going to do this without you? Who's going to be there for me, now that you're gone?"

At that moment, it seemed that the voice of God came out of nowhere. "You are all here for each other," He told me. I realized that I needed to be there for Bob, for the girls, for my mom, and that they would all be there for me throughout life. That was just how it was. But it was still lonely. Why does it seem like everyone leaves me? And how selfish of me to think this way.

Due to the weather and delays, the flight was so late getting in to Jacksonville that I missed the formal viewing. Worse yet, Sammy was getting really sick. He was burning up, with a fever of 104 degrees. I had

Mom stay with him while I went to the funeral home alone, to say my own good-bye to Donna.

It was very late when I walked into the funeral home. Nobody else was around. It was just Donna and me, and an attendant who waited for me. As I walked toward the casket, I was afraid I couldn't look at her. She was so afraid to die. She didn't want to be in a casket, but then, who did? I thought about Dad, and about our brother David. I thought about how much I already missed her, and how she made me laugh. I thought about poor Bob, and the girls, and how lost they would all be. How we would all miss her energy flying through the front door and her cooking and buzzing around the kitchen, making the house a home.

As I leaned over her casket, I looked at her lying there and I just started sobbing from my gut. She had been so lovely, so full of life. My tears left droplets on her face. A few of them ran down her cheeks, just like they were running down mine. I was so devastated in that moment.

The song from *White Christmas* came into my mind again: "*Sisters, Sisters; There were never such devoted sisters.*"

Devoted was surely the right word—we had been close since childhood, since we shared that little green bedroom just off the kitchen in the ugly pink house. Now my best friend, my wingwoman, was gone, dead. I felt incredibly lost and alone.

"I love you, Donna," I said as I brushed some of my tears off her face. "And I promise that I'll take care of Jenny and Lori. I'll be there for them the way you were always there for me. I'm going to miss you so very much." I reached up around my neck and felt for the little gold cross. I unclasped the gold chain I'd been wearing since before Sammy was born, kissed the tiny cross, and gently laid it around her neck in the casket.

At the funeral the next day, I remember wishing that we were a little better prepared—that we had written poems, put up family photos, or done any of the cool things people do to celebrate a life. Didn't happen. Couldn't happen. We were all too devastated, stressed out, and exhausted by then. By the time Donna died, there was almost nothing left of any of us.

That night, little Sammy was lying in bed next to me, but neither one of us was getting much sleep. He kept waking up because he was still feverish, and also because it had suddenly gotten really windy and blustery outside. Then Heidi, Donna's little bichon frise, started barking her brains out. Oddly, she was barking the way she did when Donna came home—very excited, scratching at her cage. I remember thinking, "That's her Donna's-home bark." It was eerie.

All of a sudden, at about 3:00 a.m., Sammy sat up in bed, wide awake and staring straight up at the ceiling. "Dondi? Dondi?" he called out.

I freaked. Dondi was his name for Donna, and when he called out, it was like he was looking at her right there above him.

I got out of bed and walked through the house slowly. I could feel Donna's essence everywhere. I wish I could say it was comforting, but I was too young and too spooked by those types of things back then.

After her death, Bob went through the house gathering up anything and everything that had to do with Donna's cancer. "I'm not throwing Donna away," he explained to me. "I'm throwing the cancer away."

I didn't blame him at all. It was something he needed to do. When someone in a house has cancer, the whole house has cancer. And as much as you want to be there for that person who has cancer, you also can't wait to get back to your own normal life. Now that Donna was gone, Bob just wanted to get on with whatever was going to be the new normal with his daughters.

Me, too. On the plane on the way home, all I could think about was how unpredictable and short life is. I realized that there was no longer anything to keep us in Oak Harbor. "Let's get out of here," I told David when I got back home. "Let's move to California."

Before Sammy was born, I'd gone to the West Coast several times to give seminars. There was the trip to San Francisco, of course, but I also went to San Diego, Santa Barbara, and then Los Angeles. I felt comfortable in each one, but I really fell in love with LA. I remember sitting in a sidewalk café on Rodeo Drive, marveling at the scene. And in the back of my mind, there was still that childhood dream of living by the ocean.

"You know," I said to David, "we would fit out there."

My husband didn't see it quite the same way. "Are you nuts?" he asked. "They have fires. Earthquakes. Floods. Crazy people. And besides, we don't know a soul. We both love this house. Our business is here. If you want to move, let's go to Florida, near Bob and the girls."

"Come on. Let's go do something different and exciting," I replied. "If we're only going around once, I want to really go around. What happened to that Bassett sense of adventure I fell in love with? Tell you what—we'll put our house on the market. If it sells by a certain date, we'll move. If not, we'll stay."

I have these landmark days, and the "certain date" I had in mind was August 10, Donna's birthday. David made it clear that he thought this was a stupid idea, but eventually I got him to go along with it. Although he never said as much, I suspect he agreed to it only because he knew the odds of actually selling the house by that date were pretty small. Houses don't usually sell in the summer, and this was a tough economy and an unusual house. It was going to take a certain type of buyer.

We listed the house with a realtor, but we got no offers. The right person had to want all that property and an old house. Then, one day, there was a knock on the door.

CHAPTER 14

California,
Here We Come

IT WAS A SUNNY, WARM, end-of-summer day in Oak Harbor. Believe it or not, it was August 10, my sister's birthday. I pulled open the heavy red wooden door to find an attractive couple in their thirties. "Sorry to just knock like this, but we noticed the For Sale sign, and, well, we thought we would just stop and take a chance. See if anyone was home." Call it manifestation or destiny, but there it was, and yes, really, on my sister's birthday. The house wasn't exactly ready for visitors, but they didn't seem to mind. After stepping around Sammy's baby toys on the floor, wandering out to the river and the beautiful backyard with all the flowers, and spending time in the country kitchen with the big cathedral ceilings and fabulous window with great views of the water, they made us an offer. We accepted it. The next day we started packing up the house, preparing ourselves for an eventual move. We were headed for California, but first we had to find a place to live out there. We gave ourselves a few extra months in Oak Harbor to get our life in order before the big move.

David left first, immediately after Christmas, driving a big truck with all our furniture and household goods, pulling our Mercedes behind it. Not quite a week later, I flew out with Brittany, now eight, and Sammy, who had just turned two, my mom, and of course Maggie, our Shih Tzu. It was New Year's Day night, 1993, and the approach over the desert, then the mountains, and into the LA basin was a stark reminder that we weren't in Oak Harbor anymore. Then the lights of Los Angeles spread out below. They were beautiful and dramatic, but a little intimidating. It was all so big, and so very different from the home we had left behind. My moment of being overwhelmed opened a crack of self-doubt that was just wide enough for a small flood of second thoughts to rush in. "Oh my God, what have I done?" I asked myself as we began our long descent into Los Angeles.

That flash of regret was over as fast as it came on—David was there to greet us at the airport. We collected our bags and Maggie. We found a place on the cement outside the airport for her to relieve herself after the long flight. Then we all climbed into the Mercedes and headed for Calabasas.

Through a friend, David had rented a brand-new contemporary little house in a gated community. We walked in, and it instantly felt like home. David must have been up for days without sleeping to get ready for our arrival, because he had the house pretty much in order. The furniture had been placed; the kitchen was set up. David knew how much I loved fires, so the fireplace in the family room was ablaze. But most important, the house was warm with the smell of David's grandmother's heirloom chicken soup with cinnamon and lemon—comfort food at its very best. He had been cooking it all day in anticipation of our arrival. He wanted us to feel "home." It worked. We sat tired but excited as we ate soup in our new California home, looking out the kitchen window at our real in-ground swimming pool, little backyard, and then to the San Fernando Valley below. What a view. What an accomplishment for Cindy Redick and David Bassett from Ohio.

After we put the kids to bed, he took me over to the window and put his arms around me as we looked out together. He took a deep breath. "I hope we never have to go backward from here," he said. My thoughts exactly.

We embraced the change, settling into the gated community and its perfectly groomed yards and homes. The people were quirky and hip.

There were neighbors and families everywhere. It was different and exciting. The weather was amazing—warm sunny days, even in January.

We had been in California for less than three weeks when all of a sudden the ground started to rumble and rock.

No, that's wrong. That doesn't even begin to describe it. The earth began to jerk and lurch violently—as if Satan himself were coming out of the ground. The noise was deafening—both the shuddering of the earth and the rattling of our house and everything in it. Everyone was still in bed, and as I was jolted awake I thought, "Well, it's either the end of the world or . . . an earthquake." I jumped out of bed, grabbed Sammy, who was sleeping in between us, and went tearing down the hall toward Brittany's room. As soon as I saw her bed, I was afraid she was dead—the quake had thrown her armoire and dresser on top of it. She also had Carly, a little girl from down the street, staying overnight, and I feared that both of them were under the pile. "Brittany!" I screamed. *"Brittany! BRITTANY!"*

"Mommeecee!"

The two girls had made themselves a bed on the floor in the corner; they were frightened, but completely fine and out of harm's way. I put my arm around both of them and told them to hold hands. I held Sammy in my other arm as we ran downstairs. We struggled to keep our balance, because the whole house was still shaking violently. I got all the way out the front door before I realized I had forgotten my mother. And where the hell was David?

When I opened the front door, Lana, Carly's mother, was standing there. "So . . . ," I began, "how often does that happen?"

"Lemme tell ya—I was born and raised here," she replied. "I've never been in one that bad."

"Take the kids; I need to go get my mother," I said as I ran back in the house.

Mom was standing in the doorway, scared out of her mind. David came running down the stairs. "Where were you?" I asked him.

"I took a quick shower and called Ohio to tell Bruce Winters we were in an earthquake. I figured the water was going to go off and the phones were going to go dead."

He was right about that. All the lights in the valley that we could see from our house at night were—gone. Now there was nothing. Pitch black. There was no running water, either. It was as if the world had stopped.

January 17, 1994: the Northridge Earthquake—my introduction to California living.

"So, Bassetts, when are you going back to Ohio?" Kenny, our neighbor wanted to know. He was out in the street, just like the rest of us, but he seemed to be pretty nonchalant about what had happened. Which is to say he was drinking a margarita and playing basketball. "If that shake, rattle, and roll scared you," he continued, "you might as well leave now. Earthquakes are a fact of life out here." He was a New Yorker with attitude.

It was a long, crazy week, and it really tested our moxie, but I knew I wanted to stay. I had the sense that my entire life in Ohio had been an earthquake; here, at least it was warm.

Eventually things got back to normal.

Brittany and Sammy were thriving in the new neighborhood with friends everywhere, riding their bikes up and down the hilly streets of Calabasas and running back and forth to one another's houses. David got on with the business of building our business and running the Midwest Center. With Brittany in school and Sammy home with us—and a part-time sitter—David was able to work out of the house to schedule infomercial shoots and strategize new ways to move the company forward.

I resumed my schedule of speaking engagements and continued my involvement with the National Speakers Association. During one of their conferences, we broke into group sessions. I signed up for "How to Articulate and Speak Well." There were about thirty people in the session. At the beginning the group leader went around the circle, asking each of us to explain who we were and what we did. When it came to my turn, I was only about halfway finished when the moderator put up his hand. "Stop!" he said. "I want everyone to listen to this woman's voice. Listen to how articulate she is."

Who? Me? I'd never had any special training, but as I thought about it, it did seem that I'd always been able to express myself in a way that people could relate to. Because it came easy to me, I just didn't understand that many people find it hard to do. It was a gift I didn't even knew I had.

At the end of the session, a woman came up to me. I had no idea who she was until she introduced herself. "Lucinda, I'm Henriette Klauser. You want to get a coffee?" Henriette is the brilliant author of *Writing on Both Sides of the Brain* and several other bestsellers, and when she approached me, I was amazed. The two of us are so very different, she with her conservative clothing, PhD, and Brooklyn accent, and me with, well, me.

But we really hit it off, and she asked me whether I'd be her roommate at the next Speakers Association conference.

I said yes, even though I dreaded it—not because of anything wrong with Henriette, but because of what was wrong with me. What was *still* wrong with me. I still suffered from IBS—irritable bowel syndrome. It can be embarrassing and difficult to control, and it was a huge problem for me in my teens and twenties. I was always having diarrhea and upset stomach episodes. And if I wasn't having them, I was afraid I was going to have them—at the worst possible moment.

Irritable Bowel Syndrome ran my life. It was one of the reasons why I refused to socialize or go places. I had to be absolutely sure there was a bathroom everywhere I went. Check and double check. At the time, I didn't make the connection between the diarrhea attacks and anxiety disorder, but when I was a teenager I drank Pepto-Bismol like it was Kool-Aid. Whenever Good-Time Susan and I took a road trip, I made sure I had bottles of the pink stuff in my purse or my bag. Even though as an adult woman I now understood that anxiety was one of the root causes of my problem, my IBS was still an issue. I continued to have powerful urges that came on suddenly. How was I going to share a room—and a bathroom—with my new friend, this highly respected writer? What would she think of me if I had an IBS episode?

That first evening there was a welcoming banquet for all the attendees. I barely ate, because I feared the consequences. After dinner, Henriette and I went upstairs to the room to chat and go to bed early for the big day ahead. We were in the room talking when she said, "Lucinda, you should write a book. I know you have a book in you."

I did a double take. She was the second person at the conference to tell me that. The first was a handwriting analyst—a graphologist. After asking me to write my name, she had looked at my signature and said, "This is fascinating. You're going to be very successful. You're going to write books, but you have to stay focused. You tend to get a little scattered."

I decided not to share the graphologist's reading with Henriette. I was skeptical. What did I know about writing a book? "I'm not a writer, Henriette," I insisted.

"Of course you are, Lucinda," she replied. "You just have to sit down and do it."

What Henriette was saying made me nervous, and I knew only too well what happened in my large intestine whenever I got nervous. My stomach started rumbling.

Uh-oh.

I jumped up and headed for the bathroom, mortified because of what was about to happen. I closed the door and locked it, just grateful that I made it to the toilet before I started to explode. But explode I did, and when I explode it gets noisy. Very noisy. I coughed. I flushed the toilet. I ran water. It was so embarrassing.

Undeterred, Henriette was on a roll and kept talking to me as she walked toward the bathroom door. I could hear her coming my way as I broke out in a sweat. Oh my God. My worst nightmare. "Write for fifteen minutes a day. Write the way you speak. Don't worry about it being grammatically correct. Sometimes less-than-perfect grammar is more powerful," she continued as if nothing were happening. Then, to make matters worse, she came over and body-slammed herself up against the door to make sure I could hear her.

Ever since I was a little girl in the house with one bathroom—the bathroom that was off-limits if my parents' bedroom door was closed—I'd had a huge hang-up about people hearing me when I was in there. Now, here I was, with Henriette just on the other side of a very flimsy bathroom door, hearing *everything*. Not only was she an earwitness to my loudest bodily functions, she also expected me to hold up my end of the conversation while I was, well, having a meltdown.

I could have died on the spot.

As I came out of the bathroom, I looked to see if she was shocked or embarrassed for me. She didn't even seem to notice.

What happens when your "worst nightmare" turns out to be someone else's "so what"? It's no longer your worst nightmare—you're over it. Suddenly it's no big deal. Henriette continued on about why I needed to write.

"But I don't know what to write about," I protested to Henriette. I took a deep breath and attempted to lie down on my bed.

Not going to happen. Henriette jumped up, grabbed my hand, and pulled me toward the door. "Come with me," she said as she dragged me out into the lobby. "Lucinda, you sit down right now and write for fifteen minutes." She handed me a blank pad and a pen. Henriette was insistent—there was no way for me to get out of doing what she wanted.

"But I'm tired. My stomach is upset."

"Write about that," she said.

"I can't. I'm not a writer."

"Just sit down and write. Something will come to you. Maybe not this minute, maybe not tonight. But it will come. Just write," she said with a smile.

So I wrote. And I wrote every remaining night of the conference. I am forever grateful to Henriette, because it was her nudging and encouragement that gave me the motivation to begin.

I came home from the conference and continued writing, fifteen minutes a day, just like she told me. Sometimes the fifteen minutes turned into four hours, then into all day or into the night. Sometimes I would journal about my day or my life; other times I would research a topic, get an idea, and run with what it meant to me. The amazing thing was, it came easily to me.

I discovered something wonderful. I loved writing. The book I envisioned was going to be an extension of the principles I talked about in my speeches, and an introduction to the problem-solving techniques that I'd included in the *Attacking Anxiety and Depression* program. And, like the program, it started from the understanding that people with anxiety disorder are amazing, gifted, and creative, not from any idea of how messed up they are. The goal was to empower people to change, to begin taking charge of their lives. That if these creative, sensitive, imaginative people could turn this type of thinking outward, where it belongs, instead of inward, scaring themselves and worrying themselves sick, they were capable of great things. I gave it the working title *From Panic to Power*.

I wasn't very far along when David went off to a marketing conference in San Diego. One of the other attendees was a literary agent named Margret McBride. They clicked, and David insisted that the two of us had to meet. Margret came to Calabasas, and I told her about my concept for the book.

Margret believed in me and in the book from the very beginning. We never even wrote up a formal proposal; she simply brought me to New York and put me in front of editors at some of the biggest publishing houses in Manhattan to verbally pitch my book. We went to lunch with Diane Reverand, at the time an editor with HarperCollins, and I pitched her the whole book off the top of my head. Margret asked for an advance of $1 million. And, OMG, we got it! It was extraordinary for a first-time author.

As soon as I finished the first three chapters, I sent them off to Diane. I was so proud of what I had written. It was pure and from my heart. My story. My voice. But I wasn't a "writer." What if she didn't like it?

One evening I was sitting in my office, all alone, writing, when the phone rang. "Is this Lucinda?" The voice on the other end of the phone was crying.

"Yes, this is Lucinda Bassett."

"I can't believe you answered the phone!" the woman said. "I didn't think anyone would be there at this time of night."

"Can I help you?" I thought the caller might be in the midst of a panic attack.

"I went through groups in Louisville with your program, with your sister, Donna," she began. "And I suddenly knew I had to call and tell you that Donna, wherever she is, is thinking about you. She wanted me to tell you that whatever you're doing, you're on the right path."

Me and my magical thinking.

I always want to believe in messages from people you love who have passed, and this was a great validation for me.

It was a huge lift—the cosmic vote of confidence I needed to keep moving forward. Fueled with optimism, I think I might have written another three chapters that very night. A day or two after that, Diane Reverand called. "Lucinda, this is exactly what we're looking for," she said. "Keep it up. We love your voice and your stories. Fabulous!"

The call that night was such a sign for me. A sign from my sister that I was going in the right direction. A sign from her that I was going to do something to make a difference—something significant for all of us. And there's nothing like confirmation from your editor that you're on the right track.

When the book came out, I was so excited. I was given a high-power publicity campaign and a multicity tour to promote the book. I did TV, radio, newspaper interviews, and bookstore signings in New York, Los Angeles, Chicago, Philadelphia, and Dallas, just to name a few. To celebrate the publication of *From Panic to Power*, Margret gave me a thoughtful and elegant gift—a beautiful gold Montblanc pen.

On the first leg of my tour, I was doing a seminar in Manhattan for the Learning Annex. As I headed into the conference room and was making my way up to the podium, a man handed me a copy of my book and asked me to sign it. It was the first time that had happened to me. I stood back, took a breath, and remembered where I had come from. I thought back to signing my name as a young girl, with the large flowing L for Lucinda. "This, this is what that was all for," I thought to myself. I still remember exactly what I wrote: "Here's to your life, an incredible journey. God bless, Lucinda Bassett."

From Panic to Power became an Amazon best seller. I was proud of myself—little Cindy Redick from the house on the dead end street on the wrong side of the tracks in Findlay, Ohio, had come a long way. And I'd gotten there by coloring outside the lines.

I was now a quasi-celebrity. *ALMOST FAMOUS*. I had the infomercial, the book, my speaking engagements; I was in *Cosmo*,

Psychology Today, and a whole bunch of newspapers across the country. I had earned the *ALMOST FAMOUS* button. Now, the big advance from HarperCollins gave David and me a chance to live out another of my big dreams from childhood. It was time to start looking for a house near the ocean.

On a beautiful Sunday we left our Calabasas digs and went for a drive over the Santa Monica Mountains. One minute we were in the valley and all its traffic. Next minute we were on a winding road cutting across the mountains, driving through a canyon dotted yellow with the flowers of wild mustard plants. About ten minutes later we came down the other side, and a fantastic view of the ocean opened up before us. Malibu, California. But not the Malibu you read about in magazines. This was country and mountains . . . on the ocean. It was open and simple and behind the times—in a good way. Lovely.

The following weekend, we did it again. This time we packed a picnic lunch of Kentucky Fried Chicken and headed for the beach with the kids. I smelled the salt air and heard the seagulls—and loved it. There we were, sitting on the beach looking at the cliffs and watching the surfers. It was unbelievable. I had this really odd feeling of coming home, of belonging. I remember thinking, "Oh my God, why did it take us so long to get here?"

CHAPTER 15

The Bargain with God

I'D ALWAYS FELT LIKE I was missing something when we lived in Oak Harbor. I couldn't quite put my finger on it. I supposed it reached back to those wild teenage days of wanting to get out and live in the bigger world. There was adventure out there, and it wasn't in Oak Harbor. When we moved to California, immediately I knew I wasn't missing a thing. In fact, the big earthquake was my first indication that California was full of new experiences and big adventures. And my career was kicking in, too. Mornings in Calabasas, I'd get into my minivan and our neighbors would ask, "Where are you off to?"

"I'm off to Hol-lee-wooood!" I'd say, as in "You got a dream? What's your dream?" *Pretty Woman*-style. I was going into Hollywood regularly now to record a new program called *Life without Limits* with an audio producer who had worked with Tony Robbins on many products.

On weekends, David and I resumed our Sunday afternoon trips over the mountains, through the canyons, and down to the Pacific, looking at houses. The California real-estate market had hit a bump, or rather a slump, so prices were down and there were a lot of homes available. One Sunday we drove up a little cul-de-sac to an open house in Malibu. It was contemporary—not my favorite style—but there was sunlight everywhere and palm trees in the backyard. The neighbors had kids the same ages as ours, and it had an ocean view. And it was in foreclosure.

With the advance from the book *From Panic to Power*, we were able to make a realistic offer; because the house was in foreclosure, we thought we just might have a chance at pulling it off. But as luck would have it, someone else had beaten us to it. We decided to make a backup offer, no contingencies, and kept our fingers crossed. David and I were in a tiny restaurant celebrating the completion of *Life without Limits* with a glass of champagne. We were also wistfully coming to terms with the idea that what might have been our dream house was going to be someone else's dream house instead. We had just clinked glasses when my cell phone went off. "The first offer fell through. You got the house!" our realtor said excitedly. Our new, almost famous, by-the-ocean life in California was about to begin.

One of the pieces of furniture that didn't really fit after we moved into our new house was our sofa. It was in limbo in the dining room, and I put an ad in the local paper to sell it. A woman named Janet came to have a look and decided to buy it. She gave me a check and said her husband would be by the next day to pick it up.

The next morning I heard someone buzz the gate. "Hello, is this Lucinda? I'm here for the couch." When I went out to the gate to let him in, the guy took off his glasses. I was momentarily speechless. "You're Martin Sheen!" I finally exclaimed.

"You're Lucinda Bassett!" he replied—a lot cooler than I was.

That was my first real-life demonstration of the fact that in Malibu, people who make millions of dollars live right next door to people who don't. Nobody makes a big deal about celebrity. Quite the opposite. Everyone sends their kids to the same schools and sits at the same soccer games and ballet recitals.

Since then it's been reinforced many, many times, beginning with when we put Sammy in the most amazing school, Point Dume Marine Science Elementary. Point Dume takes advantage of its location at the edge of the ocean to make the environment a part of how students learn—like the importance of tide pools and wetlands—and almost everything is hands-on.

The school was big on family picnics. We all got used to seeing Sammy's classmates with a celebrity parent or two. Pierce Brosnan. Kenny G. No ego, no attitude, just normal people trying to be good parents and be supportive of the school. I was "famous" as Sammy's mom, and it was the same for the "stars." They were simply hangin' out with their kids, like the rest of us. Everyone was easygoing. Flip-flops, cowboy boots, cutoffs. I loved it, and we just seemed to fit right in.

I did have to learn that the lifestyles of the rich and famous were a bit different from the lifestyle we'd brought with us from Oak Harbor, at least from a nutrition standpoint. When David and I showed up at a fund-raiser picnic with a pitcher of margaritas and a big bucket of Kentucky Fried Chicken, we spread out our blanket and started eating—only to see everyone staring at us. Without realizing it, we'd made quite an impression. The rest of the families were munching tofu hot dogs, portobello mushrooms, edamame, and raw veggies.

Oops. I barely knew what some of that stuff was, but I had to catch up fast. Foods that were considered exotic or downright weird in Ohio were healthy, normal, everyday fare in Malibu.

We never came back with KFC, but after that, David became famous—in a good way—for his warm, embracing personality, *and* his margaritas. It was a happy, mellow time. I joined the band at Sammy's school, along with Richard Page from Mr. Mister, a guy from The Knack, and a few others from the music biz. We'd play at school fund-raisers. David would circle with his margaritas, and the kids would dance around the schoolyard. Everyone had a great time. Sometimes we would all end up down on Little Dume Beach with our guitars, singing Crosby, Stills, and Nash. Oh, the people I was honored to harmonize with on those starry nights, with bonfires blazing and wine pouring! I had to pinch myself.

Life finally seemed stable, good, safe. But as the child of an alcoholic, I was always waiting for the sky to fall. Surely something bad was going to come along and ruin the dream. Surely lightning was about to strike, somewhere in my life. The first clap of thunder came in a phone call with my mother.

Although she came out often to visit, I had been unsuccessful at getting Mom to move to California permanently. She wouldn't move out of the house in Findlay, and when she was back in Ohio we spoke every Saturday morning. On this particular call, she said she wasn't feeling well but that she had an appointment with the doctor on Monday. I was concerned enough to call her back on Sunday—and again on Monday morning. She sounded funny. Her speech was slurred, and she kept repeating herself. I was alarmed—especially since she didn't seem to remember that she had a doctor's appointment.

I left for a meeting right after I hung up, but the feeling that something was very wrong with my mother kept nagging at me. I canceled my appointment and made a U-turn back for home. Then I called her doctor. "Put her in the hospital," I said to his nurse in the firmest possible tone. I was making a demand, not a request.

She put me on hold for what seemed like forever, and then got back on the line. "Doctor says you are overreacting," she replied in a condescending we-know-better-than-you voice. She sounded arrogant and patronizing, and it really got me mad—"Doctor says," like he is the final authority, the voice of God, and who the hell am I to question him.

"You tell the doctor I said to put her in the hospital immediately. That's an order from me as her daughter. I know my mother," I continued, "and I'm certain something is wrong with her."

I threw some stuff in a bag and booked a seat on the red-eye to Detroit. Just before boarding, I called my mom. By this time she'd been admitted to Findlay Hospital—at least "Doctor says" had done what I wanted.

"I'm cold and I'm scared," Mom told me over the phone, and then she started to cry.

"I'm on my way, Mom," I told her. "Just hang in there. I'll be there as soon as I can. I love you."

I hate taking the red-eye—*any* red-eye—but I hated this one more than most. I was so worried about my mother that I couldn't sleep, and I knew I faced a two-hour drive from Detroit to Findlay after I landed.

The plan was to pick up my brother Gary on my way through Toledo. As soon as I pulled into his driveway, I could tell from his face that he had bad news. "Mom's in trouble," he said as he got into the car. "They don't think she's going to make it."

I shook my head. "This can't be happening!" I shouted. "I talked with her just before I took off. She can't die!"

As Gary and I entered the ICU at Findlay Hospital, the doctor came out to meet us. Our brother Michael was with him. Both of them looked grim. "I'm so sorry," the doctor said. "She was such a lovely woman."

Was? *Was?* That really pissed me off.

"What do you mean 'was'?" I asked. He was talking about her in the past tense, like he'd written her off, like she was already dead.

"I'm so sorry," he repeated.

"She's still breathing, isn't she?" I demanded. I was not about to give up on her.

"Yes, but she's completely unresponsive," he replied.

"What exactly happened last night? What is her diagnosis?"

"Well, probably a stroke, but we're not sure," he began. Embarrassed—as he should have been—he paused and looked away.

Whatever this event was, it took place after she'd been admitted. This was "Doctor says," the one who'd said I was overreacting when I demanded that she be hospitalized. If I hadn't insisted, my mother would still be at home, except that she'd be dead by now. He knew it and I knew it.

I blew by him and raced into the ICU. "Mom! Mom! It's me, Cindy!" I grabbed her hand and started stroking her arm.

All of a sudden, her legs moved, uncoordinated, as if they were flailing. So much for "completely unresponsive."

"Well, she's obviously not paralyzed," I said. "And she's not going to die, either."

Immediately I called Dr. Phil Fisher in Toledo and asked him what to do. "Findlay is a small community hospital," he said. "Your mom needs to be in a bigger, more advanced facility. Get her into an ambulance and transfer her to Toledo Hospital right away."

She was en route within the hour. Despondent and exhausted, I followed the ambulance in my rented car, cursing at God—again—all the way up the I-75. Michael and Gary were behind me in Michael's car. My thoughts were broken and scattered. I was scared. "Why, why do I lose people?" I thought to myself. First my brother David, then Dad, then Donna. My thoughts rested on Donna. Was she trying to take her from me? At holidays and birthday times, sometimes my sister and I would fight over who was going to get Mom. "You can't have her yet, Donna!" I shouted as I raced along the dark highway behind the ambulance. "Forget it. I need her down here." And with that, I started to cry. Was anybody even listening? I wondered.

While I was en route, Phil Fisher put in a call to his close friend Jim Mackey, who was vice president of Toledo Hospital. As soon as Mom arrived there, he and Phil took over. Getting admitted was as smooth as it could possibly be. The doctors did everything they could, but it still didn't look good. A huge part of the problem was that they didn't really know what was wrong with her. It seemed like a stroke, or perhaps it was some kind of meningitis. She'd been sanding down the kitchen cupboards— which were sure old enough to have lead paint on them—so maybe some kind of lead poisoning was involved. . . . It's hard to treat the symptoms if you don't know what's causing them.

Meanwhile, my mother was comatose. She had a breathing tube in her mouth, tubes in her arms, tubes everywhere, all connected to a whole bunch of monitors and bags—bags for stuff going in, bags for stuff draining out. Gary came in and put a big sign over her head that said, "Call me Kay." I set up camp at her bedside—her hospital room became my hotel room. I sang to her and talked to her. I told her jokes. I never left her side for about three days—no shower, no change of clothes, nothing. I was exhausted. Everyone else had gone home. They had families and kids to deal with. My kids were in California with David. I wasn't leaving her until she was stabilized.

Finally I decided I really had to get some rest. The hospital had offered me an empty bed in a room down the hall, and I accepted. By the time I lay down, it was around 11:00 p.m. About four hours later, the phone next to my pillow rang. It was Mom's nurse, sounding very upset. "Your mother's blood pressure is dropping rapidly. Her breathing is shallow. I've called her doctor, but you need to get down here," she said. "I'm afraid we might lose her."

Noooooooooooooooooooooo!

I raced down the corridor. "Mom!" I said, hurrying to her bedside and taking her hand. "I need you. . . . Don't leave me!"

The hospital chaplain appeared at the doorway. "I'm here to give your mom her last rites," he said.

"Sorry, but she's not going anywhere," I replied with as much conviction as I could muster. "Thanks, but please go." I was borderline rude, but I was not prepared to let my mother go into the hereafter, and I didn't want anyone getting her ready to do that.

I leaned over her, holding her hands in mine, closed my eyes, and began to pray. "Dearest God, dear Jesus, please, let your love come through my body and heal my mother. Dearest Lord, hear my prayer and heal this woman. Let her be a testimony to your strength and love."

I put my hand on her forehead and continued to pray. I prayed with an intensity I'd never experienced before. I lost track of time, almost as if I was in a trance, but somewhere deep inside I knew exactly what I was doing. I was asking God for a miracle.

All of a sudden Mom's whole body jumped—and not just an inch or two, either. It sort of jerked up as if a giant spasm or electric shock went through her. I was so scared that I jumped back from the bed. I feared the worst. *"Oh my God! I've killed her!"* I thought.

I stood there looking down at her, frightened, for what seemed like hours. And then it happened. All of a sudden, out of nowhere . . . she opened her eyes. "Mom, Mom! Can you hear me?" She didn't respond; she lay there looking blankly at the ceiling. Then she gently and slowly turned her head and gazed toward me. But the weirdest thing was that I could tell she wasn't looking *at* me, but *past* me at something over my left shoulder. There was nobody there, but I took a step back and looked over my left shoulder again. What was she looking at so intently?

Then the duty nurse came running into the room. "What's happening here?" she asked in amazement.

"I don't know," I replied. "She . . . she just opened her eyes."

The nurse was astounded—not just because her eyes were open, but because her blood pressure and her heart rate were better, too. Meanwhile, Mom cocked her head and kept staring over my left shoulder with the most peaceful look on her face, as if she were trying to make out what she was seeing.

The nurse busied herself with her duties and called for some backup. I just stood there holding my mother's hand, stroking her forehead and telling her I loved her. "What did I do?" I wondered. "And what was she looking at over my shoulder?"

Once the room was quiet, I asked her gently, "Mom, what are you looking at?"

No answer, of course. But the peacefulness in her face was so overwhelming that it brought tears to my eyes. I didn't know what was there, but something or someone was present. We were not alone.

Suddenly, it seemed, it was morning. Michael and Gary arrived, marveling at Mom's improvement. The doctor came in and announced it was time to take her for some tests. Mom would be gone from her room for a couple of hours—long enough for me to finally get a shower. I didn't share what had happened with Michael and Gary, but I was secretly relieved and hopeful about her recovery. I was just getting dressed again when the phone rang.

It was Jim Mackey. "Look, Lucinda, I wanted to be the one to tell you this," he began. "You should know that although your mother opened her eyes and there has been improvement in her vital signs, this does not mean she will ever fully recover. It doesn't look good. They are running the tests now, but the neurologists believe it's inevitable that she will have some kind of permanent brain damage. I thought you should be prepared."

"What?" I was shocked. "But she looked at me. She is responsive, and she is doing better!" Jim was with heavy heart as he tried to gently share with me the doctors' skeptical opinions about her prognosis.

I finished getting dressed and headed for the hospital's little chapel. I never felt so alone, so deserted by God. "How could you do this to me?" I cried as I fell to my knees in the chapel. "I can't lose her. Please, God, don't take my mother. Don't let her become a vegetable. Please take . . . something else. Take my company, take my book, take my career . . . but don't take my mother." I sat down on the bench behind me and cried.

When I got back to her room Mom was back from her tests, surrounded by a circle of doctors, each one more baffled than the last. "This is unheard of," they told me, almost in unison.

Her neurologist was the most dumbfounded of all. "After being in a coma the way she was, your mother should have been left with severe neurological deficits—if she survived at all," he said. "And there's none of that, at least nothing that we can find. In twenty-five years of practice, I've never seen anything like it."

From that point on, my mother continued to improve. She started breathing on her own. She started being able to communicate—first shaking her head yes or no, and then talking. Gary, Michael, and I, as well as their wives and children, all marveled as Mom continued to recover. One by one, all the tubes came out. "Tom Hanks may have been Sleepless in Seattle," said Gary's wife, Donna, "but your mom is Tubeless in Toledo."

We made sure that Mom was surrounded with love. David flew in with Brittany and Sammy. Gary and Michael and their families were frequent visitors. There was always someone with her at the hospital every day, but I pretty much never left. One night after everyone was gone, she grabbed my arm and pulled me close. "There's something I need to tell you, and only you," she whispered. She was hoarse—her larynx and windpipe were still inflamed because she'd been on the ventilator for so long.

I sat down on the edge of her bed. "I didn't want to tell anyone else," she rasped, "because I was afraid they'd think I was crazy."

"It's all right, Mom," I said. "What is it?"

She took a deep breath, and then her eyes filled up with tears. "I don't know when it happened," she began, "but I saw my guardian angel." She began to cry. "It was the most beautiful thing I have ever seen," she said through her tears. "First there was this brilliant light. It was so bright I wanted to turn away, but it was so compelling that I couldn't," she continued. "It was such a powerful feeling of love. I just had to tell you."

I was so overwhelmed by her emotion that I cried with her. "Do you remember when you saw this?" I asked.

"No, but I think I was awake when I saw it. There was this gold presence," she said, "and then I heard this fluttering." She touched the heels of her hands together and gently wiggled her fingers. "I heard . . . *wings*."

"Did it frighten you?"

"No, not at all," she said, shaking her head ever so slightly. "It was there to comfort me. It made me feel safe."

I got chills up and down my arms and legs. I knew what my mother was saying was true, and I was pretty sure I knew exactly when it had happened—when she'd opened her eyes after the prayer and the spasm and looked over my shoulder. At the time I could feel something there, even though I'd turned around and couldn't see anything. It was eerie, but not scary. "Don't worry, Mom," I said. "What you felt was real."

So . . . my prayer for my mother—the one where I'd asked for the miracle—had been answered. I never thought I had any kind of gift of healing, but my mother's recovery had been so sudden, so complete, and so against all odds that I did wonder, just a little. Truthfully, I was a little scared by how well it seemed to work.

That left the question of the second prayer—the one I said in the hospital chapel, the one where I offered God my business and my career in exchange for sparing my mother: the bargain with God. It wasn't long before I got scared about how well that one was working, too.

The Midwest Center began to flounder. The book had been selling fairly well since its release in 1997, but now book sales nosedived. Business deals collapsed unexpectedly. My mother was alive and well and getting better every day, but it looked like God was calling in His chips and taking me up on my offer. The business and my career were coming apart.

CHAPTER 16

A Bargain Is a Bargain

MOM WAS IN A LOVELY rehab facility in Toledo, recovering beautifully, when I decided to fly to New York to put out some fires that had sprung up around the disappointing sales of the book. After that, I flew home through Detroit and drove to Toledo to once again check on my mother. She was so excited to see me, and so happy to be alive and well. She was up walking the halls now, making friends with all the patients. I gave her a hug good-bye and drove back to Detroit to fly home to California.

When I got home, I sat with David and told him about the prayer and the bargaining I'd done in the chapel in Toledo Hospital that night. At first, he chuckled. He didn't really believe in all that hocus-pocus. But then he listened as I worried, cried, and what-if'd our future—the future of our company.

"What if I really bargained with God? I mean, I am so glad Mom is well," I said. "But what if we really lose the business? How will we survive? How will I continue to help people? What if we lose our home, our security? What about all our employees?" Who knew if you could really bargain with God, but what was going on was awfully coincidental.

As the bad news continued to pile up, I was worried enough that I went to see Reverend Gregory, the pastor at our church. Greg was an amazing minister—he's much less about traditional religion, which has

191 — 191

always struck me as being built around my four least favorite things: guilt, blame, anger, shame—and much more about spirituality. At services on Sunday, Greg talked about finding God and about feeling God in your everyday life, and each time I heard him preach I came out really inspired.

This day, however, there was no congregation, just him and me and my "what-if" thinking. I told him about my bargain with God and started to cry. "Make no mistake: if that's really the deal I made, I'm okay with it. I'd much rather have my mother, but . . ."

"But . . ." Reverend Gregory sensed my hesitation and was trying to draw out the rest of the story.

"I want to continue doing what I do. I help people. That's what I do. I make a difference," I continued. "Wouldn't God want that to continue?" I looked at him, searching for reassurance. "I'd hate not to be able to do that anymore, but I just want to know so I can move on and do something else if I have to."

He took a breath and grabbed my hand. "Lucinda, you made a bargain, all right, but it wasn't with God. You bargained with Satan."

"I don't believe in Satan," I said halfheartedly.

Satan was something horrific, a threat from my past. Satan was one more evil, ugly monster that was lurking, waiting to get me if I messed up. And Lord knows, I messed up. In one of my many self-help actualizing spiritual books, however, I'd found permission to "let go" of believing in a creature called Satan. In my mind, that belief served no purpose, except to make me feel afraid. It was time for me to find real inner peace of some kind. To me, Satan didn't represent that in any way.

"Okay, maybe it's better if we call it 'negative energy,'" Greg said with a smile.

That worked for me.

"Let's think of it like this," he continued. "There's positive energy—God's energy, everything loving, good for the body, and good for the soul. And then there's negative energy. It's draining, destructive. It includes envy, worry, fear, jealousy, and pain."

I nodded.

"We choose where we want to put our energy, Lucinda. You were angry when you went into the chapel at the hospital, yes?"

"Yes, angry and afraid," I admitted. "I talk a lot about God in my books and in my program. I think of myself in a way as a messenger of God. I believe God helps people through me and through the work that we do. And for this, I guess I expected that God was going to take care of my mother. When it looked like she was dying, I got mad. How dare He let her get sick and die after all the other losses and pains in my life! What I said at the time was, 'God, if you do take my mother, I'm done talking about you. I'm done being your messenger.'"

Greg smiled and shook his head. "God doesn't bargain, Lucinda," he said flatly. "If God had wanted to take your mother, He would have. You bargained with the negative side of the force."

"Now what?" I asked.

"Now you need to stand up with God beside you as your army, as your strength, and ask Him to help you get your business back."

"How do I do that?"

"The same way you asked for your mother," he said kindly, "but this time, lose the anger. Do it from a place of love." His smile broadened. "With God as your partner, with His love and His positive energy on your side, you are ten times more powerful than you are by yourself. Begin now to thank Him for your business and its vitality. Pray from a place of thanks as though you already have your success back. Do it with others. Do it with your family. Think, work, and live from a place of gratitude. If you can do that, the negative energy doesn't have a chance."

A few days later there was a fund-raiser at Brittany's school. One of the auction items was a beautiful handmade patchwork quilt. Each of the children had contributed to it. All of the patches were different, but they had a common, uplifting theme: "Believing that You Can Fly" and being the best you can be.

An inspirational quilt made by children—that sounded like a lot of love and positive energy to me. I bid on the quilt but lost out to another mother in the classroom. As I walked over and noticed that her bid had won, she approached me. "Lucinda, why don't you buy that quilt?" she said. "I just think you should have it." I knew her, but we were just casual friends. I don't know why she felt that way or why she let me "win" it, but what a gift it was to me at that moment.

When I brought it home, it was Brittany who suggested that we say a family prayer together and that we sit on it to pray. I spread it out, and the four of us sat down and held hands in a circle. The first thing we did was thank God for one another, and for Grandma—who by now was on her way back to full health. The doctors in Toledo never did put a name on what had happened to my mother, but eventually it would be impossible to tell that she'd ever been sick. Then we asked God to help us build the business back up so we could keep helping people.

Ironically or not, surprisingly or not, in the weeks that followed, the company started to recover. Book sales rebounded, my calendar began to fill up with speaking engagements, and orders for the *Attacking Anxiety and Depression* program began to increase. It took a while, but over time the Midwest Center became more successful than it had ever been. David was networking, bringing in all kinds of new successful business relationships. We were creating new product lines and growing the company to a new level. We expanded into radio, and rolled out a more effective infomercial. Oh, the power of God.

Finally, life was beginning to stabilize again. Mom was good. The business was good. Life was good.

But there seemed to be a recurring theme in my life. Just when I thought things were going to be okay, God found another way to bring me to my knees. One of the signs of our business comeback was that in 1998 I was invited back for another appearance on *Oprah!*. Over a two-year period, I was on *Oprah!* three times. Her shows were taped in advance, and her staff always let me know when the airdate was scheduled. For a segment on women and stress, the broadcast date they gave me was a Thursday. For us that was important, because we needed to let the telemarketers know that the phones were really going to be ringing off the hook that afternoon.

That Thursday I sat down to watch my segment on *Oprah!*. It was always a bit uncomfortable to watch myself on TV, because I am my worst critic. I had my phone operators on alert, ready to go, and of course my mom was watching. To my surprise, it turned out that this wasn't my show. Instead it was about a young adult man who struggled with a debilitating condition called Tourette's syndrome, a neurological disorder characterized by involuntary physical tics and body movements, as well as by uncontrollable and often bizarre vocal noises and verbal outbursts. These outbursts often include obscene language.

I was disappointed to see that this wasn't my show, but I was in awe and disbelief of what I was seeing. I sat riveted watching this poor, tortured man and how out of control of himself he seemed to be. Obviously he had a pretty severe case. He was cursing and gyrating in public, unable to stop himself from blurting out strange sounds and rude words. He flailed his head and arms around in strange ways, and people stared at his bizarre behavior. He couldn't go to the movies or out to dinner because he was so disruptive. He couldn't even go to church. And he couldn't stop it. How exhausted and depressed he must be. My heart was sick for him. Oprah and her producers, as always, demonstrated sensitivity to this horrible malady, but there was only so much one could do. Actually there was nothing one could do, and that was the worst heartbreak of all: there is no cure for Tourette's.

I thought to myself, "Thank God no one in my family has this terrible disorder. How awful for people to struggle with something so impulsive, spontaneous, and obnoxious, and so utterly uncontrollable. How could you live with that?"

At the end of the program I sat for a moment, stunned by what I had seen, and then I remembered . . . I needed to call my phone operators and my mother. The producers must have confused the date my show was to air. I would call them tomorrow. Tomorrow would be Friday, and in addition to calling the *Oprah!* show about the scheduling mix-up, I also had a doctor's appointment for Sammy on my calendar.

By this time, Sammy was six years old. He was in the first grade, and a truly beautiful little boy. I was in the office getting ready to call Oprah's production staff when the phone rang. It was Ms. Ratliff, Sammy's first-grade teacher. "You need to come get your son," she told me. She made it sound like a command, not a request.

"I'll be there shortly," I said. "Sammy has a doctor's appointment this afternoon."

"No. Now," she insisted. "Your son is completely out of control."

"What does that mean, exactly?" I asked.

"It means," she said, with as much acid in her voice as she could muster, "that he is standing in front of the classroom and clucking like a chicken."

"*What?*" I thought to myself. I drove down to the school as fast as I could and ran straight to Sammy's classroom. I was horrified to see that Ms. Ratliff was not exaggerating. My son, my beautiful son, was standing in front of everyone, flapping his arms and clucking.

"You need to control your son, Mrs. Bassett," she said in front of the entire class. "This is not acceptable."

"Sammy! Sammy!" I shouted. He seemed to be in his own little world. He ignored me. "Come on, Sammy, let's go."

I scooped him up and ran out of the classroom with tears streaming down my cheeks. I resented the teacher's nasty tone and her lack of compassion. "Whatever it is, I'll fix it," I said to myself as we drove away. Once in the car, Sammy continued making clicking noises, but he wasn't unhappy. He was just distracted. My mind was racing as we drove across the canyon to the pediatrician's office. I hated that teacher.

I tried to think through what the problem could be. "Maybe it was what he had for breakfast or something he ate for lunch," I thought to myself. "Maybe it was that cough syrup, or maybe he didn't get enough sleep. Thank God he has a doctor's appointment today. Doctor Landin will figure it out."

I liked Bob Landin, Sammy's pediatrician. He had a busy practice with lots of fun things in his waiting room. We were shown into an examination room, and I read to Sammy as we were waiting our turn. As we waited, he clicked and tapped and jumped and bounced. It seemed impossible for him to be still.

Dr. Landin came in and observed Sammy's behavior. "Sammy . . . ," he began. Sammy didn't answer. He still seemed to be in his own little world, like he had been in the classroom. He just kept clicking away. "Sammy, how are you doing today?" the doctor repeated.

"I'm okay," Sammy finally said, never making eye contact. He ran his hands like race cars down the leg of the examination table and began making throaty engine noises with his mouth. It was as if no one else was in the room. Dr. Landin continued watching Sammy intently and asking him simple questions. After about twenty minutes, he asked a nurse to escort Sammy out to the waiting room, where he could play and watch videos. Then he asked me to join him in his office.

"So, tell me what's been going on with Sammy," he said.

"Well," I began, "he's been getting in trouble at school for bad behavior. He blurts out, and he distracts others by touching them. He'll go around and tap other kids on the head, and he gets up and moves around a lot. He makes noises and jumps and taps things constantly. He can also be obnoxious at times to other kids. He's been spitting on the playground. Sometimes he sticks his butt out in an odd way and shakes it at people. When I read to him at night, I've noticed that he makes these humming noises and clicks his mouth. Also, he has gotten very particular about his food. He doesn't want any food item to touch another item. And he has started repeating what I say. He blurts out strange noises and seems to want to repeat behaviors, like jumping or touching. Today he was standing in the classroom while everyone else was working, flapping his arms and clucking like a chicken. He didn't seem to care that the other kids were looking at him. And the teacher is really angry about his odd behavior in the classroom."

Dr. Landin seemed to be diagnosing Sammy as I spoke. "Ah," I thought to myself. "Answers. Solutions."

I scanned Dr. Landin's face, looking for reassurance. "So, what do you think?" I asked hopefully. "Is this behavioral? Could it be stress from school?" I knew he would know what to do.

He looked at me with concern, took a moment, and then said, "I'm not certain, but it appears that Sammy is showing the early symptoms of a neurological disorder called Tourette's syndrome. Now, it is not uncommon—"

"What?" I said in shock, interrupting him in midsentence. "What are you talking about?" My mind immediately flashed back to my horrific memories of yesterday's *Oprah!* show. This was a dagger to the heart. "Oh my God!" I cried. "That is NOT what this is! Those people are out of control. There is no answer, no help, no cure for that. What are you saying?" I was completely stunned. "Not my little boy—not my Sammy!"

I panicked, and my mind started to race. Scenario after scenario went through my mind, each one worse than the one that preceded it. "What if he grows up to be a person that people can't stop staring at?" I thought. "How will I cope? How will *he* cope? Oh my God. This can't be true. Please no, God . . ."

I stared at Dr. Landin in absolute defiance and denial. He was wrong. He had to be. "Are you sure? How can you be sure? I want to see a specialist." My face felt flushed. Tears welled up in my eyes, but I refused to let myself cry in front of him. I needed to be strong.

"I'll give you the name of a neuropsychiatrist, Lucinda. I think he is a pretty classic case, but you do need to see a specialist. It's going to be a long road for you and Sammy. Sometimes people grow out of the symptoms, but it's something only time will tell." And with that, he actually apologized—as if he knew what we were in for. As if we'd been given a life sentence. "I'm so sorry," he said. Then he stood up, put his hand on my shoulder, and left the room.

I just sat there, numb and overwhelmed. My heart and gut were so heavy I wasn't sure whether I could stand up. "This is a bad dream," I thought. "I don't believe him. How could he know, just in the brief amount of time he spent with Sammy today?" Finally I walked out into the waiting room; my eyes searched desperately for Sammy. There he was, sitting in the corner, humming and swinging his little legs. I just wanted to run to him, hold him, and keep him safe. "I can fix it," I thought to myself. "It will be okay."

My denial lasted almost a year. I was bound and determined to undo the diagnosis. I searched the Internet. I turned over every rock, looking for answers, looking for something else—anything else—it could be. Looking for a magic pill or potion that would cure my child. "I'm the mommy. I'm

Lucinda Bassett," I told myself. "I'm a fixer and I'm going to fix this. I fix other people. I fixed my mom. I can certainly fix my own son."

But there is no fixing Tourette's. I prayed about it often, but all the praying in the world wasn't going to take the Tourette's away. Instead I came up with some creative ways to deal with Sammy's symptoms, and to channel his ADHD—which often goes hand in hand with Tourette's—into more socially acceptable outlets. He flailed his arms a lot, so we started him in drum lessons. That way, when he started flailing, he was just practicing his drums. When he developed coprolalia—compulsive potty mouth—I taught him how to cuss in a different language.

When I told David, he was greatly concerned, but somewhat skeptical. He didn't want to believe it. We began a long journey—together—to raise Sammy and educate ourselves about the best ways to help him. David spent a lot of time with him. He taught him to ski and snowboard. Any kind of intense physical activity helped him focus. To deal with Sammy's jumping, David took him to the skateboard park, where jumping was an asset. Then the two of them took up dirt biking. Sammy became a successful dirt bike racer for his young age and won a shelf full of trophies.

Maybe I couldn't fix Sammy, but I could try to fix everyone else's attitude toward him. Every September at the beginning of each new school year, I went into his new classroom—carrying his drumsticks and skateboard and dirt bike trophies for show-and-tell—to educate his classmates and his teachers about the tics, the flailing, the sudden outbursts, and the other challenges faced by a child with Tourette's. "For Sammy, it's like sneezing," I'd explain. "When you're about to sneeze, there's nothing you can do to stop it, right? For Sammy, it's the same thing. He does things he can't help doing."

Frankly, the kids were easier and more accepting about it than the grown-ups. Many adults, including Ms. Ratliff and several other teachers at his school, either could not or would not understand that Sammy had a neurological disorder, not a behavioral problem. He wasn't acting out; he wasn't swearing or flailing or being disruptive on purpose. There were some teachers who really got it and others who really hated him and didn't want him anywhere near their classroom.

In trying to cope, we went through years of doctors, medications, treatments, more medication, and psychiatrists. I finally found a great psychiatrist for him, one who really understood Tourette's and how it affects children. We eventually chose to stay away from drug therapies, because some of the meds just seemed to make Sammy worse. Instead, we filled his life with empowerment. I went to bat for him in every way that I could, and it was always a battle. I was his warrior.

In third grade, he stood up in front of his class and recited about seventy-five pages of *Harry Potter*, pretty much from memory. This brought tears to his teacher—tears of joy. "*That's* what your son is good at!" she exclaimed. "He's already reading at the eleventh-grade level, and he has amazing abilities to retain what he's read."

Meanwhile, Brittany was building her life in high school. Eventually she was voted student body president, but she was also running the local chapter of an organization called Best Buddies, which promotes one-on-one friendships between kids with and without disabilities. Founded by Anthony Kennedy Shriver, the organization has the backing and active support of the entire Kennedy clan, including Anthony's sister, Maria, at the time the first lady of California.

By this time I had stopped taking any business trips, because I felt I had to be there for Sammy. This meant that when Brittany was invited to Washington, DC, by Maria Shriver for a Best Buddies event at the Shriver home, it was David who went with her. Brittany was a junior in high school, and it was time for her to start looking at colleges. He called to tell me all the exciting news about the dinner at the Shrivers' home. "While you're in Washington," I told David, "take her to look at Georgetown University. Let her walk around the campus, just to get a feel for it."

Georgetown University . . . It had been more than twenty years since I'd lived in DC, working as a waitress at the Key Bridge Marriott. I still remembered the day that I drove over the Key Bridge on my break and spent time driving around the Georgetown campus. I was in awe of the college, the grounds, and especially the students. They were all so sophisticated and bright looking. They looked like they came from smart parents and perfect families—families with money. "How do you get into a school like this?" I remembered wondering at the time. "What type of kids go here? How smart do you have to be? And what type of family do you have to come from? Certainly not a family like mine. Someone like me would never be admitted to a college like this." I'd sat in my car looking longingly for what seemed like hours. That rainy day was still fresh in my memory.

Back then, Georgetown University represented everything that was out of reach. Now, however, my daughter, Brittany, was making top grades in honors courses—AP everything. Besides that, she was involved in tons of activities and was literally running Malibu High School. For her, I believed anything and everything was possible. Nothing was out of reach. Not even Georgetown.

Ironically, when David took her to visit Georgetown it was raining. I was anxious to hear what she thought. The phone rang. It was David.

"She'll never get in here, Lucinda," David said.

I was stunned by his comment. It was as if he'd thrown a bucket of ice water over my head. "What did you say?"

"Georgetown is full of smart, wealthy, snobby East Coast kids. It's very much like an Ivy League school. She'll never get in," he repeated.

"You didn't tell her that, did you?" I was furious that he was selling our daughter short like that.

"No, but . . ."

"Well, don't. She's smart and she's talented and she can go toe-to-toe with anyone else trying to get in there. What does she think of it?" I asked.

"She likes it, but I think she finds it all a little intimidating. Here, you talk to her."

I heard him calling for her, and then she ran to the phone.

"Mom, it is such a beautiful school. I love it here, but it's probably tough to get in."

"You can do anything, Brittany," I said. "You are amazing and smart. How bad do you want it? If you want to go to Georgetown, you can."

The spring of Brittany's senior year, our mailbox was bursting with acceptance letters for her. Among them was one from Georgetown Business School. We were so happy, and I was especially proud.

All of us went to DC to get her settled in, including Sammy. We did the rounds familiar to every freshman parent—the bank, the computer store, Bed Bath & Beyond—and with each stop, Sammy, who was not quite thirteen years old, got more and more hyper. He started tic-ing like crazy because he was nervous about his sister being so far from home. It was late August and it was still hot, so I went to the front desk at the hotel and asked whether there was a pool Sammy could swim in—swimming always seemed to calm him down.

After a few phone calls we were set up at a local sports club, and Sammy was swimming laps under the supervision of a trainer. "You know," the trainer said, "he could be a great swimmer. He has a lot of potential."

Point taken.

When we got home, I found someone from the local college to swim with him. The guy was astonished at Sammy's natural ability. "Maybe he should play water polo," he suggested.

I convinced Sammy to try out. At first he was reluctant, because our high school has one of the best water polo teams in the state, and God knows Tourette's can really do a number on a kid's self-esteem. But he made it—and became one of the stronger players on the team. David, as he always had been, was Sammy's biggest fan. Loving and playful and nurturing, he was also an incredible support system for his son. David went to every match, home or away, and always brought the Gatorade and the water. And each time Sammy scored a point, David did a Tarzan call, just like he had for Brittany when she played volleyball. In fact, David became well known for his Tarzan calls.

David wasn't good at the homework part; that was my deal. But what he *was* good at was making sure that he was really there for his kids—for sports and for advice, and for life. And as he had for me since we started dating, he made sure there was gas in the tank and air in the tires.

While Brittany was at Georgetown I visited her often, and sometimes I would sit in on her classes. I especially remember flying into Reagan Airport and landing in the snow late at night. The snow was thick and heavy and so beautiful. The two of us headed into Georgetown to a little pub for dinner. The next morning, classes were canceled because the snow had really piled up. Brittany called my cell phone and told me to meet her in the library. I went running through knee-high fresh white snow to get there. Riggs Library looks straight out of *Harry Potter*—gothic, with a winding staircase that leads all the way up to a top floor with gorgeous arched windows. The room was set up for some official university banquet—white linen tablecloths and candles.

I loved Georgetown, and I loved the university, I always stopped at the chapel and prayed. Then I'd come home to my amazing son, the water-polo star. Brittany's time in college allowed Sammy to come into his own in high school. I loved the game of water polo and the smell of the pool— Sammy looked so strong and confident. By now he was six feet tall; he was toned and sleek, the way swimmers become, and girls were really liking him. He was popular—he had so many friends. Whenever someone asks what were the best years of my life, these were it.

The business was doing well, the kids were thriving, and I had a wonderful, loving husband. We took our "official" honeymoon to Europe, only twenty-plus years late. It was also during this time that we sold our first Malibu house and bought another house—this one was walking distance to the ocean.

We were comfortable enough that I could redo it in the style I wanted. It was a contemporary house with Old World potential. I started working with a contractor and began picking out tile, cabinets, and carpet. We redid the fireplaces in stone and put in thick hardwood floors throughout the house. We took a year to redo it and settle in. My thoughts were that we would sell it in a few years and make some money on it, but it ended up being our cherished family home. It was the place for wonderful family celebrations—Christmases, Easter dinners, and birthday and graduation parties. I felt so blessed. Finally, things seemed to be on an even keel. Finally, no one was sick or dying. There was no drama. . . . Finally, I felt safe. Finally, I could look ahead and not feel like the sky was going to fall and ruin it all.

Who was it that said, "If you want to hear God laugh, tell him your plans"?

CHAPTER 17

All Fall Down

IT WAS A RAINY SATURDAY in Malibu in 2007. I was in my office at home working on a presentation for a women's conference. "We have to close the business," David said matter-of-factly, as he walked into my office and sat in the leather chair in front of my desk. The way he said it, there was no doubt in his mind—not "maybe" close it; not "eventually" close it. We have to do it now.

My jaw dropped as I stared at him in disbelief. *"What did you say?"*

"We have to close the Midwest Center," he repeated. "It will take a year to close it down. If we start now, we might walk away with enough money to survive for a year until we both can get jobs."

It was late August and the economy had just begun the nosedive that would culminate in the huge national financial crisis of the fall of 2008, although most people didn't realize it yet. Our business was a bit off, but what David was suggesting came like a bolt out of the blue.

"What are you saying?" I said.

"The economy is tanking," he continued. "Our sales are way down, and a lot of our customers who have already bought *Attacking Anxiety* aren't going to be able to pay for it. As you know, they pay in installments. These are our receivables, but we're only going to be able to collect maybe two-thirds of what people owe us—at best."

David had a mind like a calculator—no, like a computer. As he was talking, I saw him calculating. He even started drawing numbers in the air. It was as if he had a giant spreadsheet in his brain. You could almost see the wheels turning as he was running numbers in his head. "Right now we have enough in accounts receivable to be able to pay our creditors and pay off the $5 million operating line of credit we have for the company, at the bank," he continued. "If we wait, it's only going to get uglier. With both our sales and our receivables going down, what will eventually happen is that we won't have enough money to pay back the bank."

While he was trying to explain to me why we had to close the business, he started scribbling down numbers and talking—probably as much to himself as to me: "We have this much in accounts receivable, this much in accounts payable, so much in overhead. . . ."

Overhead, I knew, was huge—we spent about $1.5 million a month just to run the company, about a million of which was spent on media—much of it in airtime for our infomercial and radio commercials.

He told me that he'd thought the data through every way he could think of, but to him it was all coming up snake eyes. "We have to stop the bleeding," he said as he rubbed the hair back from his forehead.

I was aware that we had issues with our telemarketing. Whenever our infomercial ran on TV, viewers were encouraged to call in for a free CD. When they called in, they were able to not only receive the free CD but also to talk to a skilled, caring person on the other end of the line. They were also offered a thirty-day free trial of our home-study program, *Attacking Anxiety and Depression*, and a free trial of our new supplements. If they liked either, they were put on a payment plan that allowed the customer several months to pay it off. It was an effective model, but it was extremely important that the operator who took the call understand the caller and the product well. We'd always had dedicated operators fielding those phone calls—people who knew how to connect with callers. Now, however, the call center that furnished our dedicated operators had sold out to a bigger company. The new company was refusing to assign us dedicated personnel. That was a huge problem for us. It was hurting us tremendously. We had spent six months trying to find another telemarketing company that could handle our sensitive clientele. None of them could do the job effectively.

People with anxiety and depression are already skeptical and untrusting. For us, having experienced, kind, and sympathetic people who were highly skilled and specifically trained was essential. These were operators who cared, understood the caller and his or her concerns, and had even used the product. They earned the caller's trust and made people feel confident that our program would help them. This was a special skill that takes time and patience. Now, however, the new people answering the phones just weren't knowledgeable enough about our product, and they weren't taking the time to really connect with callers to help them understand the value of the program. We tried many different call centers, but nobody would give us dedicated operators.

Over that six-month period, the marketing model that had worked so well for us for years appeared to be breaking. This was a problem, but we'd faced problems before and we'd always come up with innovative solutions. Why was this one big enough to convince David we had no choice but to go to the extreme of shutting the Midwest Center down?

Ever since David left his family's grocery store business and walked across the street in Oak Harbor to work with me, he had applied his savvy business skills and creativity to growing our company. I was the "face" of the Midwest Center, but he was the man behind the curtain—he was the Wizard of Oz. His genius brain always seemed to be moving at ninety miles per hour—David had always had a manic side to him, but he used it in a good way. He thrived on it and harnessed that manic energy positively. He was always thinking, always calculating. He operated from a place of great integrity—everyone in the direct-response business loved and respected him. And he was passionate about his faith in our product. As our CEO, he surrounded us with smart, creative people, one of whom was our CFO, Scott, a great guy. I called to talk with him about David's conviction that we had to shut down.

"This isn't making sense to me, Scott," I said. "I need to understand whether or not we really need to close down. We have ninety employees—this is their job, their livelihood. We have disabled people at Riverview

Industries who depend on the Midwest Center for their income and for their self-esteem. David and I built this business from the bottom up. He's telling me that we have to abandon the business that we've built together, let everyone go, and go get jobs."

As I sat waiting for his response, I thought about how I might have to step away from being Lucinda Bassett, who was changing people's lives, and go back to being Cindy Redick from the house on the dead-end street in Findlay, Ohio. It not only made me shudder but also made me feel like I'd been hit in the stomach. I'd been doing this for twenty years—this was now my life, my identity. Again I looked to Scott for reassurance "Is there any way that David could be right and we need to close the company?"

Scott took his time before he responded, carefully looking at the numbers on his computer. "Lucinda, David is smart, and he understands the business. But I need to work through the numbers here," Scott said calmly. "It's complicated. And it's hard to determine the actual value of the receivables over the next year. But, personally, I think we can figure this out over time, pay down debt, and come up with a plan."

We kept discussing it throughout the fall, but as time passed, David became more and more concerned and agitated, obsessing about it constantly. He would sit at his computer all day and into the night, manically talking to himself, thinking things through. It was complicated because times were indicative of a possible financial downturn, our telemarketing was not working the way that it needed to, and there were strange communications between David and an out-of-state company we had done business with, a company that he didn't trust. They, too, were clearly aware of the company's struggle and recent challenges. David was not only confused but at this point also beginning to get a bit, well, paranoid about whom he could trust and whom he couldn't. He was beginning to think this company had an agenda—that they actually wanted to take advantage of the challenging situation the Midwest Center was in.

Still, I couldn't bring myself to agree with David that we had to close down. David had always been positive and upbeat even in difficult times; he always seemed to find a solution. But now he became increasingly concerned and nervous. He spent hours poring through the numbers, calculating, talking to Scott, who tried tirelessly to understand David's concerns and mine. Scott worked twelve-hour days with David in an attempt to understand his logic of doom and gloom, while helping David to see that there was a way to scale back and continue running the company.

Back in April, before all this really set in, I had booked our annual family ski trip for the Christmas holiday. I decided to pick Jackson Hole, Wyoming. David loved Jackson Hole—he'd lived there for a year and a half when he first got out of college. In October I tried to cancel the trip, but the resort wouldn't let us out of our condo. We were booked for the week of Christmas, and they were very adamant about people paying in advance and keeping their reservation. "Well," I thought to myself, "maybe it will be good for all of us to get away." I also silently wondered if it might be our last ski trip for a while.

As fall turned to winter, David's mood got darker and darker, and he got more and more depressed, distracted, and agitated. I'd see him up at 4:00 a.m., staring at the computer screen. He sat there for hours, palms pressed hard against his temples, pushing his forehead back into his scalp till the arch in his eyebrows disappeared and the skin was stretched tight. He was constantly writing out things in longhand—two- to three-page scenarios for what was going to happen. Some of them I read, some I didn't. He seemed tortured.

"Lucinda, don't go spending any money on presents for Christmas," he warned me right before we left for Wyoming. "We can't afford it. You have to get used to the idea that our life is going to change. Things are going to get tough."

What did that mean?

"David, what is wrong?" I said, scanning his face for clues. "Is there something I don't know about? Whatever it is, we'll get through it."

At this point it felt like there was something he wasn't telling me. The problems with the company were certainly concerning, but we had a substantial amount of money in accounts receivable, great employees who really cared about the company, and a long history of strong relationships with our vendors. We were smart and had been through tough times before. I felt certain we could figure it out. What was becoming obvious, though, was that David was no longer at the helm in the way that was necessary to figure it out.

"You don't understand, Lucinda. We have to close the Midwest Center."

"David, you need to calm down. The way I see it, worst-case scenario, we sell part of the company. We'll find a strategic partner." This was our long-term goal anyway, something we had talked about a few years back. "And we can always sell the house. We have a lot of equity in our house. We'll fix this. We'll straighten things out when we get back from our trip."

We left for Jackson Hole on December 20. I bought small presents for everyone, but being there really *was* the gift. The snow was beautiful, and there were deer and elk. David showed us around the town and told the kids stories about his time in Jackson Hole right after he got out of college. The stories he told were great, but beneath all that nostalgia I could tell that he was distracted and even depressed. Usually he loved Christmas, but now he seemed preoccupied. It was like a big part of him was someplace else.

On Christmas Eve day we had a nice family day skiing together, and then David had a request. "How about we go see Howard and Eleanor?" he said. These were old friends who lived on a ranch about an hour and a half outside Jackson Hole. I'd been there when we first met, and they just loved David. Their son Randy had been David's college roommate. David and Randy had remained close over the years, and David talked often about how kind and generous Howard and Eleanor had been to him when he was really struggling to start up his landscaping business in Jackson Hole.

Snow was in the forecast, but I was happy to make the trip—I was happy now whenever David wanted to do *anything*, because mostly, he didn't. Brittany and Sammy wanted to hang at the condo, so we jumped in our rented four-wheel-drive SUV and headed over the Teton Pass, past the blinking snowstorm warning lights. When we arrived at the ranch we found Howard on the front walk, shoveling snow. David grabbed a shovel and pitched in to help, while I went inside to catch up with Eleanor. We had a great visit, then started driving home through snowflakes the size of golf balls over the Teton Pass. It was beautiful. With Christmas music on the radio, the effect was truly magical.

One of my favorite songs, "Same Old Lang Syne" by Dan Fogelberg, came on the radio. I kept looking over at David. He was wearing my favorite, worn, brown-leather Ralph Lauren jacket that I'd bought for him years back, and a woolen Scottish golf cap that he always wore backward. He had a few days' growth of a beard—he looked so handsome. I looked at him and thought about the life we had enjoyed. Twenty-five years together. He was my best friend, my children's amazing father, my partner, my lover. I just loved him. I couldn't take it if anything ever happened to him. Something was going on that was bigger than just the company's challenges.

I reached over and took his hand. "Merry Christmas, David," I said, looking at him for a response. "I love you."

As he looked over at me, he looked so sad, as if he had let me down. In that same moment, a tear rolled down his cheek. "I love you, too," he said, and then he stared back at the road. David clearly was not okay. I found myself sitting there wondering what he was keeping from me. Had he had an affair? Was he dying of some disease? What was making him so distraught?

"David, what is wrong? I mean *really* wrong? Is there something you're not telling me?"

He simply shook his head and kept driving. On a beautiful Christmas Eve, in perfect snowfall driving through the mountains, he was completely lost. He was a wreck and not himself. "Wow," I thought to myself. "I don't know what demon he's wrestling with, but something is bothering him in a way I have never seen before."

On Christmas morning we got up, shared small gifts by the tree, and made breakfast. I could sense the sadness in David's tone but we managed to make it a special morning. That night we went to dinner at a beautiful country inn just outside Jackson Hole. In spite of his mood, we had a wonderful trip. Little did we know it would be the last vacation we would ever have together as a family.

After we got back to California, David got substantially worse. He kept stonewalling me about why he was so upset, but his behavior became even more erratic. I'd started doing some telephone coaching, but whenever I was on the phone, David would come into my office and stare at me and start rubbing his forehead. There I was, trying to coach a woman through her fear of bug spray in a Kmart, and all the while David's eyes were boring into me. I gestured to him to go away because I really had to give coaching my full attention, but he sat there like he was in a trance.

He was also becoming increasingly paranoid. In late January of 2008, Brittany came home for semester break from Georgetown—she was about to start her final semester. When she came home, David told her that we had to hide all of our valuables under the house, not just our jewelry but pictures and artwork, too. "Mom, what is wrong with Dad?" she asked me. "He's scaring me and Sammy. He is acting really weird and not himself."

I realized that I had to roll up my sleeves and get involved in whatever was happening at the company. He was really not making good decisions now; in fact, he sat home in fear most of the time, telling us all that we were going to go bankrupt. He would barely shower and shave. By now the Midwest Center was clearly going through challenging times. If David had been himself I knew he'd be able to find a solution, but he simply wasn't capable. I knew we needed a strategic partner and an infusion of cash.

Through a friend, I set up a meeting for David and me with a major hospital chain in Ohio that had shown great interest in working with us as a strategic investor. With some help, I put together a business plan and strategy for working with them. I had some pretty creative ideas and a great plan, and they had deep pockets and serious interest. They were excited about the potential of going forward together—they knew who we were, and they knew Dr. Phil Fisher, who had been affiliated with us from the beginning. I was hopeful that this would turn out to be a profitable partnership for everyone.

Meanwhile, David's paranoia was more and more evident. "Don't use the credit cards, Lucinda. Pay for everything in cash," he told me. "And there's really no point in going back for that meeting. They're never gonna let us sell the Midwest Center."

"Who isn't going to let us sell it? Who are you talking about?" I asked.

"They are determined to prevent us from selling the company," David said. "They want to force the Midwest Center into bankruptcy. Once we go bankrupt, they can steal the company from us for a fraction of what it's worth. They want to own our database, our product line. They'll even own your name."

My heart sank. Now he was taking it to a whole new level. What was he even talking about? To me, his paranoia about this was no more credible than his desire to hide the jewelry under the house. I called our accountant and our attorney in California, whom we both trusted immensely. Both attempted to help David look at the numbers and understand his fears. Both tried to determine whether or not what he was saying about some type of conspiracy had any basis at all.

"Could there be any truth to this?" I asked them. "Is this company somehow going to prevent us from selling the Midwest Center and try to put us into bankruptcy? Or is he just paranoid?"

What gave David's paranoia a little validation was a bizarre contract an out-of-state company had created with us for their services. David had apparently signed it without reading it thoroughly. I was reading it now for the first time with our attorney, and the terms and conditions of the document clearly seemed to be to their advantage—lots of clauses about their rights and our obligations, and very little about *our* rights and *their* obligations. After reading it and hearing David's concerns about it, I was shocked that David had ever signed such an agreement. So was our attorney. I was certain this document was causing many of the problems in David's head. That said, it still seemed to us that most of his concerns were just paranoia.

Late in January, we had tickets to fly back to Toledo to meet with the hospital chain about the next steps to take for a possible partnership. David woke up that Sunday morning, the morning we were supposed to leave, and started shaking. He jumped out of bed, started pacing the floor, and blurted out, "I can't go back to Ohio."

"What?" I asked, half-asleep. "A lot is riding on this meeting, David. You're the president. You *have* to go."

David looked at me with great sadness in his eyes. Then he took a deep breath. "I need to tell you something," he began. I could tell that he was almost in tears. He was about to tell me something awful. I could feel it in my bones.

"What is it, David?" I said, somewhat apprehensively.

"All of our money is gone, everything. We're going to lose everything, Lucinda. We're going to go bankrupt," he said.

I sat there stunned. "What are you talking about?" I said, slowly climbing out of bed, attempting to absorb what he was saying.

"All of our savings, all of our personal money . . . gone," he repeated.

"Gone . . . where?"

"I invested in a friend's business, and, well, it didn't go well."

"Who? What? What did you do? What are you talking about?" I asked, trying to get my head around his words.

"It was my best friend from college—you know, Stu. He was building high-end housing in Florida. Planned urban developments. Remember when I went down there to visit him? He showed me the properties, and it all looked great. So I jumped in and wrote him a check. Things seemed to be going well. Then he called me and told me he wanted to expand it. I got caught up in all his excitement and started borrowing to give him more money."

As he talked, he spewed out amounts of money that were mind boggling to me. I was adding up the numbers in my head, and all I knew was that we didn't have anywhere near the kind of money he was talking about.

"But the economy really hurt the whole project, just like it's hurting our business, and it started falling apart. Now he doesn't have the money to move forward and finish it, or the money to pay me back. He's devastated, too, and he feels horrible."

David was overwhelmed.

I just stood there—stunned. Was he serious? Did he really do this? Why didn't he ask me before he did this? What was he thinking, taking a chance like that with our money without me?

"How much, David?" I asked, panicked. It was like a bad dream.

"Everything we had, and lots of money that we didn't."

"At least we have the equity in our house. We'll get a partner for the business, and . . . we'll sell our house," I said, trying to process it all and search my brain for an immediate solution—anything in an attempt to make us both feel better.

David shook his head, looking away from me. "No. We don't have any equity in our house," he said, looking at me sheepishly.

"What do you mean, 'No, we don't'?" I was stunned and felt as if my whole world was crashing down in that moment. I couldn't breathe. I started to sweat.

I knew our house was now worth a lot more than it was when we bought it. Based on that, I assumed we had a decent amount in equity. But we also had a line of credit against the equity in the house for a million and a half. From time to time, David would use it to pay taxes or use it for unforeseen expenses, like short-term media buys for the company, but he always replenished the money within a month or so. I had to sign it when we used it, and I did, because I trusted him to use it wisely and replace it immediately.

"Remember when I asked you to sign the credit line a few months ago, and told you I was going to use it to buy media for the business?"

I looked at him, preparing myself for his next horrific truth. "Yes," I said apprehensively.

"I didn't use it for media." David looked down in embarrassment. "I gave that to him, too. Along with all our savings."

My jaw dropped open.

David continued, "It's not Stu's fault. He didn't know where I was getting the money. I told him I had money to invest. He just wanted us to make money together. He says he'll pay me back someday, if he can, but it's not looking good." David was pacing the floor as he talked. "We thought we were going to make a lot of money, but it fell apart. Everything is falling apart, Lucinda."

He stepped back and began running his hands through his hair, searching my face for a reaction. I was in shock. I fell to the couch, overwhelmed. I couldn't even look at him.

"Lucinda, we're going to go bankrupt. There's nothing in our savings, I've borrowed hundreds of thousands on our credit cards, and there's no

equity left in our house. There's nothing left. Between that and the company struggling, we are fucked. And when the bank finds out we don't
have the equity in our house, they'll call the $5 million note because they'll
know we don't have any security for that money. And when they find out
we're going bankrupt, they'll call us on it. It's a demand note, you know.
They can call it at any time. We are going to lose everything, Lucinda."

I couldn't take it all in. Us? *Bankrupt*? Oh my God. So this was what
he was worrying about all along. But this was not just his money, it was
our money. I was a big part of earning that money. A lifetime of hard work,
risk, and our family home. How could he do this to me, to his children?
To all of us?

"How could you do this to us? This wasn't just *your* money, David. It
was *our* money, *our* life, *our* business, *our* children's future," I said, trembling. "Both of our names are on the $5 million line of credit as equity. We
are responsible for that money."

"Lucinda, I am so sorry." He stood there, anxious and distraught.
"We're going to lose everything, Lucinda."

I was speechless.

I was one of those women who had stayed out of the business-end
of the business, and out of the business and money-end of our family's financial situation. For twenty-five years I had relied on David to
handle everything—and he had done a beautiful job, or so I thought.
Lesson learned.

I canceled the meeting in Toledo. There was no way we could talk to
them right now. We were both too devastated. I couldn't even talk to him.
I was beyond shocked.

As the days passed I tried to calm down and realize how important it
was to assure him that we would find a solution. But, secretly, I wondered
if we could. I don't know which I was more—angry or scared.

In February 2008, we had the sad task of letting go thirty of our
employees. The opportunity with the hospital evaporated.

After downsizing the company, David's behavior became downright
bizarre. He was constantly worrying and obsessing about our company

and our personal finances. He would follow me around the house repeating his mantra of doom and gloom. He would stand at the island in the kitchen wearing an old, holey T-shirt, wringing it as if it was sopping wet. As he was twisting it, he'd say, "We're going to go bankrupt. We're going to go bankrupt. We're going to go bankrupt." He chanted it over and over.

David's paranoia mushroomed. He became fixated on his conspiracy theory about the company. He imagined they were really "out to get us." He would show me e-mails or correspondence and say, "Don't you see, Lucinda? Look how they're trying to put our company into bankruptcy and then steal it. They're going to have your name, they're going to have our product line, and they're maneuvering to be able to take it from us for almost nothing."

I didn't believe him, but sometimes I would say that I understood, just to calm him down.

David was still writing out his scenarios of how this would all take place, but now they went on for five or six pages—single-spaced ramblings of detailed descriptions of the conspiracy that he believed was going to happen. Now, each page was embellished with monsters and weird stars and frowns and scary faces that he had drawn. It took me a while to realize what it reminded me of, and when I did, it really freaked me out. His elaborate longhand scenarios reminded me of John Nash, the brilliant but delusional mathematician played by Russell Crowe in *A Beautiful Mind*.

As the days and weeks passed, he became fixated on his conspiracy theory. Here I was, trying to deal with someone who was becoming increasingly unstable and paranoid, while trying to calm Sammy and Brittany and their anxiety and fear about their father's weird behavior. At the same time I was attempting to "stabilize" Midwest Center, keeping things going without anyone learning of David's instability, and trying to find a strategic partner to purchase the company. And during this, I still had to be Lucinda Bassett, doing interviews and phone coaching. Thinking back, I truly don't know how I did it. I was constantly anxious, unable to sleep, almost unable to function. Every day was like the movie *Groundhog Day*. I woke up in the same nightmare.

I remember locking myself in my office on some afternoons, attempting to catch up on missed sleep the night before, hoping David would see the closed door and think I was on a business call. We both worked at home, so we were together every minute. I just needed a break from his constant ruminating.

I would call my mom and worry to her, with her. Thank God for her. She was living part time in a condo we had bought for her in Thousand Oaks, so she was close by. There were times I would just go to her condo and sit and watch TV with her, in an attempt to forget the moments of insanity in my own home. I remember sitting there in that small one-bedroom condo thinking, "If we all have to move in here with her, where would we sleep?" It was awful.

At the suggestion of a psychologist friend, I finally confronted David directly about seeing a psychiatrist. "You need help," I told him. "You need to go see someone." When he finally agreed to go, I was relieved. At least he had enough sanity left to know he was not well. The psychiatrist suggested he was bipolar, depressed, and delusional, and decided to put him on an antipsychotic.

This drug might work for other patients, but unfortunately it just seemed to make David worse. After being on it for a few weeks, he became very anxious and more paranoid, and started doing even more bizarre things. He would lie in his closet on the floor in the dark for hours. He would tap his hand constantly on his leg and say really strange things in weird tones. He started talking about calling the bank that held the $5 million note for our company and telling them we were going to go bankrupt. One night I found him up attempting to book a flight back to Ohio to talk to the bank! I was mortified. He started e-mailing people in our business, telling them we were going bankrupt. It was such a nightmare. All the while I was holding the family together, holding the business together, trying to "fix" it, and find an interested buyer. I was exhausted, scared, and completely overwhelmed.

If you've ever lived with someone who is mentally ill, you feel it the minute you open the door. Negative, anxious craziness permeates the house. All you really want to do is run away, except you can't because you live there. Our social life evaporated; nobody wanted to come over, except the dear close friends—like Lisa and Jonathan, and Sandra and Vincent—who diligently came to comfort me and reassure him. Vincent and Jonathan were both smart businessmen, and they each spent tireless hours poring over numbers with him, trying to understand his concerns and help me discern whether or not I needed to close the company. Sometimes David would just lie on the couch like a beached whale and fall asleep, ignoring us all. It was horrid.

The kids didn't want to bring their friends home. Living with David now reminded me of dealing with my father—in the worst possible way. As I had been in the later stages of Dad's alcoholism, I was caught in this vicious dynamic, whipsawed between wanting to stay to save him and wanting to flee to save myself, and now, my kids.

With David, however, it didn't matter how much I wanted to escape. I was stuck; we all were prisoners in our home, trapped in his world—trapped in his insanity with him. The horror of what was going on hit Brittany with full force when she came home for spring break. She was heartbroken and distraught at how far down he'd gone, not just since Christmas but since she was last home in January.

I wasn't doing so well myself. For me, every day was a struggle to clarify whether David was able to think clearly enough to help me make important decisions about our business or whether he was paranoid and not in reality. How was I supposed to believe a man who spent a lot of time wringing a T-shirt and lying on the floor in the dark? And then there was the issue of our personal finances. What credit cards had he maxed out? What did we have left in the bank?

It was so helpful that Brittany came home from college. Brittany was a business major, and while she was back, I asked her to take a look at our finances. "You know that Daddy's not doing so well," I said. "Could you sit down and see if you can figure out how he pays the bills?" I was concerned that either he wasn't paying them at all or he wasn't doing it systematically.

It was also a relief for me that she was going to be at the house for a few weeks. David and I needed to go back to Ohio again, and I didn't want to leave Sammy alone. I had found several potential purchasers who were interested in buying the Midwest Center, and I had set up meetings with them. We also needed to reassure our employees, because by now they all knew that the company was in trouble.

We were due to fly out on a red-eye but as we were about to leave, David had another meltdown. "I can't go. I can't go," he told me.

I called the psychiatrist. "I don't know what to do," I said. "He's acting so weird. But I have people flying in and my employees are anxious and need reassurance. I need to go back."

"It will be okay, Lucinda. Go get on the plane."

"He's really not doing well since he's been on this drug. I'm afraid he's going to hurt himself or something."

"Has he ever mentioned doing that?" he asked.

"No," I said, "but he just isn't himself at all."

"Go. Your daughter's there. You're only a flight away."

I flew the red-eye and didn't sleep on the plane. I drove the two hours from Detroit to our offices, exhausted and overwhelmed. All I could think about was David. I had this uneasy feeling that I shouldn't have left him. At about 11:00 a.m., I was in the middle of a meeting with some of my employees when my cell phone rang. Ordinarily I wouldn't have picked up, but I saw that it was Brittany. When I answered, she was hysterical. "Mom! Mom! I can't wake Dad up. He's in bed and he's like, really groggy." I stood there stunned but careful to watch my reaction.

"Can he talk?" I said in a whisper.

"Yes, but not very well. There's something wrong with him. I think he took pills. There are a whole bunch of pill bottles here beside him."

My heart started to pound. There I stood, feeling my daughter's panic as my employees watched my facial expressions and listened to my words. They were already freaking out. They didn't need to know about this, too. I stepped out of the room.

"Call Jonathan right now," I said to Brittany as calmly as I could, but with urgency. Jonathan was David's best friend and lived just down the street. "Listen to me carefully, Brittany. Tell Jonathan it's an emergency. Tell him what you just told me and that he needs to come right over immediately. And tell him you might need to get an ambulance to get Dad to the hospital."

Here I was in a business meeting with my distressed employees, while my husband—the most incredibly brilliant, smart, loving, happy man, my best friend, the wind beneath my wings, my children's amazing father—had tried to commit suicide in our home with our kids in the house.

Our beautiful twenty-one-year-old daughter should have been at the beach or with friends, enjoying her spring break. Instead she was doing what no daughter should ever have to do. She was driving her father to a neuropsychiatric hospital—the locked-down psych ward—because he'd deliberately swallowed a toxic combo of sleeping pills and antipsychotic medication. And he'd done it with his two kids there, knowing full well that they would be the ones to find him. That's how sick he was.

Jonathan went with Brittany to get David admitted. Meanwhile, I carried on that day as best I could, trying to reassure our employees that everything was going to be okay, trying to sell the company, and trying to manage my own anxiety. I had already lost twenty pounds over the course of six months, and I was visibly exhausted, with dark circles under my eyes. My employees had to sense something, but I couldn't tell anyone. I couldn't do that to David. He was such a proud, amazing businessman. I really believed he would eventually come back together, to us, but now this? I was so scared and alone. How would I get all of us—David, the kids, and the business and my employees—through this?

I took the red-eye back to California. As soon as I landed back in Los Angeles, I rushed to the hospital to see David. The psych ward was a brutal, scary place—locks and double locks on all the doors and windows—and waiting to get in brought one of my worst childhood fears flooding back. Little Cindy Redick, who was always scared of losing her mind, always scared that someone would lock her in a mental hospital—permanently—was now standing outside the locked ward, waiting for someone to buzz the door so she could get in to see her husband. How ironic.

Standing there, I realized that there could be a hereditary component to David's illness. I knew that Grandpa Dewey, his grandfather on his mother's side, was in a psychiatric hospital for much of his life. In fact, it was the same looming, scary gothic one in Toledo that had scared the living daylights out of me as a child. He had suicidal tendencies, and had tried to kill himself several times, I believe.

As soon as he saw David, he'd say, "How's my boy?" It took his doctors years to figure it out, but he was finally diagnosed as manic-depressive. As soon as they made the diagnosis they switched his medication to lithium, and it made all the difference. No longer suicidal, he was released from the hospital and came home to live a pretty much normal life with his wife, in his seventies. Better late than never, I guess.

Grandpa Dewey had three daughters—Dorothy (David's mother), Nancy, and Carolyn. Carolyn struggled with chronic depression and bipolar disorder as well. When they told me that her doctor had prescribed an antidepressant, I immediately suspected it was the wrong medication for her. I knew that several studies had found a connection between that medication and tendencies toward suicide—tendencies we already knew she might have, because of her father. I suggested they put her on lithium instead, but they never had the chance to make that happen.

Carolyn took her life.

It was horrifying for the whole family.

BZZZZZZZZZZ. The harsh noise startled me back to the present; I had been cleared for admission into the psych ward. I pushed the door open and walked in.

When I finally saw David, I wish I could say that he looked like he didn't belong there, but I can't. He looked as out-of-it as the rest of the patients. There was something kind of crazy in his eyes. It was clear that his paranoia had taken another turn for the worse. "Get me out," he demanded. "Get me out of here, Lucinda! I need to stop them from stealing the business!"

He was in the psych ward for about a week. Because of his family history, I feared that the antipsychotics were magnifying his suicidal tendencies. When he was about to be discharged, I asked them to put David on lithium. Again, nobody listened to me. They gave him a different antipsychotic drug instead, along with a mood stabilizer. Unfortunately, he was every bit as unstable when he was released as he was when he was admitted. After telling me that my husband was paranoid and psychotic, they sent him home.

Home? Home, where he became my nightmare—again. He didn't shave or shower for days on end; he was crying all the time. When he was sitting, his knee was vibrating all the time, as if it had a will of its own. He didn't seem to be able to make it stop. I often found him lying on the floor of his closet, talking to himself in the dark and wringing his T-shirt.

David's return home meant that we were plunged back into his world of insanity, especially his paranoia about people trying to steal the company as I was trying to sell it. He was back on the computer all day, telling our vendors and our associates—anyone who would listen, actually—that we were going bankrupt. He still wanted to call the bank where we had our note and tell them the same thing. He was sabotaging all my attempts to save us, and there was nothing I could do to stop him.

Brittany went back to school, but Sammy was home going through the craziness with me. Then Sammy got sick and began throwing up. He started having headaches and nightmares. He didn't want to go to school. He was staying away from home more, hanging at his friends' houses. He didn't want to play water polo anymore, not without his dad around.

In desperation I called the new psychiatrist we had been assigned. "I need your help," I said. "What do I do with this man? His illness is really upsetting Sammy. My son is getting sick and acting out. I am so concerned about him. And here I am, trying to sell our part of our business to save things, and David is calling the bank and our vendors and telling them that we're going bankrupt! It's all such a nightmare."

"Well, Mrs. Bassett, I don't know what to tell you about your son. I suggest you get him counseling. And I suggest that you just keep David away from the phones and the computer."

"Sammy *is* in counseling! But he can't stand to see his dad acting so weird every single day. It's tearing him apart. And how exactly do you suggest I keep a two-hundred-and-ten-pound, fifty-three-year-old man away from the phone and computer? Do I tie him down? Lock him in the back bedroom?"

"I'm sorry, but there's nothing I can do. Have a nice day, Mrs. Bassett." *Click.*

David seemed to be getting worse on these new medications. He was really paranoid and now seemed to act out in odd ways. He would say strange things and sit and stare at nothing for hours at a time. I was becoming a bit afraid of him, because he didn't seem to be living in reality. He was an avid gun collector, and one day I asked a good friend of his to come and get all of his guns. I just didn't trust his behavior.

I was beside myself about what to do to help him, and us. I was anxious myself and frustrated with my inability to "fix" him. I was talking with various psychiatrists all over the country, but the answers were the same: medication. But how do you find the right one? And how do you stabilize him until it begins working? And what if it doesn't work, or worse, makes him more symptomatic? And how do you get him to keep taking it? He would lie and say he took it. I even tried giving it to him personally. He would act like he swallowed it, but he didn't. I found his pills hidden in his drawer or under his pillow. It was so torturous for all of us.

What do you do with people who are mentally unstable and causing a living hell for themselves and their families? Where do you put someone who needs to be secured somewhere, to be properly titrated to find the right medication, and get effective therapy for what could and should potentially be months at a time? What kind of messed-up system sends a paranoid psychotic home to his family?

There are no good answers. The awful truth is that in our society today there is no place to put people like this—no place to put them for their own good, where they have to stay till they get better. And insurance coverage for this type of thing is almost nonexistent. Why isn't mental illness treated like any other disease? It is just as traumatizing emotionally and financially. And yet, very little support is available.

The worse truth is that no one seems to care.

And here I was, Lucinda Bassett, self-help guru for anxiety and depression. I felt so helpless that I couldn't help him. Anxiety and depression are one thing; psychosis is quite another. I don't treat psychosis, and when someone is paranoid and psychotic, they are too sick to reason with.

I couldn't "coach" David into wellness. The best I could hope for was to get David into the hands of a really good psychiatrist and get him on the right medication.

As a result of all the stress I wasn't doing so well, so I made an appointment with my primary care physician, Dr. Martha Liddell. She hadn't seen me in months, and she was shocked by my appearance—I was now so gaunt I was skeletal. I looked anorexic. I told her what was happening. "For your own health, Lucinda, leave him," she told me. "If you don't, it's going to kill you. *He's* going to kill you."

As I was making dinner that night, I told Brittany what she'd said. "Maybe Dr. Liddell is right, Mom," Brittany said. "I'm afraid that taking care of Dad is going to make you go crazy, too."

"That's not what you sign up for when you get married," I replied. "You sign up for better or worse, for richer or for poorer, in sickness and in health." As I was saying that, I thought back to that beautiful snowy evening in December, when David and I got married. We had written our own vows, and none of that language was included—how ironic.

And yes, I was very aware that dealing with David was affecting my own mental health. Insanity isn't officially contagious, but when you're living with someone who's mentally ill, you get a little crazy, too. It also brings up a lot of your own personal stuff. Thinking I'd find some much-needed time to clear my head, I would pick up my mom and take her out to dinner, but I couldn't eat. I felt like something was stuck in my esophagus—just like when I was a kid. And just like when I was a kid, I didn't feel safe inside my own home. I didn't feel safe anywhere. Living with someone who is consistently unstable and not in reality is like being in a constant earthquake—the ground is shaking underneath you all the time.

It was the third week in May when David, Sammy, and I traveled back to Washington for Brittany's graduation. We got through it, but it was obvious that David was unwell. Even so, there was one spark, one glimmer of who he used to be. After asking me whether it was okay, when Brittany stepped to the platform to receive her diploma from the president of the university, David let out one of his trademark Tarzan calls.

If he could still do that, I thought to myself, the man I loved was still in there . . . somewhere. Mostly, however, David had turned into someone who was virtually unrecognizable as my husband, as the father of Brittany and Sammy.

By this time, Sammy was sixteen and a sophomore in high school. Sixteen is not an easy age for anyone, but Sammy was really struggling. He didn't understand what was happening to his father—he thought David could just snap out of it and go back to being normal. One day he started arguing with David, just trying to get some kind of "normal" reaction, trying to get him to be his dad again. Whenever they argued, they would wrestle and David would take Sammy down in a headlock, playfully telling him, "Puppy, when you're old enough to take me, you'll have too much respect for me to do it," all the while laughing and wrestling with Sammy. And of course, that was something David was no longer capable of doing. On this day, the situation quickly deteriorated. And then something unbelievable happened. David opened a drawer, took out a meat cleaver, and started chasing Sammy around the kitchen. I screamed and jumped in between him and Sammy. Sammy ran out of the room.

I immediately called the hospital and told the person who answered the phone what was happening, sure that they'd take him back into the psych ward.

Wrong.

"Please," I begged. "Please come and get my husband. He just went after my son with a meat cleaver! He's only sixteen, and he's scared."

"Mrs. Bassett, we'll have to call Child Protective Services. Sammy is a minor. If your husband is endangering your son, we'll have to remove Sammy from the home."

"What the hell? I thought that if David was harmful to himself or someone else, you'd admit him. Now you're saying that you'll have Sammy taken away, but you won't take David? He . . . he . . . he didn't go after Sammy. He is just acting strange," I said, in an attempt to move beyond the issue of them taking Sammy. "Sammy is fine, but David is not. What should I do with him?"

"I might suggest you put him in Promises in Malibu. It is a rehab facility for alcohol and drug issues."

"Promises is a celebrity rehab facility for addicts, not for people who are mentally ill," I said in frustration. "And besides, he could walk out of there anytime he wants to. That is not going to help him. Please, tell me what to do. We can't keep him at home."

"I'm sorry, but there's nothing we can do. Have a nice day, Mrs. Bassett." *Click*.

After that, I began hiding the knives—just like I had as a little girl. I would occasionally look through the closets and shelves, worried that David had hidden a gun or two away somewhere.

Even with the weapons gone, I was up all night, every night, scared he was going to kill himself—or us. I would lie there petrified in bed, staring at the TV at all hours. I don't remember what programs I watched, but it seemed to me that all of them were sponsored by Lunesta, the sleeping pill. I didn't understand why, but their ads made me really anxious. I couldn't stand watching them; I couldn't even listen to them. It was the oddest thing.

In early June, I had put together several meetings with people about buying the company. Despite everything, there was still a lot of value in the Midwest Center. We had a respected brand, with one of the most successful infomercial and radio campaigns in the country. We had a database with more than a million people. We still had over $12 million in accounts receivable. And since I'd taken over, I had managed to pay the bank debt down to $2.5 million.

We were scheduled to meet with a company that I felt had tremendous potential for a great strategic partnership. Before we went into the meeting I said to David, "Whatever you do, don't tell them that you and I are going bankrupt. We're not!"

"But we are!" he replied. "You don't get it."

He didn't repeat that during the meeting. Instead he just sat there, rubbing his crotch under the table and pushing his forehead back. I mentioned that David wasn't feeling well and ran the meeting.

Despite his behavior, the meeting went well. This company was clearly interested and seemed willing to sign a letter of intent.

"See, David," I said on the drive home, "we're going to sell the company." I reached over and put my hand on his leg to reassure him. "I'll set the sails and set the ship right. Then you take the helm. It's all going to be okay."

The next day, Friday, June 6, we got a call from the company that David thought was trying to sabotage us. We put the call on speakerphone in my office, so we could both listen in. I also invited Matthew, a business-savvy friend of ours, to listen to the conversation. "We're calling to let you know that we don't think it's a good idea to sell the company right now," they said.

After a long, intimidating call we hung up, with David extremely agitated and anxious.

Matt looked puzzled. "You know," he said after the call ended, "they did sound a bit strange. Maybe some of David's concerns are valid. I really don't know what to think, Lucinda."

That lit a fire under David. It concerned me, too. Could this all be true? In that moment, I found myself wondering if there was any truth to his conspiracy theory, but I decided to do my best to reassure him that things were going to work out. In spite of my efforts, that call turned him inside out. He was extremely on edge for the rest of the day. He just kept following me around talking of doom and gloom, certain that we would end up on the street.

We were supposed to go have dinner with Brittany and her boyfriend, Justin, in Hollywood, but I was very worried about his behavior.

I called Dr. Sylvia Tuckmann, his newly appointed psychiatrist. "We need to come see you today. It's crucial," I told her. "I'm really scared. David is really, really, really agitated. He is pacing the floor and making calls to people, talking about crazy things."

She was able to see us late that afternoon. It was sprinkling and cool as we walked into Dr. Tuckmann's office. I put my arm through David's and reassured him that we were going to get him help. "I think he needs to go back into the hospital," I said to her firmly. "I'm really afraid David is going to try to hurt himself again. I also think he needs to be on lithium, not this antipsychotic."

Dr. Tuckmann looked at me with a condescending smirk on her face. Ignoring me, she swiveled in her chair to face David. "David, do you know the side effects of lithium?"

"Why don't you tell him what the side effects are of what he's on now?" I shot back.

I knew that some people on lithium experienced diarrhea and weight gain. I also knew that those unpleasant symptoms tended to diminish as the body adjusted to the drug. On the other hand, the antipsychotic he was on had a very long list of heavy-duty side effects—diabetes, hypertension, muscle spasms, man boobs, aggression, sexual dysfunction, *and* suicidal thoughts. To me it was pretty clear which was better.

Dr. Tuckmann finally agreed to a prescription for lithium, but before we could get it filled David would have to have some blood work and an EKG. "I'll take him to Malibu Urgent Care first thing tomorrow," I said, "unless you're going to hospitalize him—which is what I think you should do. I am concerned for him. His grandfather tried to take his life, and his aunt actually did."

Dr. Tuckmann's sarcastic smirk reappeared as she leaned in toward David, and then said, "David, you're not going to kill yourself, are you?"

"No way," David replied.

"Do you think he would tell you if he was?" I said in disbelief. "Please," I begged again. "Please put him in the hospital, and they can get him on lithium in there and get him stabilized."

"I don't think that is necessary. You get his tests tomorrow, and we'll start him on lithium on Monday." With that, Dr. Tuckmann stood up, shook David's hand, and walked out.

I held David's hand as we left the doctor's office. It was raining as we drove to meet up with Brittany and her boyfriend, Justin. We had a nice dinner. Justin had a hat on, and I took it off and put it on David and kissed him, telling him how handsome he was and how much I loved him. He smiled, but he wasn't really present. He didn't eat. Then we went back to Brittany's house, where David lay down on the floor in front of the fire, curled up in a fetal position. It looked strange to her, but I had seen it many times. It was his favorite position to lie in when he was in his closet on the floor.

Brittany looked at her father with concern. "Mom, why don't you and Daddy spend the night here tonight?" she asked.

"Thanks, but we really should get back," I said. Sammy had a friend staying over, and I didn't want to leave them by themselves overnight.

David was really quiet all the way home.

Then, when we got into bed, out of nowhere he asked, "What about Brittany is like me?"

I thought before I responded.

"Brittany has your entrepreneurial spirit and your business brain. She's a networker, just like you are. She is creative and smart, and good with numbers."

"And what about Sammy is like me?" he asked.

"Oh, David! Sammy has your zest for life. He's adventurous. You taught him how to take care of his girlfriend, the same way you take care of me. You taught him how to be a man, and you taught him how to love someone."

I looked over at him and I could see him smiling in the light of the moon coming through the window. "And both of them love you so much," I said. "Promise me that you'll never try to hurt yourself again. I couldn't take it; Brittany couldn't take it; and Sammy *really* couldn't take it. He needs you so much now."

"I won't do that," he said. "I swear."

The next morning I woke up to an empty bed. He was gone.

CHAPTER 18

June 7–June 13, 2008

IT WAS 5:00 A.M. AND still dark outside, but the fact that David was up wasn't completely uncommon. He sometimes got up early and went downstairs, where he put his manic energy to work cleaning the kitchen. Other mornings, he took Roxie, our goldendoodle, for a walk, or even went for a bike ride. I didn't like him walking or riding his bike in the early morning when it was dark, but sometimes he just needed to get out and release his anxious energy. On this particular morning, however, I had a sense of foreboding when I looked over at the empty pillow beside me.

I thought back to the night before. I thought it was touching but a bit odd when he asked what about Brittany and Sammy was like him. But then again, he was unstable, depressed, and on medication. "Odd" had become normal. I also thought about the promise he made, both to me and to Dr. Tuckmann, that he'd never take his own life.

Nevertheless, I just felt something was wrong. Anxiety permeated my body. I could hardly breathe. I remember walking down the long upstairs hallway, thinking, "Where is he?" Roxie was lying on the floor, so I knew he didn't take her for a walk. Then I walked into the kitchen and saw that nothing had been touched. I walked out to the garage and his bike was in there. So were all the cars.

My stomach was in knots. One by one I had eliminated the best, safest explanations for where he might be. By now it was about 5:30. I started to get panicky, and I called Jonathan. "David isn't here, and I'm concerned," I said.

"I'll be right over," Jonathan said. He arrived at about 6:00 a.m., just as the sun was coming up.

I was on the phone calling Brittany as he walked in. "Brittany, Daddy's not here," I began.

She could tell I was anxious. "Mom, what are you thinking?"

"I don't know. Maybe he just went for a walk, but Roxie is here. So's his bike."

"I'm coming home right now," she said. "I'll bring Justin." Brittany lived in Hollywood, about an hour away.

Meanwhile, Jonathan and I got into my truck and drove around to all the places David and I usually walked. We left Sammy and his friend Jake asleep upstairs.

I was hopeful that we would find David out walking. My biggest fear was that we'd find him walking around not knowing where he was, or maybe walking around delusional. I knew his medication wasn't right; I also knew that we were going that very morning to get the tests he needed to start on lithium on Monday.

When we didn't find him, Jonathan and I drove back home. At that point I decided to call the police. "I want to report that my husband is missing," I said.

"How long has he been gone, ma'am?"

"Just since this morning. When I woke up, he wasn't here. I am very concerned. My husband has just gotten out of the hospital and has been diagnosed as paranoid and psychotic. He's on medication, and he's not well. He's had a real rough couple of days here, and I'm very worried about him. Would you please send someone over? We really need to find him."

By now it was almost 6:30. I called David's brother, Mike, in Ohio and told him I couldn't find David. I was just hanging up when the gate rang. A police car pulled into the driveway.

"Thank God they're going to look for him," I thought to myself.

A police officer got out of the car. Jonathan followed me out into the driveway to talk with him. "Lucinda Bassett? Your husband is missing?"

"Yes."

"Can you go get a picture of him?"

I turned to Jonathan, who was standing behind me. "Jonathan, can you go grab a picture of David out of the family room?"

Jonathan went back into the house to get a photo of David. I figured they wanted it so they would know who they were looking for. Then I started describing him. "He's about five foot nine inches tall," I began, "with dark, curly hair, green eyes, and he's a little stocky. He's been hospitalized. He's on Risperdal. He's not doing well. . . ."

Jonathan came back out and handed the photo to the policeman.

"Is this your husband, ma'am?"

"Yes. Yes, this is him. When can you begin looking for him? We drove around and didn't find him. I am afraid he is wandering around, not knowing where he is."

He looked down at the photograph, then took a deep breath and stepped back from me. "We found your husband, ma'am," he said. "It was a little earlier this morning. A man was found up in the mountains. He shot himself. This is the man we found. I'm sorry, Mrs. Bassett, your husband is dead."

In that moment, the world as I knew it . . . ended.

I stood there in complete and total shock. I refused to believe it. I immediately went into denial. I started to scream. *"No! You're lying! That's not my husband!"* I cried. *"What are you saying?"* I started hitting the policeman, pounding him with my fists. He put his arm up, stood there, and just let me hit him.

"Noooooooooooooooooo!" I screamed as I kept pummeling him in a fury. I then started kicking him, too. I was completely ripped apart to my core. David wouldn't do this to Brittany and Sammy. He promised me.

I have no idea how long I did this, but finally Jonathan came up behind me, wrapped his arms around me in a bear hug, and attempted to pull me back. I tried to fight him, too.

Right then the gate opened, and Brittany and Justin drove in. Brittany jumped out of the car and came running down the driveway toward me. I could see the tears streaming down her cheeks. "Mom! Mom! I saw him, I saw him!" she cried. "I found Daddy! I found Daddy!"

There was a place that David and I used to walk, a place I hadn't thought to go to, but for some reason Brittany had gone straight there. Justin was driving, and she directed him right to it. As they drove up, she saw all the cops. She jumped out of the car and went running toward them.

She arrived to see David and the whole horrific scene. Traumatized, she was now running down the driveway toward me as more police cars were coming through the gate.

Jonathan was joined by others in the effort to hold me back and hold me up. "*Let me go!*" I yelled. I felt pain from the deepest part of my gut, from my soul. I needed to go to David, to find him, to save him. "*Where is he? WHERE IS HE?*" I screamed through my tears.

Just like when I was four years old and they were taking my father off to jail, I was sure that if I could get to David, I could save him. "I *have* to go to him!"

"*NO!*" Brittany screamed. She put her arms around me. "No, Mom, you can't," she said. "You shouldn't see him. He's not . . . he's gone." The two of us just stood there sobbing. Still more police cars arrived. So did Jonathan's wife, Lisa. Everyone tried to comfort me, but there was no comfort to be had.

Wave after wave of remorse and second-guessing washed over me, part of the tsunami of grief that was pulling me under. "There must have been something I could have done or said last night to prevent this," I thought to myself. "Why didn't I see this coming? Why didn't we stay at Brittany's?"

All of my life energy drained out of me. I was drowning. I honestly felt like I wasn't going to live through the next minute, the next hour, through this dreadful day. I couldn't even find the strength to comfort my own daughter. Then Jonathan very gently put his hand on my shoulder. "Lucinda," he said softly, "we need to get Sammy up and tell him."

Oh my God! Sammy! He had slept through the entire thing. How was he ever going to handle this? He was already falling apart over David's illness.

Jonathan went upstairs and woke Sammy and his pal Jake. Jake left quickly, but he overheard the police talking about what happened as he made his way past them. Then Sammy came downstairs and out to the driveway. He looked around at the police cars and at Jonathan and Lisa. He knew something was wrong.

As Sammy walked toward me, I just wanted to vomit. "Mom, what's going on?"

In that moment, I had to tell my son, David's son, this sensitive, already overwhelmed sixteen-year-old, that his father was dead, and that he had taken his own life. I didn't know if I could get the words out without throwing up.

"Sammy . . . " I began. "Sammy, Daddy killed himself."

His face went white. Then he lost it.

Sammy let out a scream that came straight from his soul. "*Noooooooooooooooooo!*" He threw himself to the ground and began pounding it violently with his fists. When he stood up, he turned, and Brittany's boyfriend, Justin, threw his arms around him as he sobbed.

Suddenly he broke away from Justin. "Where is he?"

My son had exactly the same reaction that I did. Jonathan and Justin quickly grabbed him and restrained him.

"*NOOOOOOOOOOOOOOOOO!*" Sammy's cry was visceral. He started hitting Jonathan. Sammy was strong. Then he ripped himself away and ran into the house. I could hear him kicking in the door to his room and screaming.

Just the beginning of his life without his father, but I couldn't do anything about it in that moment. I couldn't walk, talk, or function.

I have no memory of how I got there, but it wasn't long before I found myself sitting in my living room with Brittany and Lisa, trying to answer the brief, emotionally detached questions the sheriff was asking about David. "How long has he been sick? What medication was he on?" he asked. I thought there would have been a whole investigation, but after

I answered his questions his job was done.

As he was about to leave, there was a knock at the door. It was Bruce Wisnicki, Jake's dad. He came in, immediately went upstairs, and sat with Sammy for what seemed like hours. I will never forget that act of kindness. At that time, we really barely even knew each other. He was one of many who "showed up" for us during that weekend.

I just sat there in the living room with the life sucked out of me. I was a zombie. My husband was dead. My children were devastated. What was I supposed to do next? I didn't have a clue.

God bless all the friends. Malibu is really a small town, and word of David's death spread quickly. Everyone knew David and loved him very much. The next thing I knew, people started coming to the house. It seemed to me that the whole community showed up. The house literally overflowed with people—people who I didn't know cared about us were sitting beside me, holding me. Someone opened the door to one of our more affluent neighbors—I didn't know him that well, but he arrived with four housekeepers, all carrying food. There must have been over two hundred people in my home that day, holding me, holding Brittany, holding Sammy, bringing us food, and taking care of us.

One person who came to the house was my realtor, Chris Cortazzo. David and I had put the house on the market, and Chris had just sold it. He arrived with the sales contract—which had already been signed by both David and me. "Lucinda, your kids need stability right now," he said. "*You* need stability."

I nodded numbly—I couldn't really speak at all. "The last thing you need to do is to sell your house," Chris continued as he ripped up the sales agreement in front of me. It was an act of extraordinary kindness and selfless generosity that cost him several hundred thousand dollars in commission. Then he took out a pan and started making pasta on my stove.

By late afternoon, friends and family started arriving from back east. They'd jumped on the first flight they could get, as soon as they heard the news. My sister Donna's two daughters, Jenny and Lori, arrived with Bob, their dad. Bruce and Pat Winters flew in from Oak Harbor with my mom. My mom was devastated—she had loved David so much. One of my best friends, Tammy Elliot, flew in from Atlanta. And Bob and Darla Van Horn also flew in from Ohio. Darla worked for us for years, and Bob and David had been good friends.

The next thing I remember is Brittany sitting on the sofa opposite me with some of her friends and Debbie Weiss, a good family friend. Debbie is an amazing woman, so generous of spirit. "We'll have the funeral service at my home," Debbie offered. Brittany and two of her friends began planning out a video tribute to David. I don't know where her strength came from at that time. She certainly had more than I did.

The obituary they wrote to put in the local paper was a fitting tribute to her father, the man who had shared my life and love:

> *Malibu resident David Bassett died on Saturday. He was 53. Bassett was born in Toledo, Ohio, on Sept. 28, 1954. He moved to Malibu with his family in 1994. A husband and father, Bassett was said by friends and family to be a man who "made a difference in the lives of everyone he knew" because he was able to relate with others and showed an interest in their needs, hopes, dreams, and aspirations. Bassett snowboarded, skied, and rode motorcycles and mountain bikes. He was a gourmet cook who was known for his congenial dinners and parties. Bassett had great enthusiasm for his daughter Brittany and son Sammy's accomplishments, as well as the accomplishments of their peers. He and his wife Lucinda were married for 25 years.*

They were also putting together a little memorial booklet for the service. Brittany said, "We want to put a quote by Daddy in here, something he always said. Mom, can you think of anything?"

I couldn't think of anything. I couldn't think, period—my mind was a blank. Just then Sammy came walking downstairs, and Brittany asked him the same question.

"Yeah," he answered as he walked into the living room, wiping his face. "Daddy always said, 'I'll walk and I'll meet you there.'"

"Oh my God, of course!" I thought to myself. "Yes, he always said that," I said out loud.

Often when we went to a restaurant down the street or when we were on a family trip heading back to the hotel, David would choose to walk instead of riding in the car with us. It was his way of getting some exercise and burning a few calories. I started to cry . . . again. All I could think was that was just one of the many things he did or said that we would never experience again.

In the booklet there is a picture of the four of us walking on the beach—just the back of our legs and feet. Underneath it, it says, "I'll walk and I'll meet you there."

I don't know how I got through that day. Brittany and Sammy were very worried about me, because I was mostly catatonic. They were so worried, in fact, that they started acting like they were going to be okay—even though they weren't. They were pretending because they were scared that I was going to go crazy, just like their dad. It was a reasonable-enough fear—I was emotionally gone, unable to cope with anything at all.

What I remember most about that day and the several that followed is the huge number of people coming and going. Brittany, Sammy, and I were surrounded by so much love and support. Everyone knew how important it was that we not be alone. Many stayed the night with us—my nieces, Bruce, and Pat. Sammy had about four kids sleeping in the room with him. His friend Jake Wisnicki, who'd stayed over the night before, came back dragging his favorite pillow and slept on the floor in Sammy's room.

I slept with Brittany in her room. I just couldn't sleep in our bed without David. I was lying in her bed, overwhelmed and scared to death. Scared to death of living without David. Scared to death of having to deal with the financial mess David had left me. Scared to death of having to deal with all the nasty people David was so worried about. Scared to death of what it would take to save what we had, all by myself. I knew the task in front of me was enormous. I don't think I have ever been so overwhelmed, anxious, and terrified in my life.

"Mom, why did I find him?" Brittany asked as she lay beside me with her little dog, Louis. "Why did I know to go to the place where he was?"

I lay there exhausted, searching in my mind for something to tell her that made sense.

And then it came to me. "When people die a horrific death, their spirit hangs around for a while," I said. "Brittany, I think Daddy brought you to him because his spirit was still there, and he didn't want to die alone. He needed you to be there when his spirit went away. I know it's awful, and I'm so sorry that you saw him—but Daddy always knew you were the strong one, and I think you were there when his spirit left him. He didn't die alone."

Brittany started to cry. "I didn't want to see that." I held her, but there was nothing I could do to help her wipe that dreadful memory away.

With that, I immediately felt angry at David. How, how could he do such a selfish, horrific thing to her, to Sammy, to me?

There must have been six or seven hundred people at Debbie and Steven Weiss's house for the memorial service. David's family stayed in Ohio and held a service in Oak Harbor for local family and friends. For our service, I wore a simple black dress that was now so big it hung on me, a hat to cover my face, and a shawl to cover my shoulders. I just wanted to hide inside myself. How awful a thing to go through. How painful, shameful, and hurtful. What was he thinking? What was everyone thinking?

I was in awe when Brittany got up to speak. She was both eloquent and powerful. I couldn't have done it. How she was able to hold it together, I'll never know. As she was talking about her father, a soft wind suddenly came out of nowhere and blew through her hair. Everyone saw it. It was like David was there. I certainly felt his presence.

Person after person got up to say lovely things about David that celebrated his life. Some told funny stories. Bob Sherry, one of our neighbors and one of David's close friends, recited a beautiful poem he had written.

One of the most moving moments in the service was when our friend Richard Page, who wrote and sang "Broken Wings," got up and sang "Amazing Grace" a cappella. It was so incredibly beautiful. After the service, I stood in the living room as people filed through to share their condolences. I was so overwhelmed I could barely stand there. The line of people was never ending. Everyone loved David so much. Brittany was with me. She was warm and gracious, but I was still numb, frozen. All of a sudden, the girl Sammy was dating at the time came up to stand beside me, without Sammy. I looked around and realized I didn't see him anywhere. "Where is Sammy?" I asked her.

"He left," she replied. "He said he couldn't handle it."

"Well, you go find him and tell him I can't handle it, either," I said to her. "Tell him he needs to get back here, right now." Within about ten minutes Sammy reappeared.

From what little I remember and from what I was told, we had a beautiful memorial service for David. I only vaguely remember any of it, and I never did see the family video. I couldn't even go in that room.

Thank God for all the people who sat with us, loved us, and gave us their support. But as anyone dealing with the sudden death of a loved one will tell you, the hardest part starts when everyone goes home. And little did I know that this was only the beginning of a year of tremendous loss and heartbreak.

CHAPTER 19

Lunesta and the Perfect Storm

AFTER THE MEMORIAL SERVICE, Bruce Winters stayed to help me start figuring things out. There was so much I didn't know about our finances—like, everything. I didn't know how much money or debt we had—or where it was. I didn't know which bank held the mortgage for the house. It took Bruce a while to discover that the title to our home was in a trust with a company that had gone out of business a few years earlier. Our financial situation was a tangled web of confusion.

David had left a suicide note. Much of it was about how much he loved me and Brittany and Sammy. But he also reiterated in the note what he'd been saying for months—that there were people involved in a conspiracy to hurt us professionally. He referred to at least twenty people and various companies in different parts of the country that he thought were involved.

But, of course, David's head was full of demons, and as Bruce dug, he found more evidence of how sick David really had been. I thought I knew all about David's handwritten scenarios. Turns out I didn't know the half of it. Bruce found tons more, pages and pages of notes that he had written, with weird pictures drawn on the sides of the pages.

240

Bruce and David had been friends since high school. When we were still living in Oak Harbor, we saw Bruce and his wife, Pat, often. As much as I valued their friendship then, I cherished it even more now. At a time when I was struggling to breathe from one moment to the next, they both did so much to help me survive.

Bruce knew all about how much money David had given to Stu. In fact, he knew about it before I did. On one of his trips back to Oak Harbor, David had invited Bruce to come over to his parents' house. (They were at their winter home in Sarasota, Florida.) He sat there knocking back straight scotch as he told Bruce how he had given Stu all of our money behind my back. It was Bruce who insisted that he had to tell me what he'd done, and David confessed to me shortly thereafter.

It was Bruce who sat at David's desk right after he died, going through the Rolodex and phoning everyone about what happened. And then it was my brother-in-law, Bob, who came out for two weeks and helped me go through David's office and our personal finances. Brittany helped so much as well. As all of us worked to get through it, there was just a mountain of bad news everywhere we looked, and the deeper we went, the uglier it got. We found that David had borrowed another couple hundred thousand on various credit cards—at a ridiculously high rate of interest. There were unpaid bills. The situation was far worse than I already knew.

And the hits just kept on coming. One of the top potential buyers who had shown significant interest in acquiring the Midwest Center before David died called to offer me their condolences. On that same phone call, they also rescinded their offer for a letter of intent. They said they might consider reinstating the offer, but since the president of a company specializing in anxiety and depression had just killed himself, they wanted to see how the situation played out over the next several months.

The Midwest Center didn't have another several months, and neither did I. I needed a partner to help me get through this; I was just too exhausted to handle it all myself. I had to do something about selling the company right away. The way David died, I wondered whether I'd be able to sell it— even at a significant discount—or whether I'd have to shut it down and declare bankruptcy, thus fulfilling David's prophecy.

As the days unfolded, I spent the hours and minutes afraid that we really *would* lose everything, and that brought back another tidal wave of old childhood fears. I was terrified that I'd have to move back to Findlay. Back to the old shingled house by the railroad tracks on the dead-end street. Back to the place where, as a kid, I was always afraid of getting stuck for the rest of my life. There were times I got so scared that I would lie in bed shaking.

I sure as hell wasn't sleeping. The charcoal-purple circles under my eyes looked like craters on the moon, and I went to see my doctor. "Lucinda, you need to take something," Martha said. "I'm giving you a prescription for Lunesta."

Lunesta—how ironic! While David was sick, their TV commercials made me so anxious I would literally cover my head with a pillow when they came on. Was that fear some sort of premonition, a warning sign of what was to come? I'd never taken a sleeping pill before in my life; now the green moth and I were going to be a team.

Every night. It was the only way I could get any sleep at all.

I also began having recurring nightmares that David walked into the house and said he was still alive, but he was not stable and still, well, crazy. I was so glad to see him, but I was anxious that he was still crazy. I wanted him back, but not like that.

To my surprise, a week after David's death there were still two companies that were interested in buying the Midwest Center. They each sent someone to talk with me at our home. "They're probably not going to offer you a lot for the company, Lucinda, but I think you should take the meetings," Bruce advised.

"I don't think I'm strong enough to do it unless you and Brittany are with me," I said.

So, there I was, one week after David's death, taking meetings to sell a company that was now left without its president but with the legacy of what he had done.

As Bruce had predicted, the price both were offering for the Midwest Center was far less than what we would have wanted before David died, but it was better than nothing. At the meetings, one of the companies reassured me that they were committed to doing everything possible to retain our employees in Ohio, and to maintain our relationship with Riverview Industries. That mattered to me—I really felt an obligation to honor their loyalty and do what I could to protect them. They also wanted to keep me on as the voice and brand. The Midwest Center wouldn't be my company anymore, but at least I'd still have my job.

I agreed to sell the company to this second group. As we moved through the sales process, however, I wondered if any of David's concerns would become a reality. The only way to find out was to move forward with the sale.

As all this was going on, I sensed that David's spirit was still around. It wasn't long before I got proof delivered in a most unusual way. I knew a woman who was very connected to the supernatural. Her name was Sandy, and one of her friends was a chef who lived in a home where a very famous person had died. Sandy rang my doorbell on her way to a séance there. With her was her eight-year-old daughter, Allegra.

While I was speaking with Sandy, she handed me a piece of paper that was folded like Japanese origami. "Allegra gave this to me," she said. "She told me it was a letter from David."

Confused, I looked back and forth between mother and daughter. "Allegra wrote this," Sandy explained. "I really think you need to read it."

I unfolded it to see the large, round handwriting typical of an eight-year-old girl. "Dear Lucinda," it began. As I read, my jaw dropped open. There were things in the letter that only David would know, things only David would say. "I'm okay, and don't worry about the company. The company will take care of itself. I love you, Dancing Bear."

I was stunned. Dancing Bear was one of David's nicknames for me. Allegra had met David once or twice, but there was no way that little girl would know any of what was in the letter. I wanted to keep it, but Sandy told me she wanted to take the letter to the séance. She left with it and I never got it back—a regret I have to this day.

As I started taking the first baby steps toward selling the company and moving through the due-diligence process, David's words of delusion

and paranoia kept echoing in my head: *"They'll never let us sell it. . . .*
They'll never let us sell it. . . . They'll never let us sell it. . . ." Over the last
eight months or so, he had repeated it to me over and over. Less than a
week after the funeral, and just a few days after meeting with the new
buyers, people from around the country who were associated with that one
particular company began contacting me.

I was afraid to check my e-mails. I didn't want to answer the phone.
Anytime UPS came to the door with an envelope, I panicked. I was now
forced to deal with David's demons and fears, alone. I didn't know what
was going to happen next, whether I'd be able to sell the company, or
which, if any, of David's anticipated scenarios of doom and gloom would
come true.

It was a real effort to push those thoughts out of my mind, but I had
to—there was no time for what-ifs now. Less than two weeks after David's
death, I became a frequent flyer on the red-eye back to Ohio—the red-
eye was all I could afford. The sale of the Midwest Center was starting to
move forward, but there were all kinds of details to be worked out. When I
wasn't in Ohio trying to reassure our employees about their futures, I was
in meeting after meeting as the buyers probed into every financial detail
of the company. In spite of David's fears, the sale seemed to be heading
toward completion.

All I knew back then was that I was in overload, but I was about to
find out how much my already overloaded plate could really hold. On July
15, Richard Bassett, David's father, my children's grandfather, had a coro-
nary and died. I think when he found out that his son David had committed suicide, it was just too much for his heart to take.

So here I was. My husband had committed suicide. My mother was at
my house, depressed and tired, and needing me desperately. David's father
had died of a heart attack. My kids were in denial and overwhelmed. And I
was on the edge of sanity myself, balanced between being Lucinda Bassett
by day and Lunesta Bassett by night. What else could possibly go wrong?

I had just returned from another red-eye trip to Ohio when I got a
phone call that put me right back on the next flight. It was from Mary, my
brother Michael's wife. Michael had had a seizure in his swimming pool.

When they discovered him, he was at the bottom, alive but unresponsive. His son called 911, but the paramedics couldn't resuscitate him. Now he was in Toledo Hospital in a coma.

When I went to see him, Michael was on a ventilator; regular beeps from the equipment he was hooked up to kept track of his vital signs, and there were tubes coming in and going out everywhere.

It was now late summer, 2008. I was flying back to Ohio sometimes twice a week. I was plodding through due diligence and trying to stabilize my employees in Oak Harbor during the process. Once the meetings ended, I headed for the hospital to see Michael. I had to do whatever I could to support my mother, Mary, and the three boys while Michael was lying there in a coma. By the time my head hit the pillow, there was nothing left of me at all.

I was really drained when I went with my new, almost signed "partners" for the annual ERA D2C—that's Electronic Retailing Association Direct-to-Consumer Commerce convention in Las Vegas. For people in the direct-response business, this convention is like the New York Stock Exchange. The buyers and sellers are all in one place; simply put, it's where you go to do business.

For me, no matter how badly I was reeling from all the death and disaster in my life, being here was imperative. In years past, David had always come with me. Now I was here with Brittany, running the gauntlet through the convention hall, feeling like everyone was staring at me, pointing and whispering.

Representatives of marketing powerhouses like QVC and Home Shopping Network set themselves up for twenty-minute face-to-face appointments with people who were pitching new products they wanted to sell on their shows—like speed dating. They were the most coveted appointments at the convention.

Right after David died, my friends Bill Guthy, of Guthy Renker, and his wife, Victoria Jackson, had hooked me up to meet with a representative from QVC, who set me up to meet with one of their top buyers. Now I had twenty minutes to sell this woman a product I had thought of creating, called *The Solution*. If I was still going to be the face of the Midwest

Center after the sale went through, resuscitating my image was imperative. I was still Lucinda Bassett, albeit a bit of a beaten-up brand.

While I was talking with the QVC rep, all I could think was, "Does she know that my husband committed suicide?" I didn't ask, and neither did she. I must have pitched the new product idea well, because she bought it. There was just one small problem—at the time I pitched it, there was no product. It was like when I sold my first book. It was all in my head. I knew what it was going to be, but it didn't exist yet. This was September, and she wanted me to be selling it on the air in January.

I went from Las Vegas back to Ohio, to have more meetings to prepare for the final due diligence on selling the company, and to see Michael. He had been in a coma for two months. At first the doctors had given us some hope that he might pull out of it, but now it was clear that his brain damage was too severe. Michael Redick died on September 16, 2008—just over three months after David killed himself.

My mother, who was already not doing well, was beside herself with grief. She had kept a vigil by his bedside; now she was ripped apart. She had already lost my other brother, my sister, and her husband. She also felt the loss of my husband, David, deeply—she had adored him, and he was always very good to her. Until he got sick, he took care of her the way he took care of all of us. And now Michael was gone, too.

Once again, I was overwhelmed with grief. But I had to get on with the business of attempting to save things. I knew it was going to be a tremendous amount of pressure to meet the deadline for *The Solution*, but I didn't have a choice. This was one way for Lucinda Bassett to get back on her feet, and to prove my value to the new owners of the Midwest Center. I had to write the new material, get into the studio, record it, and get it manufactured in a matter of months, all on the heels of my husband's suicide, my brother's death, and selling my business.

Little did I know that there was still more death and devastation to come. Three months after my brother died, we received word that my mother's favorite sister, my auntie Jean, had cancer. By the time she was diagnosed, it was already well advanced. She died eight weeks later, in February 2009 in Findlay, Ohio, where my mother had her home.

By then my mother was totally destroyed with grief and sadness. I brought her out to California to stay with me again. I thought it would be good for her, and for me as well—as I had been since David's death, I continued to be profoundly afraid of being alone. But after about a month in Malibu, she insisted that she wanted to go back to Findlay for a while. I sensed she wasn't doing well and tried to convince her to stay, but she said she just wanted to be in her own town and her own home. She was simply worn out.

I flew her back to Ohio. Two days later, I got a call from the local hospital. She had been admitted with severe abdominal pain, fever, and nausea. The diagnosis was diverticulitis, a disease of the large intestine, and they needed to operate immediately. The doctor told me that diverticulitis was often associated with a low-fiber diet, but I think Mom got sick because she was reeling from David's death, Michael's death, and her sister's death. All the loss was too much for her, and it made her body vulnerable.

I jumped on a plane to Ohio—again—and sat by her bedside for seven days, praying she would be okay. They put her on antibiotics; at the end of the week, the doctor said she was recovering well, so I flew home. Days later, he called to tell me my mother had pneumonia.

I flew back right away. When I arrived at the hospital, they were transferring her into the ICU. I got there right before they put a ventilator down her throat. I could tell she was frightened. "Mom," I said, "what are you afraid of?"

"I'm afraid I'm going to die," she said.

Those were the last words she ever spoke. When I close my eyes, I can still see the fear in her face. That fear made me terrified—terrified for her, as she was scared to death of dying, and terrified for me. I couldn't imagine life without my mother. She was my wingwoman, my biggest fan. She was the one I called when I got a book deal, or when I got on *Oprah!*, or when my kids did something to make me proud. She was always there to talk to on the phone, always there to give me advice. I loved hearing her talk about her crossword puzzles and TV shows and what flowers were beginning to bloom. Maybe some would call it small talk, but to me it was so much more than that. Sharing the joy she took in these simple pleasures grounded me when I got overwhelmed by my own too-hectic life.

I stayed in her hospital room around the clock. I set up camp, just like I had the last time she got sick. This room had a little couch, so I brought in a pillow and a blanket. I also had my laptop and my cell phone with me—this became not only my temporary bedroom but my temporary office as well. With the ventilator she couldn't talk, but she was by no means comatose. Even though she was sedated, she could see and hear me. When she wasn't sleeping, I read to her and talked to her. Most days, I never left her side. On a couple of evenings, dear friends Carolyn Dickman and Pat Winters took me out for dinner and a brief change of scenery.

For almost a week the doctors were optimistic, but suddenly Mom started going downhill. Her breathing became heavier, and her hands started to discolor. She was fading in and out of awareness. Her doctor advised me that she wasn't tolerating the respirator well. He wanted to remove it to see if she could breathe on her own. Nobody could tell me for sure what would happen when they did.

My mother was a high-energy, bright, active woman. She loved to dance, drink cappuccino, and enjoy a sunset. She was afraid to die, but I knew she didn't want to live this way, either, with a feeding tube in her stomach and a breathing tube in her throat. She had an advance directive, and I was the executor. Her life was in my hands.

I was once again supported by my wonderful friends. Carolyn Dickman, Pat Winters, and Dr. Phil Fisher came to help me make the decision to take her off the respirator. Her blood pressure and her heart rate started bouncing around, but they were still there, so I kept talking to her. "Mom, you're going to be okay," I reassured her. "You're going to go home soon. You're going to get out of here."

Late that night I went back to her home, a few miles from the hospital, to rest and take a much-needed shower. I opened the door and stepped into the house I grew up in. It was eerie that my mother wasn't there to greet me. The silence was dreadful. I walked slowly around. Mom had family pictures everywhere—on the piano and the cabinets and the bookshelves—a testimony to her devotion to her children and grandchildren.

The details of her daily life were just as she'd left them when she went into the hospital. Her half-unpacked suitcase was still in the bedroom. Her coffee cup was still on the kitchen table, together with her crossword puzzle magazine opened to a puzzle she hadn't quite finished.

The possibility that she might never come back to complete that crossword, to unpack the rest of her clothes, struck me like walking into a wall. I crawled into her bed for a few hours' sleep before I returned to the hospital. Her scent still clung to the pillow.

I woke up early and went back to the hospital. As I was setting up camp again, the doctor pulled me out into the hallway to speak with me. "Lucinda, your mother is dying. You have to give her permission to die, or she could go on like this for days," he said compassionately.

"What? I'm *not* going to let her die!" I said in a raspy, whispered shout. "First of all, she doesn't want to, and second, I need her. You know that my husband died last year. And shortly after that, my brother. If I lose her, too, I'll never make it." As soon as the words left my mouth, it was clear to me how selfish that must have sounded.

The doctor put his hand on my shoulder. "She's showing all the signs, Lucinda. She's ready to die. She's very uncomfortable. You have to let her go."

I was devastated. I walked back into the room, sat on the edge of her bed, and there she was, looking right at me. Her eyes were so tired.

All of my support systems had left the hospital by then. Carolyn, Pat, and Dr. Fisher were gone. Brittany, who had come for a few days, had flown back to California. I was there alone. And being alone is what I have always feared most.

I started to cry and took her soft hand in mine—Mom always had the softest skin.

I took a deep breath, stroked her hand, and began. I knew what I had to do. I told her what a great mother she was, and how much I loved her— how much we all loved her. I told her that her sons David and Michael; her daughter, Donna; her husband, Ikey; her sister Jean; and my husband, David, were all waiting for her on the other side, and that she was going to be safe there.

The next part was the hardest of all. I brought my face close to hers. "Mom, you need to let your body do what it wants to do. If you need to move on, it's okay with me that you do that. That guardian angel of yours will be with you all the way. Gary and I are okay. All the grandkids are going to be fine—we'll take care of them. I promise." Then I squeezed her hand and added, "I will be there with you someday."

The doctor held my other hand. The nurse monitored Mom's vital signs. Within moments, her heart rate plummeted. So did her blood pressure. All the while, she kept looking into my eyes. I didn't take my eyes off hers as I said softly, "It's okay, Mom. It's okay to let go."

And then, she died. It was July 10, 2009, a year and a month after David's death. She was eighty-seven years old.

Her passing was both the most painful and the most beautiful experience I've ever witnessed. My mother loved life so very much, and to watch her surrender like that, to let go, and be willing to let herself die was a powerful thing to see. She totally knew she was doing it. She knew it was time. "If she had the strength to do that," I thought to myself, "then I can get through what I have to get through."

Witnessing her die with such grace and dignity was an incredible gift my mother gave to me, especially after the horrific death experience I had been through with David. But it wasn't her only blessing. A feeling of transference of her energy and her strength came over me. I sat in that hospital room holding her hand for at least two hours. I wasn't frightened. It wasn't the slightest bit morbid. I could sense her presence all around me.

I was going to need every ounce of my mother's strength to keep going. I walked out of that hospital with her purse on my arm and her watch in my hand. I had never felt so alone in my life.

CHAPTER 20

It's Heart Related

HERE I WAS, PLANNING another funeral. It was unbelievable to me. I was beside myself with grief. I was so sad and so tired that I just put myself on autopilot. All I knew was I needed to get it done and get out of there. I was spent and emotionally drained, but I wanted to do it right for her. I went straight from the hospital to the funeral home to make arrangements for my mother's cremation and memorial service. Mom died on a Friday; I wanted to hold the funeral on Sunday. I had been in Ohio off and on for over a month. I needed to get back to my life and my family. It was all surreal, like a bad dream. I just wanted to go home.

I called Christopher, one of the guys in my brother Michael's band, and asked him to play guitar at the service. I went back to Mom's house and, as painful as it was, gathered up all of the pictures scattered throughout her house that represented her life. I blew up one of her on a trip to Hawaii with me. She was decked out in a Hawaiian skirt and a lei. She looked so happy in that picture. It reminded me of all the great trips we took together. I placed that beautiful picture up front on an easel beside a beautiful heart-shaped flower arrangement made up of white roses. The rest of the pictures I placed all around on the podium, where the casket would have been. There were so many pretty flowers. It all looked beautiful. I knew she would have loved it.

It was actually a lovely and moving service. Friends who had known her for seventy years, women who had worked with her at RCA, all were there. Many of them got up to speak. I read some cards that the kids had given her over the years. My brother Gary got up and spoke as well—how strange that out of her five children, we were the only two left now. All of the grandchildren were there, too—all of them except Brittany and Sammy. Brittany had just been to see her in the hospital, and Sammy was still completely overwhelmed by all the death in our lives. His grandmother's funeral would have been more than he could handle.

When Mom had insisted on going home a few months earlier, I was frustrated. It was much easier for me to look after her when she was close by me in California. With her in Findlay while she was sick, it made life more difficult for me to have to be gone and fly back and forth. God knows, things were tough enough already.

But at her memorial service, I understood the importance of her being home in Findlay when she passed. In Findlay, she had lifelong friends. There were over two hundred people at her funeral; if she'd died in California, none of these people would have been able to attend. After the service, we had dinner at her favorite restaurant and told more stories. Then I went back to the brown-shingled house at the end of the dead-end street by the railroad track and closed it up. I knew I would have to come back to deal with her belongings and sell the house, but I was burnt, spent, sad, and done. I was on a plane for home that same night. I cried all the way back to California.

I felt like I'd done right by my mother, but I came home to Malibu feeling completely abandoned and alone. It had been almost fifteen years since I had written about how to go from panic to power, but now I felt like I had no power left. I felt vulnerable and completely adrift. My husband and brother and sister were gone. And now, so was my mom.

And my company was gone—or at least, it was no longer mine. Even though I felt good about the new partners and their intentions going into the deal, it was strange to have no say in what was taking place managerially at the Midwest Center. The sale had been completed, so I would have some money coming in, but I would be getting it over the course of three years. So for the moment, I was still financially challenged and feeling very insecure. Meanwhile, I had become an employee of the company I had founded and owned for over twenty years—a company that had been my life and a huge part of my identity.

I was hit by a depression like I'd never known. How could I go on without my husband and my mother? How could I go on when everything in my universe kept falling apart? So much loss and change. It was as if I had PTSD—post-traumatic stress disorder—except I never got to the P, because horrible stuff just kept happening. It was then that I remembered what PTSD used to be called: shell shock. After David's death, it seemed there was always another bomb dropping for me, something new and terrible to deal with. Almost two years later, I was still taking live fire.

Even the everyday stuff stopped working right. My housekeeper of many years had been like a member of my family, but while I was in New York on a business trip, she suddenly moved all of her belongings out of the house without saying anything. Someone else, someone I had considered a friend of mine, had offered her more money. And she quit without notice. I came home to a dirty house and a dead bird. It was very, very depressing. As an added aggravation, I started going through menopause. There's a saying that the hot flashes of menopause are your inner child playing with matches. Mine was using a flamethrower.

One of my biggest goals now was to get Sammy stabilized. Despite being in therapy—we all were—he was falling apart. As angry as I had been with David about the financial mess he left behind, I was even angrier about what his suicide had done to Brittany and Sammy. Sometimes I would think to myself, "David, how dare you kill yourself and leave your children with this horrible legacy? How could you do this to Sammy? You knew how vulnerable he was. How much he counted on you."

Two years after David's death, Sammy still couldn't get it together to go to school. It seemed some of his Tourette's symptoms had gotten much worse. He was tic-ing like crazy. His OCD got worse, too. He also got verbally and physically abusive, and was getting into fights. He was being homeschooled by necessity; he was so overwhelmed by losing his dad that he was still throwing up every morning.

Life was just one challenge after another, but I was working hard trying to save everything and to "heal" all of us. At times I would see a smile from one of the kids, hear them laugh, and I would think, maybe just maybe, they are healing. Or I would have a night out or a day with a friend and temporarily forget the nightmare we'd all been through. But we were still far from stabilized.

We were now coming into May 2010. It was almost two years after David's death, and I was hoping and praying that things were calming down. But Mother's Day was looming, another painful holiday. I used to love the holidays; now I dreaded them. So did Brittany and Sammy. Holidays meant . . . no David. Holidays were a reminder of what David did, and the way he died. Father's Day, his birthday, and the anniversary of his death were the worst, but Christmas, Thanksgiving, and the rest of them weren't much better. By committing suicide, he robbed us of the joy of the holidays, and left us with no good way to observe them. If we stayed home, the walls closed in and we were overwhelmed by memories of our own past celebrations, celebrations when David was still alive. If we went out, it seemed that everywhere we went we'd see families—*intact* families with fathers—having fun together, which only made David's absence more painful.

Anyway, this particular Mother's Day became one we would never forget. I got up feeling bummed not only because of David but because it was my first Mother's Day without my own mother. I went for a walk—I figured that was something I could manage. I took Roxie, David's golden-doodle, and Elvis, my little spunky twelve-year-old Yorkie, with me. The contrast in size was always humorous, because Elvis never really understood how small he was. In his heart, he was as big as Roxie. Near the end of my street there is an open field, and I let them off the leash to run through it.

On the corner beyond the field is a house with high walls and a huge iron gate. The guy who lives there is a very bizarre man who keeps to himself. He is very "security minded"—three big German shepherds patrol the property. These are killer guard dogs, definitely not house pets. They were barking as we walked through the field, and Elvis, thinking he was as big as they were, went right up to the gate to bark back at them. I immediately ran to get him, but I wasn't fast enough.

Within a matter of seconds, Roxie and I watched in horror as one of the German shepherds put his head through the gate, clamped his jaws around Elvis's neck, and dragged him inside. He retreated up the driveway with Elvis in his mouth.

I ran home as fast as I could, yelling for Sammy. "Sammy! Sammy! Sammy! The German shepherds have Elvis!" Sammy grabbed a BB gun impulsively—thinking he could use it on the dogs if he had to. He, his girlfriend, and I went running back to the house and the ominous gate. The dogs were nowhere to be found.

The three of us climbed up on the gate and peered over the top. To our surprise we could see a housekeeper standing in the kitchen, staring at us and looking stern, with her arms folded across her chest. "Please open the gate!" I shouted. She just stood there shaking her head.

I took a moment to call the sheriff's department, explaining what was going on. It was then that they told me the housekeeper had also called them. I was glad to hear that she at least did that.

Thinking maybe it was a language problem, Sammy and his girlfriend started screaming in Spanish. "*Perro! Perro! La puerta, por favor!*"

Finally the housekeeper came out of the house and down to the gate. "You didn't have to scream at me," she said. Her English was perfect.

As soon as she opened the gate, we went running in. There was a trail of blood leading to the body of Elvis. He was torn to shreds.

As Sammy handed the BB gun to his girlfriend so he could pick up Elvis, we heard, "Drop everything and turn around!"

We turned around and found ourselves facing several officers from the sheriff's department. Their weapons were pointed at us. "Whose gun is that?" one of them asked.

"It's mine," Sammy said. "It's a BB gun."

Two of the sheriffs moved forward, grabbed Sammy abruptly, handcuffed him, and slammed him against the police car. "You're under arrest for attempted assault with a deadly weapon. You have the right to remain silent. . . ." They finished reading him his rights, put their hands on his shoulders, pushed down on his head aggressively, and threw him in the backseat of the black-and-white.

"Why are you arresting my son?" I asked in panic.

"Ma'am, the housekeeper said that he pointed the gun at her and threatened her with it."

"We were screaming at her to let us in to get our dog. We were not threatening her."

"She says she doesn't speak English. She says she didn't understand you," he replied.

"She speaks English! When she came out and opened the gate, she said, 'You didn't have to scream at me.' She is lying."

Another officer then pushed me against the squad car. "Ma'am, if you don't calm down and remain quiet, I'm gonna place you under arrest as well."

"Wait! That's my dog—dead—over there, and you're going to arrest *me*? What about the man who owns this house? His dogs just killed my little dog. They reached through the gate and grabbed him. What if that had been a little child?"

"Ma'am, you need to shut up and calm down, or you're going to jail, too."

True story.

Not only did they not care about my dog, they wouldn't even let me take him home right away. For the time being, Elvis was "evidence"—to be used against my son. It was awful.

Brittany arrived just in time to see the sheriffs hauling her brother off to jail. She got in her car and drove away in tears. Another wonderful holiday experience. I spent the day home alone, trying to reach my lawyer. He finally returned my call.

"Lucinda, you've got to get Sammy out of there as soon as you can," he warned. "By tonight, at the latest. Sammy just turned eighteen—he's no longer considered a juvenile. They've set bail at $50,000. You don't want him to be arraigned tomorrow. Sammy could end up going to prison."

Sammy? Prison? I was horrified and outraged. "For a BB gun?" I shouted. "Those dogs ripped my dog apart. Elvis was outside their gate—

one of them reached through it and grabbed him. We just brought what was left of him home in a garbage bag. And you're telling me that the sheriffs think a kid with a BB gun is more dangerous than a grown man who keeps vicious killer German shepherds? He's not facing any charges over this?"

"That's the way it's looking, yes."

I didn't have $50,000. And anyway, it was Mother's Day—where was I going to get that kind of money on Mother's Day?

Just then Bruce Wisnicki, the wonderful man who sat with Sammy for hours and hours on the day David died, called to wish me a happy Mother's Day. I started sobbing into the phone. I was crying so hard that it took a while to make Bruce understand what had happened.

Thirty minutes later, Bruce was at my door with a bag full of money. I don't know how he had managed to come up with $50,000 cash, but he did. We drove to the sheriff's station in Agoura and posted bail for Sammy.

The arrest ruined the last few months of Sammy's senior year. He was consumed with worry, and as a result started vomiting more often. We were both a wreck, caught up in something that was simply wrong and unfair. Soon after the arrest, we were faced with the second anniversary of David's suicide. It was agony for all of us, Sammy most of all. He did make it to graduation a week or so later—barely—but bolted as soon as he was handed his diploma. Didn't even stick around for pictures. All he could think about was the possibility that he was going to prison for a BB gun.

My lawyer was as mad as I was about what happened—and as puzzled. "I don't get it," he told me. "This ought to be a no-brainer. No way the charges will hold up in court. First of all, a BB gun is not a deadly weapon. That's their first screw-up. Second, it wasn't loaded. Go figure. Third, Sammy's got witnesses who saw the whole thing."

You'd have thought that as soon as these facts were confirmed, it would have been over. But instead, it dragged on. My son, who could barely function, whose Tourette's symptoms were flaring, who had lost his father, was now living with the threat of prison over his head. We had to hire a private detective in an attempt to interview the housekeeper and investigate the scene. This went on for months. It was another nightmare for the Bassett family. At this point I was beginning to think we were cursed.

Finally, in late September, the case was dismissed due to lack of evidence. Seems the housekeeper wouldn't show up for court, or even to be interviewed. But just as that came to closure and Sammy was attempting to get on with his life, he came to me enraged.

He'd been looking for something on the Internet and found a blog full of speculation and misinformation about how and why his father had killed himself. An aggressive blogger, a guy who apparently likes to write vicious, untrue blogs about people in an attempt to provoke a response, wrote that David committed suicide in our own backyard. Then he said that he killed himself because he knew our product was a sham.

Yeah, right. That would do it.

"Mom, get that stuff about Dad off the Internet!" Sammy shouted through his tears.

"I wish I could, Sammy, but I can't."

Oh, the price of being *ALMOST FAMOUS*. Why, why do people want to hurt others and make up nasty lies about them? People who don't even know you. As if losing David to suicide weren't enough?

No one but close friends and family knew the torture we lived through with his mental illness. No one but close friends and family really knew how he died and what demons he dealt with. No one but someone who has lost a loved one to suicide understands the guilt, blame, anger, and shame that the surviving family members must live with.

Suicide leaves questions that can never be answered. But that doesn't stop people from asking them. It also doesn't stop people from making things up about what happened. I couldn't come out and confront the blogger, or even refute the lies. My company—or what used to be my company—didn't want me to, and in any event, I wasn't ready to take on this kind of thing or put my family through it.

Unfortunately, the Internet is a blessing and a curse. It is amazing that on the Web, anyone can say anything about anyone and no one can stop them. Do these heartless people have any idea of the anguish they put my family through?

And why do people think they have a right to even ask you how a family member died? You look at things differently when someone you love commits suicide.

"How did your husband die?" That was the question people asked when I told them that my husband had passed away. What happened after that was always awful. Though I rarely did it, telling people that my husband committed suicide was a real conversation stopper. There was an awkward silence, followed by a shocked facial expression that wasn't entirely sympathetic. Their eyes went all squinty, and behind those narrowed eyes it was easy to see all the questions they were dying to ask. *Why did he do it? What dark secret was he hiding? And were you part of the problem?*

Some people even had the nerve to ask those things out loud, in a nicer, roundabout way, of course. No matter how they put it, each question felt like an interrogation, and it stabbed. Every time the question came up, the wound was reopened.

"What should I do?" I asked my therapist.

"Just tell everyone it was heart related," she said with compassion. "You don't owe anyone that kind of intimacy about your personal life right now, Lucinda."

The truth is, David was a bright, successful, amazing guy who had a predisposition for manic-depressive illness. Then, due to some very stressful circumstances, many of which he created, he set himself up for a serious episode of ongoing, tortuous emotional instability. I believe that David became overwhelmed with financial concerns—some real, some imagined. I think he felt he betrayed me and our family; he felt betrayed by others, real or imagined. He then became increasingly untrusting and paranoid and thought people were out to get him. It was all too much for him. It broke his heart, in a way. So, saying his death was heart related wasn't a complete lie. As a result, he got very sick. But all that said, I do believe the biggest reason he took his life was because he was on the wrong medication. I believe to this day that if he had been put on lithium, he would still be alive.

It became time that the truth be told, in honor of David and our family, so that people would know what really happened to this beautiful man. So that people who don't even know him or us stop putting hurtful stories on the Internet. And so that David's legacy is positive, for him and for us.

Also, it's time the truth be told because it is important for those who have struggled with a loved one's suicide to understand that there is life after the loss of a loved one to suicide. But it takes a great deal of time to get there. And here's the rest of the story.

CHAPTER 21

Surviving Suicide

TIME HEALS, EVEN WITH something as horrific as suicide, but it heals a lot better if you get as much help and support as possible. David's death and my mother's death left me without the two key people I had always counted on for emotional support. As down as I was, as adrift as I was, at least I knew enough to reach out to friends and others for help.

I'm sure it wasn't easy to be around me at times. With generalized anxiety disorder, one of the hallmarks is motormouth, the need to talk and talk and talk. After David's death, I talked incessantly about my worries and all the issues I had to deal with. I was fortunate enough to have "walking partners," friends who would take the download as I went on and on about everything that was causing fear and stress, and especially about my apprehension regarding what was happening in my life. They would walk the dogs with me and listen to me worry. They would sit and talk with me on the phone for hours—or should I say, listen to me talk for hours.

Friends from across the country all took turns coming out to be there and talk-talk-talk me through my angst. There was Bruce Winters, my husband's best friend from Ohio, and his wife, Pat, who is to this day one of my dearest friends, as well as my wonderful brother-in-law, Bob Wittenmyer, and his daughters, my nieces Jennifer and Lori. Also flying in several times was one of my oldest and dearest friends, Tammy

Elliot from Atlanta, and my beautiful friend and wingwoman Carolyn Dickman, who worked with me for years at the Midwest Center. Then there were my wonderful friends from Malibu—Del, Kerrol, Lisa, Sandra, Shirley, Deb, and many, many more. I don't know how I would have made it without all of them. They came to hang out with me when I couldn't stand to be alone; they let me panic and talk about my fears. I would talk-talk-talk, worry-worry-worry, and they would try to help me problem solve and think things through. The idea was not to look at the big picture, just to fix what I could.

The most important mantra for me was, "One thing at a time, one minute at a time." Eventually it became "One day at a time," and then "One week at time." That is how I managed my life for three years, and it was a tough, emotional, fearful roller-coaster ride, with very little control over the future. But I stayed in the moment, took one thing at a time, lived one day at a time, worked with a great therapist, and spent time with my children and friends.

And little by little, I worked through it all. I sold the company David had said I'd never sell. I paid down the debt and eventually put my family on a sound financial footing once again. Stu found a solid partner for his company and has finished two developments. He brought me into his business as a silent partner, enabling me to recapture some of the money David invested, and to even eventually, someday, see a profit.

In working through the loss, stress, and uncertainty of the last four years, I learned I couldn't look at the big picture or look too far into the future. I had to deal with what was in front of me, put one foot in front of the other, one minute at a time, one hour at a time, one day at a time.

I reached out to Margret McBride, my literary agent on the book *From Panic to Power*. She cried as I sat with her and told her not only about David's death but about everything that took place after that. I told her I thought there might be a book in what happened to me.

We went to New York to pitch it. I wanted to write a book about surviving suicide, but publishers told me that no one wanted a book on that—the audience would be too narrow. But I knew they were wrong. Right after David died, I looked for books about coping with suicide and life after traumatic loss of a loved one. Nothing I found was uplifting or empowering. There was nothing that said what I most needed to hear—nothing that said, "You can get through this, you can live again, you can laugh again, you can love again." Someone actually gave me *The Year of Magical Thinking*, Joan Didion's book about the death of her husband and her daughter. I pored through it, hunting for clues, anything that would make me feel better. It was beautifully written, but it made me so depressed I had to put it down. By about halfway through, all I could think was, "I'm doomed."

The publishers were still adamant that the book not focus on suicide, so the idea of a book about suicide morphed into a memoir—and this is the book you are holding now. At first I was uncertain. I wanted to honor David, but I also wanted to protect my family. For me, writing a memoir meant that all the dirty little secrets in my life would come out. With a great deal of thought, I came to realize it would help my children understand why I am who I am, what I did to get where I am, and why I do what I do. I was also hopeful that it would provide some closure by giving them an appreciation of what a loving, beautiful man their father was, despite the pain he caused us by taking his life.

Suicide still deserves its own book, and I intend to write it. Don't tell me no one wants it—that's what they said about *Attacking Anxiety and Depression,* after all. Those who are left behind when someone takes his or her life are the forgotten ones, the ones who survived. We walk around with our heads hung down, tormented about what happened. We feel the guilt, blame, anger, and shame. We try suicide support groups, and they suck. We try to talk to our doctors, but none of them have anything to tell us because they haven't been there.

Someone has to have the guts to step up and talk openly about suicide and mental illness. Why not me? I'm a person who has to have a purpose, and it has to be a purpose that makes a difference. I want to write the kind of book I wish had been there for me and my children right after David died. One of my biggest goals is to help people see the light at the end of the very dark tunnel of suicide and understand that it is possible to survive it. If I can do it after everything that I've been through, especially coming from where I was, then anyone can do it.

EPILOGUE

Keep Looking Up

IT WAS THE SUMMER OF 2011 when a very special friend took me camping in Yosemite. Despite the fact that the scenery was lovely and the water-falls were full and beautiful, I was distracted and having trouble getting out of my own head. My mind was swamped with thoughts about the new book, about my clients, about money, about Sammy and Brittany and how they were doing—thoughts I should have put aside to be in the moment and enjoy the beauty around me.

This had been a great year for rain and snow, and my friend knew how spectacular the falls would be. As we hiked to the waterfalls and floated down the river in a raft, I tried to enjoy it, but he saw that I was still worrying. One of the best things about this man was that he was great at staying focused on the here and now. He helped me enjoy living in the moment and to appreciate the simple things.

After a few days of tents and community showers, I finally let go of my worry and let myself wallow in the incredible beauty all around me. It took my breath away. Waterfalls were everywhere. It was pure and fresh, and so beautiful my heart leapt.

At one point we pulled the raft up onto the riverbank and just sat and looked up at Yosemite Falls for hours. It was amazing to see the force of the falls and smell the crisp, fresh air. All my life I looked up, to God, to a higher power. I looked up for guidance and support to those who had left me—my dad, my sister, my brothers, and finally my husband and my mother. I looked up for positive universal energy, and I looked up to find the sunshine behind the clouds, the rainbow after the storms of life. Sitting there on that riverbank, it all just made sense.

In Yosemite, you see the bigness of God like you've never seen it before. Before David died, I'd spent my whole life looking up to God, trusting my faith in even the worst situations. Somewhere along the way, I had lost touch with God . . . given up on God. Now it was time to look up once again. The trip made me realize how much of life I still had ahead of me, how precious it was, and that I had to forge a new relationship with God. The old one, based on structured religion, had stopped working. It just wasn't feeding my soul.

When I got home, I decided to start looking for an alternative church and eventually found my way to the Agape Spiritual Center. Everyone there was so gracious and happy. They are peaceful with each other—and with themselves. When I first started, I was sure I'd never get to be like them. After all that had happened, I was way too messed up.

Wrong. As I began attending services there, what I realized was that it didn't matter that I was anxious and depressed. I could accept myself as I was, because God loves me that way.

In fact, God loves me no matter what. I came to a new understanding of my relationship with God. God isn't this up-there deity, sitting in almighty judgment and keeping score. God is right here, not just in pristine nature, like in Yosemite, but inside each and every one of us. Agape and Michael Beckwith's teachings helped me realize that I was *already* good with God. For someone carrying as much guilt-blame-anger-shame baggage as I was, this was huge.

I became newly open to the presence of God in things big and small. It strengthened an idea I already had, which is that we can all be instruments of God. I never believed that I was any kind of laying-on-of-hands miracle worker, but I did believe that God had given me this really special gift of being able to help people with anxiety and depression.

What evolved through Agape, however, was my understanding of what drove me in that direction, and my understanding of the relationship between my wanting to help others—to rescue them—and my unmet need to heal or rescue myself.

You can't rescue anyone unless there's an emergency, right? And one giant downside of being a rescuer is that you may operate—as I did—from a place of perpetual crisis mode. That's been me, my entire life. I had never fully understood how damaging that is, but when your life is one 911 after another, there's not much time for inner peace or personal growth.

I went through life being a rescuer—that's what I always meant by "fixing people"—but I was a rescuer coming from a place of needing to be rescued myself. Now I realized that there was some work I had to do to heal myself—to come to grips with the darkest parts of my childhood—before I could move from rescue mode to healing and empowerment mode.

It meant that I had to let go of all the dirty little secrets, but that doesn't mean it was easy to do. During one session with my therapist, he asked me whether I'd ever been sexually molested as a child.

I tensed up as all the old defense mechanisms deployed. "Why do you ask me that?" I said.

"Because you have several of the classic symptoms. . . ." which, of course, in summary included issues with guilt, blame, anger, and shame. No surprise.

I took a deep breath and nodded. "Well, actually . . ."

I proceeded to tell him the story of my "blackout time" between the ages of seven and nine, when I was left home alone and at the mercy of my abuser. Finally, after all these years, I felt safe enough to tell someone. Finally, I might stop blaming myself for what happened to me when I was a child. Finally, I might be able to get beyond guilt, blame, anger, and shame—and let myself love myself.

That was a huge step toward being able to come to terms with the past. It enabled me to look to the future with a new, open heart. I started to dream again. Ironically, it was around this time that I was invited to a dream-board party. A dream board, also called a vision board, is a manifestation of your future created by your own subconscious.

Making one involves sorting through a variety of pictures and words, usually from magazines, and pulling out the ones that set off some kind of strong positive reaction in you, spontaneously. Not in your head, but in your gut.

The idea here is that you don't overanalyze why a certain picture or sentence or group of words appeals to you. In fact, don't analyze it at all. The pictures or words you choose could represent love, inspiration, excitement, joy, adventure, relationships, family, spirituality, material desires, health—anything—but you won't know what they represent till you see them all together. The final step is to glue or tape the pictures or words to the board itself. Allow your intuition to place the images on the board—don't force any particular design or arrangement. This is a visceral, not an intellectual, activity. The whole idea is to let your deepest hopes and aspirations come forward without your deliberately control-ling the process.

I had talked about the process of making a dream board in my last book, *The Solution*, but had never actually done it myself. I thought this would be a good experience for me.

I almost didn't go to the dream-board party. I was supposed to go with a friend, but she canceled on me last-minute because she was sick, and I really didn't feel like going by myself. I knew that when I got there, I wouldn't know a soul. Besides, it was too far; I looked fat; I needed a manicure; and I was having a bad hair day.

Despite all the roadblocks I was putting up for myself, a nagging voice inside me kept telling me to get off my butt and get dressed. My time in Yosemite had shown me the importance of looking up and looking for-ward, but it also raised questions that I needed to answer about my future and what I really wanted. Who was I going to be now that David was gone, my company was gone, and my children were getting on with their lives? I had to find my new normal, and to do that I had to get out there. Normal wasn't going to show up on my doorstep and ring the bell.

I grabbed my car keys and headed out to Barnes & Noble. Everyone who was invited to the party had been asked to bring ten magazines with lots of pictures in them. I picked up ten that dealt with the things I knew I wanted in my life—good health, healthy children, and spirituality. Surely, I thought, I could pull enough stuff from my stack of magazines to make a dream board. On the way to the party I got lost, and wandering around hilly, twisty streets of the Hollywood hills was so frustrating I almost turned around to go home. I was about to give up when a couple on the sidewalk waved at me. "Are you going to Rolonda's?" they called out. "Just park. Then come with us. We're going, too."

Once I got inside, there was fabulous food, a great fireplace, and about sixty really interesting and accomplished people. Many of them were writers and producers and other successful people from what we in Los Angeles call "the business"—movies and television. When I realized who was around me, I started feeling pretty small. Who was I to think I belonged here? The urge to flee had just crossed my mind when someone asked me what I did for a living. I was starting to explain when another guest turned around and said, "Oh my God! You're Lucinda Bassett! I have your program and it saved my life!" That made me feel good, like maybe I wasn't so out of place here after all.

Our hostess, a beautiful and spiritual woman named Rolonda Watts, assembled us all and had us stand and introduce ourselves. "I'm Lucinda Bassett, and I'm really honored to be here," I began. "I help people overcome depression and anxiety. I have an infomercial, I'm on the radio, and I have three books out. I know this all sounds pretty good but "—I paused and took a deep breath before continuing—"three years ago my husband David, my lover, best friend, and business partner committed suicide. My whole life fell apart. My kids and I have never . . . will never be the same. So, that said, I don't know where I'm going, but I'm hoping that someday down the road my family finds happiness again. I hope I find happiness again."

I started to cry. This was the first time I'd announced out loud to people that David had killed himself. I was emotional, but at the same time I was struck by an odd sense of relief. Finally, *finally* I told the truth about it. It felt so freeing.

When I sat down again, you could have heard a pin drop. After the rest of the group was finished, I stood up to get a drink and was bombarded with people. They came up to give me hugs, press their business cards into my hand, and share their own stories of loved ones who had taken their lives or had died. I was overwhelmed by all the empathy in the room.

Meanwhile, Rolonda started passing out blank two-by-three-foot posters so we could begin working on our dream boards. By the time I was done speaking with everyone who came up to me, I looked down to see that all of the magazines I'd brought were gone. But, of course, this is how it is supposed to happen. I immediately laughed at my own ridiculousness, thinking I'd be able to control this process—or anything else in my life, for that matter. There was no point in my trying to control the dream-board experience—just the opposite: it's supposed to be random and instinctive.

There were plenty of other magazines to work with, and I started looking through them and impulsively tearing out pictures. Someone handed me a glass of wine. While I was pulling images, a woman came up to me. "Here," she said as she handed me something she had torn out of a magazine, "you need to put this in the center of your board." It read, "When you've been through hell, you tend to appreciate heaven." I glued it to the center of my board.

After a few of hours of great conversation, coupled with randomly ripping things out of magazines and gluing them on, my poster board was finished. I stood back and gasped. I was shocked. Wow! *That's* what I want?

I didn't think I was at all ready to be in a long-term relationship, but the whole right side of the board was about a guy—a guy with kind of long hair and a business brain. Next to him I'd glued down a couple of interesting places—Italy, and a Caribbean-looking place with bright turquoise water. The left side of the board was about spirituality. It said, "God wants to talk to you."

After that night, I let go of the idea of telling people that David's death was heart related. I found that the more open I was about it, and the more comfortable I was with telling people that David killed himself, the more people responded to me. Just like at the dream-board party, arms and doors opened up for me in a very loving way. People shared their stories with me. Everyone knew someone, either in his or her family or a close friend, who'd struggled with mental illness or who had committed suicide.

Suicide is like AIDS or cancer. It's uncomfortable, and it scares people. And so, for the first few years, none of us really talked about it too much. It was another secret in my life, and I knew how to keep those. But now, I am a grown woman with children to set an example for.

I had learned that secrets are toxic, and eventually they eat away at the lives of those who keep them bottled in. When you say that your husband or father committed suicide, people look at you with surprise and even in some odd way, suspicion. But it's up to you how you take it from there. It is up to you at some point to make the decision to accept it and yes, even talk about it. For me and for my children, it has been so freeing to tell the truth about it.

The real secret about suicide turns out to be how common it really is. The best thing about talking about it is that you will touch someone who knows someone who has been touched by suicide and, in turn, help him or her heal. And of course when you do this, you are helping yourself heal as well.

Months after the dream-board party, I wandered into a café on a Saturday afternoon. I sat at the bar and ordered a glass of sauvignon blanc and some guacamole. There was a side patio attached to the restaurant. All of a sudden, two attractive guys entered from the outside patio. One was Italian-looking, had long, dark hair, and had two little boys with him. He smiled at me.

"Your boys are beautiful," I said, looking at the kids, who were clearly enjoying being with him.

He laughed and motioned over his shoulder to his friend, who was just about to join him. "Not my boys. *His* boys."

We talked, and he told me about himself. He was business savvy, a world traveler, smart, edgy, and quite successful. He was also the father of older boys.

We continued talking, and I have to admit I was intrigued. Then he said, "You're cute. There's something about you that seems familiar.

Anyway, I'd really like to take you out."

"But I don't even know you," I said.

"Google me," he replied.

Hmm. Who did he think he was?

"Well, Google *me*," I countered with a smirk. Who did he think *I* was?

I told him my first name and that I was an author. Then he asked for my phone number.

When I got home, I was looking for something in my closet and randomly pulled out my dream board. I had completely forgotten about it. To my surprise, there, all over my board, was the guy I had just met. Long hair? Check. Business brain? Check. World traveler, spiritual, and successful? Check.

"That's him!" I exclaimed to myself.

That evening my phone rang. "Are you really Lucinda Bassett?" he asked when I answered the phone.

"Yes."

"Really! I saw you on TV ten years ago and thought how beautiful you were and what amazing energy you had. "

Possibilities.

It's been four years since David died. I still miss him as if it were yesterday, and yes, the holidays still suck. And yes, at times, it is still painful beyond words.

When someone you love takes his or her life by suicide, they also take part of yours. And the hurt they leave behind never goes away. Often, the hurt catches you by surprise: the welling of tears that can erupt at any given moment at the mention of their name, of a memory, or a song; the knots in your stomach that can never completely be eradicated; and the hole in your heart that can never be filled.

It would be a lie if I told you I am not angry, or that it is not a selfish act—because I am, and it is.

And try as you may to forgive and forget, you never quite can, completely. And that is the true, painful secret of suicide that someone who takes his or her own life never bothers to consider. The selfish act that took away their pain leaves the surviving loved ones with a lifetime legacy of pain to bear. We are left to hold the pain in our hearts forever. And so the memory of the loved one who chose to leave is, unfortunately, bittersweet. As if losing them forever wasn't enough.

But, I am learning life for the living *must* go on.

Understandably, and with caution, I once again have decided to share my life experience to help others. I've started a new business and a new brand. I am now focusing on helping those who struggle not only with anxiety and depression, but also with grief, tragedy, and loss, and, of course, suicide.

The kids are moving on, too. Brittany has a great new job and a solid, loving relationship with her boyfriend. Sammy is living on his own, going to culinary school, and has a wonderful girlfriend. And it appears that he has, for the most part, outgrown Tourette's and is symptom free.

If someone had told me four years ago that I would be writing a memoir, that I would be starting a new business, that my kids would be getting on with their lives, and that we would even experience joy again, I would have said it was impossible—even though I believe that's what David would have wanted for us all.

As I am in the final editing stages of this book, we have just passed another milestone in the "left by a loved one" grieving process, David's fifty-eighth birthday in September. But this birthday was different from the last three, which we didn't acknowledge. The kids weren't ready before; it was simply too painful. This year, however, Brittany and her boyfriend Justin, Sammy and his girlfriend, Ashley, and I all went to dinner in honor of David.

Brittany complimented Sammy on his shirt when he sat down at the table. I recognized it immediately as one of David's favorite shirts.

"It was Dad's," Sammy said, tugging at the shirt with a certain sentimental sadness and appreciation.

As the night unfolded, we spoke of David, toasted to him, and then continued with our dinner. I sat, admittedly, in a somewhat somber sadness, but also in gratitude for these two beautiful people who sat before me and who share my life; they are my gifts from David.

As I watched Sammy interact with Brittany and be affectionate with his girlfriend, I thought back to the night before David left us, when he asked me what about Sammy was like him. "His voice, his gestures, his analytical mind, his gentleness, his lovingness toward women," I thought to myself.

Then I looked at Brittany, mothering Sammy and giving him advice. I remembered David asking, "What about Brittany is like me?" I watched her and thought, "Her confidence, her directness, her sense of responsibility, and her laughter." All of these were David's traits.

In that moment I said a prayer to him, and I thought to myself how the two of them, in their own unique and beautiful ways, would keep the spirit of David alive for many, many years to come.

Lucinda,

Pardon me if I stare,
It's maybe my way of saying I care, I care,
And I love you, both today and tomorrow.
I've sure had things my way,
Happiness and love every day,
Seems as if you've blown away all of my sorrows.
Well I think of you all the time,
Be it filling your gas tank,
Or making up silly rhymes.
Just to let you know how I feel about you,
Here I go again: My heart starts to tremble,
My love bashes, like cymbals,
My eyes seem to float away,
I lose touch; don't know what to say,
But I feel it in so many ways.
I want you tomorrow, and I want you today;
I just love you.
Please accept my gift; let it show,
I want everyone to know,
That my love, it is always about you.

—David

Acknowledgments

A VERY SPECIAL THANK-YOU goes to my literary agent Margret McBride, for knowing David and me, our relationship, and our family so intimately—and for caring so deeply. Also, for helping me to understand that this story eventually needed to be told. You cried with me and grieved with me, but kept reminding me of my life's mission: helping others who struggle. The mission is the same, but the struggle comes with a new and different message.

A special thank-you to all the people at Sterling Publishing. Michael Fragnito, for getting me, and my message, from the moment we met. Your kind heart, clear vision, and determined style helped bring this book to what I believe was a predestined place. Pam Horn, who worked diligently and from a place of integrity to make sure my desires and needs for clarity were understood in representing my life and my story, in my way—in my words, my writing style, and from my heart. John Foster, who caringly shepherded the final manuscript into print.

A warm and loving thank-you to Kay and Digby Diehl, a wonderful team of collaborators who always showed up with a great attitude and dropped everything to totally tune in to my world for months. You were nothing but a true joy and pleasure to work with. When I couldn't think of the right word or phrase, you could. When I cried, you cried. What a team we were. I remember saying to you, "You've worked on some incredible memoirs. Isn't everyone's life story this intense?" You both looked at me

278

with bewilderment and simply shook your heads and said, "Not even close." I couldn't have done such a wonderful delivery on this book without you.

A very special thank-you to my children, Brittany and Sammy, for agreeing to let me tell this story and for understanding the importance of the reasons behind sharing it. Thank you to both of you, for loving me even when I was shattered and shaking, and for helping me to believe in myself, and my mission, again—even when I didn't.

Thank you to my very dear friends and family who helped me walk through the fire: Del, Tammy, Kerrol, Carolyn, Pat, Bruce, Lisa, Bob and Darla, Shirley and Lloyd, Bob and Mary Ellen, Richard Miller, Jesse, Bill, Deb and Kenny, Sandra and Vincent, Lisa and Jonathan, and Mark. A special thank-you to my brother-in-law, Bob, and my nieces, Jennifer and Lori, who have been so loving and supportive, and who have become my extended immediate family. Thank you to my brother, Gary, and my cousin Jerry, along with some of the others named above, for being there to walk me through the death of my mother. You were all so important over the last four years. You kept me going, kept me believing, listened to my worry, my fears, and insecurities, and always gave me something to believe in and to look forward to. Most important, you helped me live in the moment and believe there was still a future, even though in my darkest hours I couldn't see it.

A special thanks to one of my dearest friends and business associates, Dr. Phil Fisher. You have walked my walk with me from the beginning, and I love you so much for always loving me and believing in me, and for being there for me.

Thank you to all the professional friends and business associates who helped me patiently and diligently untangle the Web: Marc Akerman, Greg and Sandy Hutchins, Michael Crum, David Ruth, and Neil Jannol.

A loving thank-you to all the employees of the Midwest Center who stood by me during the darkest hours and continued to believe in the message. I could never have moved forward with selling the company without your help and dedication. Although I no longer own the Midwest Center, I will always hold the memories of working with all you wonderful, dedicated people in my heart forever.

Thank you to James Kinney, my marketing director for this project, and for the social media strategy surrounding it. Your energy, enthusiasm, and diligent, clear strategy helped to spread the word and the message to hundreds of thousands of people who needed encouragement for dealing with all types of tragedy before the book was even released.

And finally, a special thank-you to all of my clients and followers who stood by me during this difficult time. Many of you took the time to respond to the negative blogging and Internet entries that happened after David's death, which were incorrect, inappropriate, and hurtful. I appreciate that more than you will ever know. Without all the support and love I received, I don't think this book would have come to be. I thank all of you from the bottom of my heart and soul.